Hunting in the Arctic and Alaska

HUNTING IN THE ARCTIC
AND ALASKA

Photos. A. M. Collins

POLAR BEAR IN THE ARCTIC OCEAN

When this bear was first seen swimming toward the ship it resembled a small piece of ice. Only the black spot of its nose moving from side to side betrayed it. The polar bear ranges far over the ice in search of seals and young walrus. This animal was 72 miles east of Herald Island, the nearest land.

HUNTING IN THE ARCTIC
AND ALASKA

BY
E. MARSHALL SCULL

WITH 126 ILLUSTRATIONS FROM PHOTOGRAPHS
AND 11 MAPS

PHILADELPHIA
THE JOHN C. WINSTON COMPANY
1914

AUTHOR'S NOTE

The frontiers of the world are now all but gone, for the feet of men have trodden almost every trail and the beaks of ships have blown into every sea. Blazes on the trees, keels buried in the beaches meet us wherever we adventure. But this does not necessarily sadden a man who leaves for the time a more crowded civilization to seek refreshment in the wilderness. To him the smell of the woods and the salt taste of spray are sufficient.

This story of a hunting trip pretends only to tell of a summer cruise through, beyond and around Alaska in search of sport with the rifle and the freedom which gives that sport its zest.

The photographs have been selected from a large number taken by members of the party and each bears the name of the man who took it, except those by the author. Special portraits of various related game heads, lent by the owners for comparison with those shot on the trip, have been reproduced on the same scale, and each bears the owner's name. No retouching has been allowed on any illustrations.

For advice, criticism and assistance I am grateful to Alfred M. Collins, Wilson Potter, Gilpin Lovering, Dr. Arthur W. Elting, Dr. William T. Hornaday, Allen I. Smith and Charles R. Wood. None of these gentlemen is responsible for any shortcomings of the text.

E. M. S.

Philadelphia, April, 1914.

CONTENTS

(9)

ILLUSTRATIONS

GENERAL MAP SHOWING ROUTE OF THE TRIP

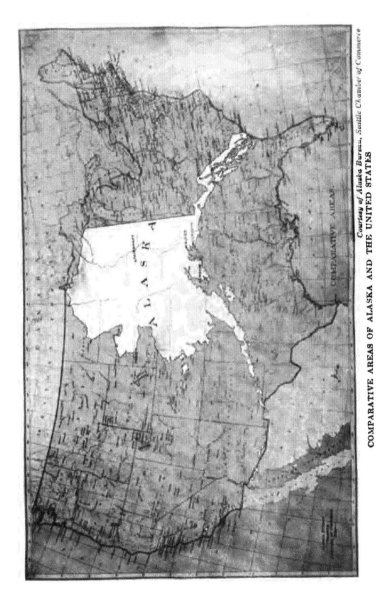

Courtesy of Alaska Bureau, Seattle Chamber of Commerce

COMPARATIVE AREAS OF ALASKA AND THE UNITED STATES

MAPS

CHAPTER I

W E lay under the fly of our tent one sizzling December noontide just south of the equator in British East Africa. A little thermometer, basking in the sunshine, was filled with mercury clear up to the top, beyond its highest figures. A quivering haze of heat-waves lay above the earth, twisting distant objects into uncouth, lively antics. Zebras and gazelles dozed in the scanty shade of thorn bushes.

"It would be a pleasant contrast to this winter climate," remarked Collins, as he sipped his lime-juice, "to spend a summer in the Arctic."

Fancy played with this thought until the idea was not only born but well nourished.

On our return to temperate latitudes there followed an extensive investigation of various routes and means of making an expedition into the lands of ice and snow. We corresponded with Arctic explorers, hunters, whalers and sportsmen. Norwegian mariners offered to take us north of Iceland; Scotch whaling captains would show us their trade, with some hunting thrown in, on a six months' voyage between America and Greenland; we could charter a steamer at vast expense and cruise perhaps as far as Ellesmere Land, toward the regions which Peary had made his own. The Antarctic we left quite out of consideration because of its comparative dearth of big game.

Finally all other localities were brushed aside and we decided to put our hopes on the Arctic Ocean north of Bering Strait, north also of Alaska and eastern Siberia.

It might be interesting to set down some of the reasons for this choice.

The big game of the Arctic is polar bear, walrus and musk-ox. Whaling is, of course, a most thrilling sport, but hardly in the category of game hunting.

The polar bear inhabits the vast ice-packs extending southward in all directions from the pole, breeding by preference on remote coasts and islands which are seldom ice-free and are therefore unmolested. He preys chiefly upon seals and young walrus. We would have reasonable chances of finding this great animal either on the Atlantic or Pacific side of America.

Of walrus two sorts are recognized by naturalists: the Atlantic and the Pacific. They differ in the shape of the head and in other less conspicuous ways, but most strikingly in size. The Pacific variety is larger and bears far longer and heavier ivory tusks than its Atlantic relative. This fact helped to turn us toward the west.

Musk-oxen are seldom brought to bag by sportsmen. They exist in northeastern and northern Greenland, Grantland, Ellesmere Land and the Arctic coastal countries west to Great Bear Lake, nearly as far west as the Mackenzie River, north of 64 degrees. By no planning could we promise ourselves a shot at these strange cousins of the sheep during a summer hunt. Therefore we left them out of our reckoning.

Other men had made trips to Greenland and the eastern coasts of arctic America. So far as we knew, no sportsmen had yet carried a simple hunting expedition

through Bering Strait into the fastnesses of the western
Arctic and hunted in Alaska in one summer.

Now at the right moment came Captain Kleinschmidt
from Seattle with the charter of a suitable ship, with
some personal experience, and with very dazzling plans
for a full summer and autumn among the big game of
Alaska as well as the frozen north.

We were to shoot walrus and polar bear in the Arctic,
look for a wild sheep in easternmost Siberia as yet
unknown to science, try to get tundra caribou and great
brown bear on the Alaska Peninsula, and hunt the giant
moose, the white sheep and the black and brown bear of
the Kenai Peninsula—four distinct hunting trips in a
space of five months. We were to furnish the funds for
the hire of ship and crew and purchase of all necessary
stores up to a fixed sum, and could share the expense
with not more than two other hunters. Kleinschmidt
would be responsible for unforeseen extras. His interest
lay in obtaining motion pictures to complete a series
begun two years before.

It did not take long to make a contract on these
terms. It was then late in April. Kleinschmidt hurried
west and we telegraphed the money ahead of him to pay
for the outfitting. He had to sail from Seattle at the
first of May and work up the coast, where we were to
join the ship at Nome, in northwestern Alaska, by the
middle of July.

How should we go to Nome? A fast steamer from
Seattle would deposit us there after a voyage of eight
days, to be sure, but it would be purely a sea trip, over
much of the same route that we would take in our own
vessel. Happily we made arrangements to travel down
the long Yukon River, through the heart of "the great

country," in company with a large party of business people from Seattle, visiting all the principal mining camps on the way. We would arrive on the distant coast in time to meet Kleinschmidt's vessel.

Dr. Arthur W. Elting and Gilpin Lovering, both sportsmen of wide experience, made their wills and arranged to be our companions. Alfred M. Collins and I were the rest of the hunting party.

We traveled from the eastern seaboard of the United States, three thousand miles to Seattle, as the first stage of our journey. Thence we threaded the Inside Passage for one thousand seven hundred miles to Skagway, at the head of Lynn Canal.

To go through this maze of waters we embarked at Seattle, June 21st, on the little steamer "Jefferson." Dr. Elting and Collins were with us; Lovering was to come later direct to Nome. Mrs. Elting was also going with her husband through Alaska and back to Seattle.

Now we found ourselves in a company of more than one hundred, the first party that had attempted to make a thoroughly comprehensive tour of Alaska in a single summer.

There was no particular difficulty of traveling in Alaska, but the facilities were so irregular, particularly on the lower Yukon, that it would be hardly possible for the independent voyager to cover the ground that this excursion set for itself. Special steamers had been chartered, schedules of transportation companies devised months beforehand to make close connections for our convenience and arrangements made for us to inspect all the mining and other industries at every point we visited. It was an exceptional opportunity to see the country.

THE WHITE PASS AND THE UPPER YUKON

Above: Over the White Pass, which presented great difficulties to the early prospectors, a railway now runs. This view was taken part way up, looking back to Skagway.

Below: Two Yukon River steamers taking on wood at Eagle City on the boundary between Canada and Alaska.

Photo. A. M. Collins

PROSPECTING AND DREDGING GOLD

Above: Illustrating how a prospector pans out gravel to see if he has struck pay dirt.
A few yellow grains remaining after he has washed a shovelful indicate the presence of gold.
Below: One of the largest gold dredges which wash gravel at the lowest cost. Both of
these photographs were taken on the Klondike River.

Briefly, the itinerary before us was as follows: to traverse the Inside Passage by steamer, cross the White Pass to the head of the Yukon River, take steamer to Dawson and see the Klondike gold fields, go down the great river across the boundary into Alaska, to Fairbanks, the chief interior town, and emerge at Nome, formerly the greatest Alaskan mining camp.

There we were to board our own hunting schooner, sail across to Siberia, up to Wrangell Island in the Arctic, back to southwestern Alaska, and return to Seattle by the south coast. It would have been hard to plan a more thorough tour of this part of the world for so short a time as we had.

We landed from the "Jefferson" at Skagway and went directly into the interior of Alaska.

It was a fateful trail in the earliest days of the rush of '96, from Skagway to Dawson and the Klondike. Many a man lost his outfit and many a one his life. But these were, for the most part, inexperienced gold-seekers who brought useless weight of unsuitable things or too few necessities.

There were four well-marked stages in the long journey of 571 miles; first, packing over the pass to Lake Linderman; second, the lake and river voyage nearly to White Horse; third, shooting Miles Canyon and the White Horse Rapids; fourth, the long drift down the river to Dawson. At first the trail from Dyea over the Chilkoot Pass, which was shorter but steeper, was much used to reach the head of Lake Linderman, but eventually a wagon road constructed through White Pass, a short distance eastward of the Chilkoot, won the traffic. Thousands of horses fell dead by the roadside and tons of abandoned provisions littered the trail.

Once safe at the first lake over the mountains from Skagway, the adventurers felled timber, cut planks with a whipsaw and nailed together a rough boat for the rest of the voyage.   Not often was there at hand to advise them anyone who had made the whole trip, and, as one of the old rapids pilots put it, "They expected us to run them through the tall water in every kind of vessel, from rafts to coffins."

Pilots at the head of Miles Canyon steered the boats to White Horse for sums of twenty-five to fifty dollars. The distance from Skagway to White Horse was 111 miles.   The rest of it, 460 miles to Klondike River, was not so difficult.   In fact the whole route presented no terrors to a party properly outfitted and guided by experience.

But now we traveled this famous trail in luxury.   A train carried us twenty-two miles up to the summit and thence by easy gradient past the dreaded rapids to White Horse in one daylight.   Observation cars enabled the old-timers to point out each historic spot to wife or stranger. Lunch was served at Bennett, a halfway point.   It was told us that no one could buy a meal there unless possessed of a railway ticket.

The train halted at Caribou Crossing on Taku Arm, whence steamers plied eastward and made connections with the productive gold camps on Lake Atlin.   In a few minutes we had discovered Shorty Austin, a tall, lank guide for the neighboring country, in which he promised good hunting for sheep, goats, moose, caribou and bear.

No sooner were the details of a possible trip in this locality noted down than we were shunted down a branch line to an iron and copper mine at Pueblo belonging to the White Pass Route. The ore, which was mined from levels several hundred feet below the surface, contained copper enough to pay the expenses of shipping and smelting in Tacoma. We were told that the property had yielded a very large profit in the first year it had been operated.

Ptarmigan, one of the beautiful northern grouse, abounded in the neighborhood; but it might not be so much longer, for the men slaughtered the defenceless birds for winter food. In a two or three days' hunt they would load a half dozen pack horses. One photograph showed 3,000 ptarmigan thus secured.

We drew back to the main line and passed the narrow gorge of Miles Canyon and the Rapids into the town of White Horse, which came into existence as a refitting station, after the perilous rapids, for the river journey to Dawson. Nowadays it is the head of navigation on the upper waters of the Yukon drainage system. This fork of the Yukon is called the Lewis River, until it joins the Pelly.

Before going on, however, we saw a boat run the Rapids and visited a fox farm.

Dr. Sugden, an old-time river pilot, sent a dory by rail up to the head of Miles Canyon, and a large crowd walked out to the Rapids to see him come out of the gorge and go through the swift water. Merl la Voy set up a motion-picture camera. After a long wait the boat shot out of the canyon into the rapids. The pilot steered with an oar at the stern and kept bow downstream, choosing the round back of water where the current ran swiftest and deepest. Though the angry wave-crests seemed from our point of view to be curling frequently into the open dory, the boat came through with very little water aboard.

We ventured the opinion that a strong swimmer might go through the White Horse Rapids. "No one has ever succeeded," replied Dr. Sugden. "Every time that a boat capsized, or a man fell out and lost hold of the craft, death followed. The current probably draws downward in places. I once saw a large spruce tree, about seventy feet long, come through. At one place it was whirled up on end, drawn down straight out of sight and cast out below the rapids, broken into three pieces."

On the river bank, below the steamboat docks, a very old man was making dories of rough lumber, the seams calked and smeared with tar. "I have been doing this for nine years," he said, "and have built nearly a thousand boats, ranging in value (at present prices) from fourteen to thirty dollars."

We rowed across the current in one of these, to a fox farm on the opposite side. The two proprietors led us through the alleys between the cages, which were about four feet high. "We have invested some twenty thousand dollars in our breeding stock," they explained. "If one of the black ones gets away it is like losing $1,500 in the river; consequently we have buried the lower edge of our wire fencing about four feet deep." A number of foxes were running loose in the alleys. At this moment one of them climbed upon a cage and jumped for the top of the outside fence, which was some nine feet high and six feet from the cage. He just missed enough foothold to make his escape. "More wire on top of that fence, Jim," said the man, looking significantly at his partner. These men were bitterly critical of the policy of the White Pass Route. It charged, they said, exorbitant freight rates if the goods were valuable.

Fur farming, particularly fox farming, was thought by many persons to have a lucrative future. But the high price for breeders, the liability of loss or death, and the probability that the price of these furs would come down rapidly when many farms began to ship, discouraged not a few.

White Horse being one of the outfitting points for big game hunting at the head of White River, we interviewed Charles Baxter, a professional guide. He said it took two weeks to go in, and two weeks to come out, which, added to a forty days' hunt, made at least nine weeks. He would follow a trail to Kluane Lake, traverse the lake in boats and look for moose, sheep, caribou and bear in the country between the Donjek and White Rivers. We also heard of a well-recommended guide, Tom Dickson, Kluane, Yukon Territory.

We, however, boarded the steamer "Dawson," an old stern-wheel, wood-burning, shoal-draught river boat, and headed farther down the stream. The swift current wound through the hills, forming bends and shoals, which required careful handling at many points, and a rather spectacular passage at Five Finger Rapids.

Here four gigantic rocks sat in the stream, towering above us, and made five channels, in roaring through which the water dropped four feet. The captain chose the right-hand pass. He brought the steamer opposite to the rock which divided it from the next channel, back-paddled and held her till she had shifted out fairly to the passage, then drove her through at full speed. The vessel swung as she made it and each end nearly touched the vertical cliffs.

The Rink Rapids, a short distance below, were quite different and more feared. This was a considerable fall

of water, curving to the left in a bend. Rocks lined the
right hand, a beach made out on the left. As we
approached it many passengers crowded the deck just
before the pilot house, talking volubly. "Not a word
while we are going through!" roared the captain. He
reversed and held the vessel's stern as close as possible
to the left-hand side, sweeping along in the current,
letting the bow swing wide. The water presently brought
the bow inshore and then he drove ahead, watching the
left shore so fixedly that his eyes seemed bulging from
his head.

Four days out of White Horse we drew up at Dawson, the famed city of the Klondike, now a struggling
village of about 2,000 people, one-tenth of its one-time
population. The Klondike River and its tributary
creeks had yielded almost all their richness and were
now being picked over by giant dredges which let no
gold escape. In two years, we were told, they would
finish the Klondike.

A thirty-mile ride up the local railway, on flat cars
furnished with plank benches, revealed no great activity
aside from the dredging operations of two large companies. The most impressive monument of the former
workers was the vast piles of dirt torn from the hills and
creek bottoms, sluiced of their richest pay and heaped
aside. On these the dredges were working.

The largest gold dredge in the world sat in a muddy
pond, feeding itself in front from the bed, venting
itself at the other end, like some fabulous, prehistoric
monster. We crossed a gangway and entered its
resounding vitals. The noise stunned our ears. An
endless chain of great steel buckets tore loose the dirt
forty feet under water, biting a foot into bed-rock, and

fed their loads into a great steel cylinder perforated with holes. Larger stones clanged down this tilted cylinder and were carried directly out to the dump in the rear over a long elevated tail board; smaller dirt sifted through the holes and the heavy gold was caught at once in riffles. They said that the machine recovered five thousand dollars a day.

By name the Yukon began where the Pelly flowed into the Lewis, halfway between White Horse and Dawson. Below that, two great tributaries, the Stewart and the White, added a large volume to its main stream. We were now on a considerable river, which moved no longer hurriedly over steep rifts, but majestically, if still rapidly, boiling on the surface as its muddy water surged from the depths of its uneven bed.

The steep mountain heights, which pressed the upper stream into a narrow bottom, softened in outline at Circle City and drew back from a wider valley, which became eighty miles wide at Fort Yukon. The river broadened and was choked with low islands. A few houses on the bank formed a town, with a name printed boldly on the map. Such were Eagle, on the boundary, and Circle City. Other names on the map were mere epitaphs of a forgotten cabin: as Star and Nation.

We crossed the Arctic Circle for the first time at Fort Yukon, a naturally desirable site for a settlement, near the mouth of the large Porcupine River. One of the earliest trading posts in Alaska, of the Hudson Bay Company, Fort Yukon remained an important fur dealing center. To it the trappers brought each spring their winter catches of fox, marten, mink, weasel, bear and lynx, from the Porcupine and Black Rivers countries. Through the valley of the Porcupine was also a prac-

ticable route, nearly all by water, from the delta of the
Mackenzie River to the Yukon, with a portage of only a
few miles.   One trader had about 800 fox skins ready
for shipment.   Another resident had shot a large moose
about 300 miles up the Black River.   Shrunk considerably by drying though it was, the widest points were
still 68¾ inches apart.

A long distance to Fort Hamlin we threaded the shifting channels of the broad Yukon Flats, until the hills
pinched the stream together again at Rampart.   The
principal sight here was the cabin of Rex Beach, author
of stirring Alaskan stories.   Here we met Captain Mayo,
the trader in Beach's "The Barrier" and one of the most
famous old-time Yukon characters.

On we went, and at Tanana turned up the shallow
Tanana River toward Fairbanks.   If the Yukon was
tedious to navigate, the Tanana was worse.   The flat-
bottomed "Dawson," drawing less than four feet, habit-
ually brushed the bottom and frequently ran hard on the
edges of the channel.   Almost immediately she slid off
again, except once when it looked as if we might stay a
long time.   All these river boats carried long spuds,
great wooden beams, standing upright, one at each side
near the bow.   If fast aground they would set the lower
ends of these overboard, raise the bow by hauling on
tackles made fast to the upper ends and walk her off the
sand.   Only once did they cast off the stops and get
ready to use the spuds; but before they were lowered,
the current had washed her free again.   It was slow
going, for the pilot had to steer by reading the surface of
the water and often tried several courses before finding
one clear.   Then there was a wood pile to stop at about
twice a day, here, as well as on the Yukon, and several

FISH DRYING AND AGRICULTURE ON THE YUKON

Above: Salmon, split and hung to dry on frames at the river bank. Numerous dogs are usually tied to stakes at all villages to minimize their frequent quarrels.

Below: A government experimental farm at Rampart, where suitable plants and grains are being developed for the vast areas of favorable soil.

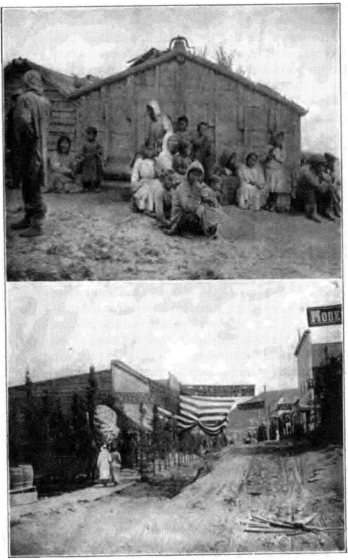

VILLAGE SCENES BY THE YUKON

Above: Athabascan Indians and one of their cabins in an interior town of Alaska.
Below: The main street of Ruby, a bonanza mining camp on the lower Yukon. The placer mining was done on creeks 30 miles north of the village through which all supplies were handled.

hours were spent loading fuel. Thick-skinned passengers debarked and took a walk at these points; others remained on board out of reach of the mosquitoes which swarmed on the river banks but not on the boat.

It took two whole days to beat the sand banks and the swift current up to Chena, some twelve miles from Fairbanks, and we were carried to the larger town by train.

Fairbanks housed about 2,000 persons, who received us hospitably and took our money readily. Prices were rather high: the smallest coin in circulation was a quarter dollar. It was immaterial whether one purchased a newspaper or a ten-cent cigar, or had one's shoes polished: "Two bits, please." Two boiled eggs in the restaurant were sold at seventy-five cents, reduced from one dollar.

A train ride to some of the placer mines made clear the scarcity of water which prevailed all summer throughout the country. Yet besides all this it was also evident from other sources that Fairbanks was declining. The many business men with whom we talked, optimistic though they must appear publicly by compulsion of popular sentiment, admitted, in a corner, that the future was dark. "If we only had the railroad from the south to develop the country!" But they gave the impression that they would be glad to sell out and try other fields. Some quartz had been found around Fairbanks, but not as yet in quantities warrantable to support a town like Juneau. The placer mines had, apparently, passed their period of great production, and would eventually be worked out. Strategically the city was placed badly, except only as a center for a large population profitably engaged in mining. A worked-out placer camp generally fades away, unless on some logical highway of commerce. Dawson might continue to be a stopping place on the Yukon long after its gold had been cleaned up, but there would be no geographical excuse for a railway touching Fairbanks.

"But you ought to see the wonderful fruit and vegetables raised here by So-and-so," someone, interested in agriculture, told us. We hunted him up at his greenhouse, in which a profusion of tomatoes, melons, cucumbers and other plants were thriving. Fresh tomatoes sold at seventy-five cents a pound. "I can't keep anything over the winter," he said, "except one or two flowers. Everything must be planted from seed and the summer is so short that they hardly have time to ripen, except by forcing under glass. I have made a living, but no amount of money."

Inquiries about the game of the neighborhood all led back to Harry Karstens. When one tried to locate a person in this, as in other towns, the answer frequently was, "You'll find him at the Northern, or the Palace," or one of the other bars. But not so with Karstens: "You'll probably find him at Hall's bookstore." Finally we tracked him down; a tall, strong, clear-eyed young man. He had been a partner of Hudson Stuck, the missionary, in their successful attempt to climb Mt. McKinley, and he told us that he had shared the expenses of the expedition.

Stuck seemed to have gotten all the credit in the newspapers for the achievement, but when we met him a few days later at St. Michael, Stuck said that he could not have made the ascent if Karstens had not pulled him through, and repeated this in his own published story. People in Fairbanks told us that Karstens was the man who brought the party back alive.

As for hunting, Karstens had made the Mt. McKinley region his own. He had spent much time there, hunting, trapping and studying animal life, with Charles Sheldon, of New York. For a congenial companion Karstens was willing, if he had leisure, to undertake a trip to the head of the Toklat River, about sixty miles east of Mt. McKinley, in the fall or winter, though he did not make a business of acting as guide. The game was moose, sheep, caribou and possibly bear.

When ready to evacuate Fairbanks we found the steamboat had been brought up the Chena River to the city. We turned skillfully in the narrow stream and reached the Yukon in half the time it had taken to come up, not without numerous bumps on the shallow flats at the mouth of the Tanana, and transferred to the steamer "Sarah," a larger ship of the same type as the "Dawson," but of a different line, the Northern Navigation Company.

Ruby had been heralded as a bonanza mining camp. It had produced a million in its brief career, but when we reached the town it gave every sign of an early demise. There was no bank in the place and we could not learn that one was expected; an indication that the knowing did not look for long-continued prosperity.

The rest of the lower Yukon was a repetition of what we had already seen for many days, save at Holy Cross Mission, where a roomful of native youngsters recited verses and songs of welcome, at the beck of a fluttering sister of the Roman Church.

Four days after leaving Fairbanks we anchored in the mouth of the Yukon, awaiting the flood tide to let us over the bar. Some of the young men on board put on bathing suits, one of them a woman's gear, and plunged overboard for a swim. Two Eskimos had come out in kayaks to trade ornamental needlework, and their narrow canoes were tried by the swimmers. When the man in female dress had crammed his legs and skirts with difficulty into the little round hole and pushed off, the kayak promptly upset and he had to paddle desperately with his hands to keep his head above water until the others reached him and helped him get out of the craft.

At St. Michael, some sixty miles from the river mouth, we finished the long journey in river boats on July 15th. We had traveled 2,651 miles on the Yukon and its tributaries in fifteen days since leaving White Horse, visiting many places in the interior of Alaska and had covered 7,563 miles from our homes on the Atlantic coast. But the real sport of the summer was not yet begun.

CHAPTER II

A S we entered St. Michael harbor on the river steamer "Sarah," the three-masted schooner "Abler" was one of the conspicuous boats at anchor there. She had come from Nome to meet us. A skiff was made fast astern of her; otherwise there was no sign of life.

"Where are your friends?" asked the fellow passengers of the "Sarah."

"Probably on the dock," we replied. But there was no Lovering or Kleinschmidt among those gathered to greet us.

We walked up the main street and down again to the harbor. Still no one emerged from the "Abler." Elting shouted; but in vain. From a warehouse he then got a megaphone, and hailed the schooner. A voice answered. Elting mentioned his name. "Well, what do you want?" came the reply.

"Collins, Scull and Elting are here, and we want you ashore," he answered.

"All right!" And presently the launch towing a dory put off, and brought Lovering, Kleinschmidt and two or three of the crew to the dock. Barely tasting our pleasure at this long anticipated meeting, we hurried to inquire the plans made, as we had only an hour. It had been our idea to go to Nome in the "Victoria," which lay ready to take on the "Sarah's" passengers, and then have the

3   (33)

"Abler" follow and pick us up there.   But Kleinschmidt objected to loss of time in lightering and possible prolonged delay if bad weather prevented this promptly, because landing must be effected at Nome on the open beach of the roadstead, for there was no harbor or shelter of any kind, and the big seas came in from the open water directly upon the strand.

Presently all our baggage was lowered with a rope over the "Sarah's" side into the dory, and taken out to the schooner.   Elting and I went on the "Sarah" to the "Victoria" to send off last letters and say good-bye to friends we had made and left.

On returning to St. Michael town we ran across Archdeacon Stuck, who had just made the first complete ascent of Mount McKinley with Harry Karstens of Fairbanks.

Collins and Lovering were meantime in the Northern Commercial Company's store buying mukluks, parkas, kamlaikas, and a few odds and ends which would be necessary to us in the far north.   Mukluks are Eskimo skin boots, made of seal or reindeer hide, most carefully and accurately sewed together by the native women, so that they are waterproof.   They are always worn over several pairs of stockings, and fitted with a removable felt or straw insole to keep the feet from getting damp. A parka is an Eskimo shirt, made of fur, with a fur hood which can be drawn over the head.   A kamlaika is a waterproof overshirt, with a hood similar to the parka, but the garment is made of the intestines of the walrus or seal, sewed together in strips with fine stitches.   These kamlaikas are made very large so that they will slip over a fur parka or other garment worn by the natives, and reach below the waist.   Their fullness permits them to be tied around the edges of the opening in the kayaks, or skin canoes, in which the Eskimos hunt seals and walrus during the spring and autumn months, when there is considerable ice in the water. By thus fastening their outer garment to the little boat, the natives are perfectly secure against dampness, and are able to perform extraordinary feats in rough water in their frail crafts, even to capsizing and righting themselves on the other side. A well made garment of this kind, which would completely cover a man down to his knees, weighs only a few ounces and is most convenient to carry in the far north, where every man has to take upon his own back all the things which are necessary for him to use in living for days or weeks away from a base of supplies.

The town of St. Michael is one of the oldest settlements in Alaska, built on the island of the same name, and is the best harbor near to the mouth of the Yukon River, from which it is sixty miles distant. The town, originally founded by the Russians as a trading post, has fallen into the hands of the Northern Commercial Company, which practically owns it. It is the headquarters for Alaska of this large corporation, which deals in furs obtained from the natives, supplies them and white settlers with provisions and other goods, and operates the only important line of boats plying regularly on the waters of the lower Yukon River. The town is picturesquely situated, and rises gradually from the beach to a slight elevation back of the docks, at which the steamers land.

Several stores appeared to be in fairly flourishing condition when we were there, but the town contained at most only a few hundred inhabitants. A considerable number of abandoned river steamers had been drawn up on the beach facing the outer harbor to end their days by gradually decaying at the mercy of the weather. The policy adopted by this Company in its business dealings seemed to be that of exacting all that the traffic would stand. Numerous complaints reached us of the extortionate charges, of tyrannical methods in dealing with people who fought its policy. The stories were similar to those told us about the White Pass and Yukon Route on the upper reaches of the river. These two concerns practically monopolized the trade of the interior of Alaska, and for many years worked in harmony with each other, but at this time were engaged in a bitter rate war, which affected chiefly the part of the river between Dawson and Fairbanks, where their lines overlapped.

As an instance of extortion, Elting was asked in St. Michael to pay the Northern Commercial Company three dollars an hour for the services of one of its half-breed carpenters to build a crate for his Arctic specimens.

St. Michael proudly possessed the most northern lighthouse in American territory, the nearest one being about 700 miles farther south, at the entrance to Unimak Pass, at the extreme western end of the Alaskan peninsula.

Captain Larsson, the sailing master of the "Abler," dearly loved to prolong his stays in port and not hurry out to the high seas. It took several hours to get our clearance papers. But eventually we weighed anchor about 4.30 P. M. of a beautiful, calm, clear day, and headed northeast to clear the harbor, and then westward toward Providence Bay on the coast of Siberia. The "Abler's" gasoline motor pushed us through the water at a rate of six miles an hour, and the island and town of St. Michael gradually faded away in the distance. Our course was laid in a straight line to Provi-

A HERD OF REINDEER ON THE YUKON

Several hundred reindeer were driven to water on the river bank and appeared nearly as tame as domestic cattle. The government restricts their ownership to the aborigines, and several individuals have become wealthy. The meat alone gives each animal a value of about twenty-five dollars.

MAP OF ALASKA SHOWING RAILWAYS AND STEAMSHIP LINES

Courtesy of Alaska Bureau, Seattle Chamber of Commerce

dence Bay, passing by the northern side of St. Lawrence Island, the largest isolated island in Bering Sea. It did not turn out that we were destined to follow this exact route, as indeed happened on almost every occasion when we drew a straight line upon the chart; but at the time of starting we were blissfully ignorant of what the "Abler" could do or could not do, according to the stress of wind and weather.

Meantime we unpacked our things and stowed them in our cabin, where we could use them at once, or in the hold of the ship, whence we could get them in case they were wanted. There were two staterooms in the after cabin house designed for the use of the four hunters. Elting and I drew the larger of these, with three bunks arranged in a tier, one above the other. Collins and Lovering obtained the smaller, with two berths.

Our neighbors' room measured six by six feet, of which the bunks left a floor space about four by six feet. There was a door communicating with our room, and we invited them to use so much of our apartment as they needed to put away their things. But after they had unpacked and hung up everything that they had on the walls of their cabin, and upon strings ingeniously rigged between all available projections of the walls and ceiling, there was hardly space to get into the room from the deck door, to say nothing of being able to open the communicating door into our cabin. They had a little stool to sit on, but generally crawled into their bunks and lay down, for lack of standing room on the floor. Everything in their stateroom was so behung with articles that their going to bed reminded me of an oriole retiring into its nest.

As promptly as possible we changed the clothes of

civilized bondage for the free and easy garments of the
wilderness.   A flannel shirt, breeches, boots or shoepacs, and a cap or cloth hat, were to be our outer shell
for the next few months.   We packed away in trunks
in the hold of the ship all the fine linens and carefully
woven textiles of the white man's existence in the centers
of fashion, and set ourselves to sorting out the articles
we had brought for real use and enjoyment.

When a man goes off on a long trip to a new country
he canvasses the things it will be necessary to take,
and after obtaining the information from the people
best informed or, if these are not available, from the
literature written about the country, makes up a list
of indispensable articles for that region.   After whittling
this down to its simplest elements, he gets its items
together.

Now the ideas of each man vary as to what is indispensable on a hunting trip, and the indispensables of
several men when added together make a good deal more
than are necessary to any one.   Consequently, on every
trip into new country, the traveler finds himself loaded
up with more than he really needs.   All the articles are
good and serviceable as a rule, but he finds afterwards
that he could have managed with less and thereupon
makes a resolve not again to furnish himself with so
much.

I still hope some day to realize the ideal of having
an outfit which is exactly sufficient, and not too much;
but it is not always easy to do in going into countries
where the conditions are very varied, and where they
are rather different from one's previous experiences.
When everything that we did not need on the ship was
stowed away below, there remained a considerable out-

fit in the cabin. Rather than recite the whole assortment, which contained many useless items, a list is given of what I would take on another summer cruise in the Arctic.

Personal Outfit.

Two United States Army flannel shirts, two suits woolen underwear, three pairs heavy woolen hose, three pairs light woolen hose, one Duxbak or Burberry hunting jacket, one suit of oilskins (hat, short coat, trousers), two pairs mukluks (Eskimo skin boots), one fur parka (Eskimo hooded fur shirt), one pair calked boots, one pair shoepacs (rubber soles and vamps, leather uppers), one pair slippers, one suit pajamas, one cap with ear flaps, one soft hat, three pairs woolen gloves, three pairs cotton gloves (as windbreaks over woolens), two pairs trousers (preferably of jungle cloth), one necktie, one belt, six handkerchiefs, one sleeping bag, books, toilet soap, tooth brush and dentifrice, talcum powder, razor, brush, shaving soap, hand mirror, brush and comb, three towels, two pipes, five pounds tobacco, pouch, cigarette papers, needles, thread, buttons, knife, pocket whetstone (coarse on one side and fine on the other), tape measure, green spectacles of fieuzal glass, head net, binoculars, kodak, twenty films, exposure meter, note book, pencils, fountain pen, ink, fly dope, brass tags for trophies, scales, clothes bag, a dozen small oiled bags for duffle, one fine tooth comb, insect powder, pocket compass, ten yards cheese cloth, simple medicines.

Arms.

One high-power rifle, 50 hard-point cartridges, 50 soft-point cartridges.

One .22 rifle, 1,000 cartridges.

One shotgun, 50 shells No. B.B. shot, 200 shells No. 4 shot, 200 shells No. 8 shot, 200 shells No. 10 shot.

Gun oil, rags, and rods, assorted fish hooks and lines.

Camping Outfit.

One light tent, one pack cloth, one folding lantern, one canvas bucket, two frying pans, three pots, plates, cups, knives, forks, spoons, can opener, one hatchet, 100 ft. $\frac{7}{16}$ in. rope, one pack bag or harness, one kerosene hot-flame stove, two 1-gallon oil cans.

Trading Goods for Small Curios.

Assorted needles, red, blue, black, white thread, leaf tobacco, plug tobacco, chewing gum, matches, best quality small tools.

Trading Goods for Furs, Ivory, etc.

Flour, sugar, automatic rifles and cartridges, saws, drills, vises, clocks, watches, sewing machines, cotton duck (white, brown and blue).

Among the most useful things was a series of charts of the coast of Alaska and Siberia, together with detailed charts of the various harbors which we expected to enter. It soon appeared that all those aboard the "Abler" were old, at least older than those we had just brought from Washington, and many of them were torn so that their use was difficult. Most of the work of navigation was therefore done with these new charts.

We put into the uppermost bunk, which was chin-high, all the clothing and things which we did not need to have at immediate hand. Elting took the middle berth; I rolled into the lowest one, which was on a level with the floor. The springs of these beds consisted of thin slats laid upon cross pieces at the ends. On these was spread an old blanket, and upon this we arranged our sleeping bags, unlaced, so that we could crawl into them without difficulty. In a few weeks, after I had got accustomed to this bed, I slept very comfortably. With the compulsory life-preserver, folded up and placed at the head of my bed, the space between that and the other end was exactly long enough to fit into. At the outer side of the bunk, a board about six inches high served to keep the occupant and his bed together. This good fit proved to be useful. When the "Abler" was performing her acrobatic feats in a storm the would-be sleeper wedged himself firmly at head and foot and, by drawing up one leg, braced himself sideways, with the knee against the board, reducing to a minimum the danger of battering his brains out by longitudinal motion, or of joining, by lateral rolling, the loose articles which were sliding about the stateroom floor.

Supper was served at five o'clock in the afternoon, according to ship's usage. To approach our food was a simple matter in smooth weather, but if a high sea was running it required something like the following maneuver:

Grasping the stateroom door knob, of which the latch was broken, one pushed stoutly outward against the strong wind, stepping to the narrow deck, which was about three feet wide, and seized the low rail, about two and a half feet high, to prevent one's self from being thrown overboard. Still holding the rail firmly, one shut the door with the other hand; then, by means of the rail making way along the deck a few yards, to the saloon door, one grasped this and pulled it open. Carefully choosing the right moment one made his spring into the dining saloon and pulled the door to after him with a bang.

The dining saloon was about fifteen feet long by eight feet wide. Forward on the port side a door opened into the captain's cabin, and on the starboard side a door into the galley. From the latter issued forth the dishes and the perfumes thereof, convoyed by the cabin boy, a young Eskimo. Down the two or three steps into the galley we could catch occasional glimpses of the Japanese cook, who in all kinds of weather managed to have a meal ready at the proper hour. An ingenious system of wires strung across the top of the stove kept the pots and pans in their places and prevented any wholesale destruction of food even in a severe storm. Under his ministration we never lost more than one or two dishes at any one time. The crew and the Eskimos lived in the forecastle in the extreme bow of the ship, and ate their meals somewhere there. All the rest of us, passengers and officers, dined at one mess in the saloon.

The full sitting of the mess was twelve souls, packed around an oblong table, close to one side of the saloon. Between this and the wall five of us sat on a narrow wooden bench. At one end of the table Ed Born, the owner and engineer of the "Abler," had his accustomed seat on a little, old iron safe.

Ed Born was a powerfully built man, with a handsome Roman face, black hair, and a good-natured smile. He was full of humor and enjoyed a joke, even if it was on himself. As owner of the ship he might have taken everything much more seriously and been a "kill-joy," but he left the navigation to the captain and mate, and asserted himself only a few times when things looked threatening to his interests. He was a force that lay in the background, and yet carried the responsibility.

All the rest of the men drew up stools to the table. At the opposite end to Born was Captain Larsson, a tall man, rather bulky at the belt, from vigorous abstinence from exercise, with mild, blue eyes, and a sandy moustache. He was deliberate in movement and very scrupulous in performing the legal requirements which enmesh the procedure of a ship entering and clearing port. He was born in Sweden and educated as a mechanical engineer, but early ran away to sea and worked up to the rank of master. Among other things he had been a salt trader between Portugal and Brazil, a yachting captain in southern California, a sealer in Bering Sea, and proprietor of a machine shop in Seattle. A more polite man never drank whisky.

Ed Born's brother Frank was assistant engineer. Dark like Ed, Frank was smaller and slighter. He had a short leg, which had been broken when he was a boy and badly set. Frank always had a hearty laugh ready, and never carried anybody's troubles except those of his own watch below in the engine room. An evening in port would make him open his soul to his friends.

At Captain Larsson's right hand, figuratively and literally, sat Mate Carl Hansen. Born in Norway, the mate had spent thirty of his forty-six years at sea. He had been counted dead of yellow fever at Santos, Brazil, had been caught in a tidal wave at Shanghai, and had been stabbed in the head at Singapore. On the Pacific coast somewhere he had been a successful pugilist: an excellent training for mate of a ship. "Mate," as every-one called him, was of medium height, compactly built, self-possessed in every emergency, a thoroughly experienced seaman; cautious, yet full of courage. His thick hair and moustache were rather bright red, and a week's growth of beard gave him a florid appearance. He was inclined to be ready to manufacture an offence out of a fancied slur. The mate proved to be the best man on the ship for navigation and emergency, and more than once pulled us out of tight places when the captain had given up the job. He was at home in the ice, in which kind of work Captain Larsson was inexperienced, and we came to have great confidence in the mate's judgment and seamanship. He used as a panacea for all ills "Quaker Balm," guaranteed under the Pure Food and Drugs Act to be a combination of opium and alcohol, but for sociability's sake preferred a mixed drink called "smotherins," half port and half whisky.

Captain Kleinschmidt sat on Larsson's left. Of middle size and age, the manager of the expedition was impetuous himself and impatient of others not equally quick. This was his misfortune apparently, for he tried hard to accomplish everything and stood a lot of bad knocks without much grumbling. He looked, as he was, a native of Germany, and had long been a sailor before making a stake at Dawson. Subsequently he carried mail at Teller, Alaska, had spent considerable time in Kotzebue Sound, and had also been in the Arctic. Latterly he had taken up bird collecting for museums and motion-picture photography as a business. Captain Larsson declined to recognize his title, which was that of a river skipper, and punctiliously called him Mr. Kleinschmidt.

MEMBERS OF THE HUNTING PARTY   *Photo. A. M. Collins*

Left to right: Alfred M. Collins, Dr. Arthur W. Elting, Gilpin Lovering, Capt. F. E. Kleinschmidt, E. Marshall Scull

PERSONNEL OF THE "P. J. ABLER"   *Photos. A. M. Collins and Gilpin Lovering*

Frank Born, Assistant Engineer   Ed Born, Owner and Engineer   Captain Larson
Cabin Boy   Cook Ikede   Cook Meyer   Rev. S. Hall Young, D.D.   Taxidermist Kusche

Mate Hansen
Taxidermist Albrecht

One of the most entertaining of our companions was the Rev. S. Hall Young, D.D. Small and thin, with a sparse, gray beard and hair, his eyes quickly observant behind spectacles, Doctor Young's insistent voice penetrated every conversation on any subject, and since he had spent most of the time in Alaska as a missionary since 1879 he had a storehouse of information. But a boundless optimism for the country's resources and prospects tinctured his opinions, and laid them sometimes open to argument.

Young was a strong chess and checker player, a tireless reader, an enthusiastic hunter of every kind of bird and animal, large or small. He killed a good caribou on his sixty-sixth birthday, packed the head four miles, wading an icy stream in doing so, and was consequently flattened out by lumbago. He was superintendent of the Presbyterian missions in Alaska. His daughter was Mrs. Kleinschmidt, and he was the guest of his son-in-law for the summer.

Collins, Elting and I sat on the bench against the wall; and on the opposite side of the table Lovering was placed between the two taxidermists. These were "Professor" Kusche and Albrecht. Kusche was short but strong, with rosy cheeks and a heavy moustache, and was quiet and deferential. He laughed off and avoided any argument, except those about birds or insects. Kusche spent most of his time aboard skinning the birds which Kleinschmidt and Dr. Young brought in to be prepared, and in tramping for beetles and birds when ashore. He was by profession a landscape gardener in charge of the grounds of an institution for the feebleminded in California. He was the only man of our mess who foraged with his knife.

Albrecht, on the other side of Lovering, was a student
of the University of Iowa, working in a museum at the
same time. He was a tall young fellow of sallow complex-
ion, rather inclined to take things easily, since, as he put
it, "I thought I was coming on a vacation."

To the reader 'who, after the foregoing description
of the "Abler's" personnel, still does not understand
the organization of our expedition, I may say that we
ourselves never fully comprehended it either, as the
hierarchy shifted rank according to circumstances. We
four hunters were called "passengers." The other *dra-
matis personæ* were as follows:

Captain Larsson, sailing master; Carl Hansen, mate;
Ed Born, owner of the "Abler" and chief engineer;
Frank Born, assistant engineer: Captain Kleinschmidt,
lessee of the ship and manager of the cruise; Dr. Young,
father-in-law and guest of Kleinschmidt; Kusche and
Albrecht, taxidermists; Ikede, Japanese cook; Jimmie,
cabin boy; four or five ordinary sailors (who frequently
deserted and were recruited anew).

All of these men had lodgings in different parts of the
ship from that which we occupied. Captain Larsson
and Dr. Young lived in the little cabin just off the dining
saloon on the port side. Ed and Frank Born and the
mate occupied a cabin off the engine room, immediately
below the dining saloon, and Kleinschmidt, Albrecht
and Kusche had a stateroom underneath ours, at the stern
of the ship. Doctor Young spent most of the time on
board, lying on his back in the upper berth of his stateroom, reading a book, or playing chess or checkers when
he was up and about. Albrecht was the other chief sufferer
when the waves ran high, but instead of remaining below
he sat about the saloon, often with his head in his hands.

There were times when the rest of us found it more comfortable to keep to our beds, and, in truth, there was nothing much to get up for, if one did not feel like eating.

For the first meal, and for some time after that, the cabin boy ran around the deck ringing a bell. We all gathered in the dining saloon. Delicious steaks were served from two reindeer carcasses that had been shipped at St. Michael; salmon cutlets and sundry vegetables, coffee or tea, fruit and pudding augured well for the future.

The morning of our second day on board dawned bright and calm. We were making good progress toward the coast of Siberia. Jimmie, the cabin boy, called us at six-thirty, and breakfast was served at seven. Dinner at noon was announced by a hand-bell, like supper of the evening before. Jimmie was most attentive to our comfort. He saw that the little tin bottle, which contained water for our toilet and was placed in a little washstand, was always filled; and that the waste can under the tin basin of the stand was always empty. I think on one of those early days I saw him also making an attempt to sweep out our stateroom. After much tossing in the sea had worn off the keen edge of Jimmie's finer feelings we did all these things for ourselves.

It will be seen from the foregoing description that the "Abler's" cabin house was a high affair of light wooden construction placed on the poop deck, and contained our two staterooms, the dining saloon, galley and captain's room. Just forward and pressed up against this cabin the pilot house rose a few feet higher into the air. Forward of that the main deck stretched about eighty feet up to the bow. The main deck was about three feet above the water line, and protected from the combers by a stout bulwark with scuppers at the deck edge. There were two hatches on deck. The forward hatch lay between the fore and the main masts; the after hatch between the main and the spanker. A large iron tank holding five hundred gallons of gasoline was firmly fastened to the deck just forward of the after hatch, and there were various loose barrels on the deck at all times, together with some large iron drums in which Klein-schmidt had brought up low grade gasoline or distillate, for engine fuel. More of these iron drums were stowed in the hold, and he had deposited a number of them at St. Michael and also farther south in Pirate Cove in southwestern Alaska, to be used upon the return voyage. At the end of the trip, therefore, the decks were almost completely full of gasoline drums. In addition to this bulky cargo a launch on the starboard side and a large dory on the port side were lashed in place.

Provisions, trading goods with which to pay off such natives as we might hire, and the thousand and one other things found on every ship were stowed in the hold under the forward and after hatches, in such a manner that after they had been sorted over a few times it was almost impossible to find any article that might be required.

CHAPTER III

THUS we were on our way to the coast of Siberia at its extreme eastern point, the Chukchi peninsula, which juts out from the great mass of Asia nearly to the shore of North America. Our course lay in a direct line some 220 miles from Nome, and therefore about 335 miles from St. Michael, to Providence Bay. But hardly had we been twenty-four hours on board when the wind began to freshen and the barometer showed an inclination to fall. The breeze kept increasing from the northwest on our starboard bow. In the evening the sails were eased and we had to change our course to three-quarters before the wind, to pass south of St. Lawrence Island and get under its lee. Captain Larsson looked for a blow, and if it came upon us close to the northward of St. Lawrence Island, we could not claw off the lee shore. This was our first intimation that the "Abler" would not make way to windward against a breeze and a moderate sea. She could do only six knots an hour under gasoline alone with her eighty-five horse-power motor, and a head sea combined with the windage on the high cabin house made progress little or nothing against a good wind.

All hands turned out for supper, but soon after that Elting took to his bed, Dr. Young to the rail, and Collins to the fresh air. Elting exchanged bunks with me, as the lower one was easier to get into. All through the night the "Abler" drove through the quartering sea and occasionally a great wave would slap against the house. I rose three times in the night and went on deck in my thin pajamas to see if the island was in sight. A piercing chill was coming down from the distant northern ice, the thermometer recording 37 degrees, F., and I returned to my blanket quickly. To me, ignorant of the "Abler," and peeping through the little pane of glass at my bed head, the crested seas seemed vicious, and kept me uneasy all night, for fear that we should be unable to work up to the island if we were carried off too far to leeward, and that we should be blown far south of our course. As the blow increased to forty miles an hour, and might have been able to rise to one hundred and forty for all that I knew, it crossed my mind several times that we might possibly be in for something serious. After we got used to the "Abler" a trifling breeze like this never annoyed us. The captain kept her to it with the fore sail on, and at six next morning land was sighted. During the forenoon we rounded under the lee of Southeast Cape, St. Lawrence Island, where the sea was still choppy, but not menacing, and proceeded on our way about three or four miles from the shore. Here it was much more comfortable. The wind slackened somewhat; the sun came out and warmed us a bit. Several of us did not get up for breakfast, but all enjoyed some more reindeer meat at lunch.

The bold Southeast Cape of St. Lawrence Island looked forbidding, and the snow-capped mountains cooled off the wind so that it was about 44 degrees, F., in our cabin in the morning. We held outside the reefs, several miles off shore and the south coast trending northward in a great sweep, to jut out again at the Southwest Cape, took the land out of sight as we plowed along, except for the loftier mountains on the promontories.

We were now headed N. W. by N., making about four and one-half knots with the motor, and the foresail set. "Jenny," the engine, palpitated every now and then, but caught her breath again in a moment and churned patiently on.

Elting turned out for dinner, feeling fit again, and Dr. Young, who, the evening before, nearly let himself be knocked overboard by the main boom without a protest, also came out. Jimmie, the cabin boy, had served breakfast between his spasms of eructation, and omitted all his other duties. The smoother water, gentler if chilly breeze, a fine red sunset at 10 P. M., cheered all hands. It was decided to buck the sea around the west end of the island and make for Providence Bay against the wind and the presumably heavy swell. About midnight we passed the Southwest Cape and headed north in a gentle ground swell and light northwest breeze. The gaunt, rocky cliffs, flecked with snow in spots down to the water's edge, moved slowly by as we turned into bed.

Breakfast the next day found us still going comfortably on our course in a light northwest wind with West Cape astern, and Cape Chibukak abeam. To keep our jib, foresail and spanker full, we had to lay considerably off our proper course. The water changed in color from dark green to blue as we drove over the thirty fathom depths, and again to green as we shoaled up to ten or twelve fathoms. The bold headlands of St. Lawrence Island sank as the crags of the Siberian coast lifted above the horizon, both being plainly visible most of the way. Like those of the island, the latter stood steep from the sea with snow fields in their ravines.

Birds frequently passed us or rose from the water as we approached; red-legged guillemot, lesser auk in little flocks skimming the surface, phalarope and fulmar.

During the afternoon three sailboats hove in sight, a few miles off the coast. Two of them were taken in tow of our vessel at once, and with one we held converse. The bow man spoke English, and as he tended the walrus-hide tow line, told us they had killed three walrus in the neighborhood. The meat of two was in their boat, and presently we came up with the seal-skin float which marked the third. Jimmie said they spoke "nearly Japanese." He could not understand them in Eskimo. The Japanese cook looked on them with disdain. These natives were Chukchi.

"You make good trade?" inquired their spokesman.

"Yes," replied Kleinschmidt. And while we were meditating what rare values we might get from the innocent native he asked,

"How much whalebone a pound gold in Nome?"

"About ninety cents," was Kleinschmidt's answer.

This caused some consultation in the whaleboat. Thinking to make the quotation understood, Kleinschmidt held up a silver dollar.

"You sabe dollar?" he asked.

"Me sabe; yes."

Kleinschmidt made as if to tear a small piece out of it. "Not dollar; ninety cents!" he explained.

"Oh, yes; me sabe ninety cents," the man replied; and continued, "How much for walrus ivory?"

But about this time the Chukchi cast off from us and went to the float of the remaining walrus, which had already been skinned.

The wind had forced us, in order to use our sails, to head somewhat eastward of our course, and as we approached the Siberian coast it was seen that we had to turn and crawl toilsomely against the light breeze for

Photo. A. M. Collins

CHUKCHI UMIAK AT PROVIDENCE BAY.

The boat is a framework of wood covered with walrus hides, used in summer, when the water is free of ice, for long expeditions, walrus and whale hunting. The owner's whole family and dogs usually accompany him.

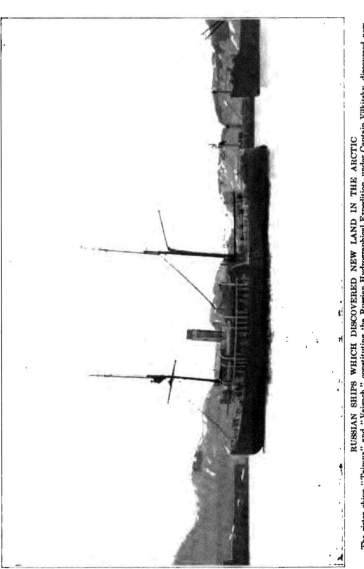

RUSSIAN SHIPS WHICH DISCOVERED NEW LAND IN THE ARCTIC

The sister ships "Taimyr" and "Vaigach," constituting the Russian Hydrographical Expedition, under Captain Vilkitsky, discovered new islands north of Cape Chelyuskin in the summer of 1913. They were photographed in Emma Harbor where they were coaling from a supply ship.

about ten miles to the entrance of Providence Bay, keeping a mile off the end of Bald Head to avoid the reefs there.

Once inside the jaws, a splendid fiord opened ahead. The rough, rocky sides of the hills appeared to have been cleared of earth, except where delicate yellow-green grass tinted the soil, filling the lower parts of many ravines. Here and there snow patches persisted, even close down to the water.   Not a stick of timber or brush was to be seen in any direction either on mountain or valley.   The grayish-brown mountains, flecked with ochre-colored earth and dirty snow, were inhospitable and dreary in their majesty.

A few miles within the entrance we made out a half dozen huts and fish-drying stands on a low sandspit to starboard. This was Plover Bay; a safe anchorage except in northerly gales.   On we went, however, as the sun dipped below the western hills, and where the fiord bent to the west entered the better mooring ground of Emma Harbor.

A black steamer lay ahead.   To our glasses she gave no token of nationality or purpose, but hardly had we sounded the bottom and let go a mud hook when a boat put off from her and came toward us.   Meanwhile a few glances took in all there was to see of the tiny settlement on the eastern beach.   A substantial and even pretentious house of squared logs, with scroll-work eaves jigged from planks, sat between two other outbuildings, and was the residence of Baron von Kleist, Governor of the province northward to East Cape and under the Kamchatka Governor.   A few other light spots indicated tents, occupied by the native inhabitants.   Save where the harbor entrance gave a vista to the west side of Providence Bay, and to the south, where a low reach of tundra extended to the sea, barren mountains shut in the port completely, openings in them being blocked by more distant ridges and peaks.

The boat from our neighbors arrived and discharged on our deck several sailors, a second officer in uniform, an interpreter who spoke German, and the Russian servant of Baron von Kleist. It turned out that the vessel was a Russian supply ship, awaiting the arrival of two ice-breakers, which were on their way north, and were expected next day. The Baron was absent in Anadyr, about two hundred and fifty miles west, on his boat with his young bride, and would not be back for two weeks. The officer looked at Collins' and Elting's passports, and declared they would not permit us to shoot, collect butter-flies, or stay in the harbor except to take on water. As for obtaining hunting licenses that was out of the question.

"You might try tomorrow," he said, "to telegraph to Anadyr Bay and ask the Baron to give you a permit, if the captains of the ice-breakers are willing to do that for you by wireless."

It looked dubious when we went to bed, but the ice-breakers offered a hope.

Two able-looking black vessels now lay near the supply ship. Their bows rockered up from the water about eight feet abaft the stem, and, with an over-hanging rounded angle, rose vertically to a high forepeak. Their torpedo sterns showed a loaded draft of twenty feet. They constituted the Russian Hydrographical Expedition, which had been for several seasons surveying and charting the eastern and northern coast of Siberia.

Kleinschmidt, Elting and Collins boarded them to

prospect the ground; Dr. Young and "Professor" Kusche landed, taking lunch, butterfly nets and bottles to gather insects and birds, for which purpose the latter carried a walking-stick cane.

Kusche had this weapon made for him by a gun-smith in Los Angeles in 1892. It consisted of an out-side barrel, of steel which was originally Damascus swords, to shoot .55-90 shells loaded with birdshot. Inside of this fitted a .38-55 Winchester barrel, turned down to slip in, and within this a brass tube for firing .22 cartridges. The small right-angle handle contained a trigger and folding hammer. It was necessary to un-screw the handle from the barrel to load or to slide out what barrels were not to be used. The steel was wrapped with black tape to disguise its object. "The gun was originally as long as a walking stick," explained the Professor, "and I carried an oak plug in it to keep out dirt when in use as a cane. One day, however, I fired it off hastily, without removing the plug and several inches burst off the end of the barrel. It got damaged again in the canyons near Los Angeles when my burro kicked up a wild cat and the beast got me by the leg before I could pull the cork out of the gun. I hit the cat a blow with it; the gun went off and killed it, but blew several more inches off the barrel. Another time I got into a lot of rattlesnakes. After shooting two in the head, a third appeared and I said to myself, 'there's too many of them,' so I clubbed that one with the gun, and one after another until I had killed six. The barrel was considerably bent by this, but I put it through the fork of a tree and straightened it out and it shot as true as ever." Kusche used the weapon for getting birds, and could hit remarkably well with it. He said he had killed a wild goose at 160 yards, and once brained a deer with a .22 bullet. He used only shot in the .55 and round balls in the .38 barrels.

Captain Larsson and Ed Born went ashore while Lovering and I stayed aboard. During this time a couple of skin boats floated out with a half score of Chukchi visitors. They wore mukluks, red wadded close-fitting breeches and loose parkas. The men had the central portion of the top of the head trimmed very short over a patch about four inches in diameter, and the rest of the hair, left long, was combed down uniformly on all sides, giving a rather attractive style to their head dress. Word was passed around to lock doors and leave nothing portable exposed, as the natives would steal whatever they could. This lot, however, stood about patiently, offering, when asked what they had to trade, a few seal skins and coils of walrus-skin rope.

We did not put temptations in their way, but perhaps they were not so bad. When Nordenskjöld wintered in 1878 at Kolyuchin Bay, on his famous voyage through the Arctic from Europe, he said this of the Chukchi: "All who came on board were allowed to go about without let or hindrance on our deck which was encumbered with a great many things. We had not, however, to lament the loss of the merest trifle."

Their skin boats, or umiaks, were flat bottomed, somewhat like a dory, but sharp at both ends, with raking stems and no rocker of the keel. A flat kelson ran the length of the floor, the bilge stringer was sprung out by floors at the bottom; the frames flared and were held by thwarts midway to the gunwale, all being lashed in place with sinew. Several light stringers at each side of the kelson and others at the overhanging sides served to prevent the skin covering from caving in.   This was of raw hide, stretched over the outside, carried inboard over the gunwale and laced to one of the stringers just above the line of thwarts.   At bow and stern the gunwales did not meet, but ended about four inches beyond the end of the stem, and half that distance from each other.   The skins were fitted and sewed to stretch taut and waterproof.   Oarlock sockets were lashed to the gunwales and the oars fashioned from a single timber.   These Chukchi boats at this harbor were about twelve feet long.   Those used in the Arctic for whaling and walrus hunting farther out at sea were as much as thirty feet long.

Kleinschmidt and the launch party soon returned from the Russian vessels with the information that we should come back about noon and learn if we could use their wireless.   In the interval all went ashore to see the town.   The Baron's servant watched our every move. He objected to our cameras; when Elting, Collins and Lovering started out across Rosene Creek toward some native tents, he seemed uneasy but could not convey his thoughts to them, so they paid no attention to him.   To ease his mind Albrecht put his camera in the launch before joining the others on their walk.   Kleinschmidt and I waited at the house, observing the lace curtains and such other evidences of woman's care as showed through the windows.   It was a forlorn post for a young woman to live in, and I pitied her.

Noon found us at the gang-way of the "Vaigach," one of the Russian ice-breakers.   A group of officers welcomed us cordially and the ship's doctor, a short man with long reddish moustache, introduced all hands in excellent English.   "Will you kindly come to the ward room," he invited, and we filed below.   Elting conversed in German with two of them and I discovered two more who spoke French. A steward soon began to piece out the table and in a few moments we found ourselves at lunch with the hospitable fellows. We were a dozen at the board. Commander Vilkitsky in charge of the expedition, the captain of the ship Lieutenant-Commander Peter Novopashenny, Lieutenant Nicolas Helchert, the doctor Eduard Arnhold, the chief engineer and the two navigating officer were our hosts. I sat between Elting and Helchert, who spoke French. On the other side of Elting, the chief engineer fed him in German. Across the table the doctor held forth in English and there was a constant undertone of Russian.

Vodka whetted the appetite; sardines and other appetizers foretasted a formal banquet. Soup, chicken, vegetables, marsala, madeira, beer, salad, ice cream frozen with snow, coffee and liqueurs, interspersed with cigarettes and followed by cigars, completely satiated us and left us torpidly hearkening to the strain of Russian songs on the phonograph.

"You have been very kind," some one remarked, "to share your luxurious fare with us. You must live high if it's always like this aboard."

"Oh, we are very glad to see you," one of the officers replied. "We never have anything to drink unless we have guests."

The officers reassured us considerably about our liability of getting into difficulties if we landed in Siberian harbors without a permit from Baron von Kleist, or other official source. On account of the high mountains they could not telegraph by wireless to Anadyr. We should have cleared and obtained our papers at Petropavlovsk in Kamchatka, some twelve hundred miles distant.

To lay down the law to the Baron's servant, the chief engineer went ashore with us and the poor fellow, Zolotoroff by name, was uncomfortably placed between two fires. Collins and Lovering took a little rifle and revolver to blaze away with on a walk up the creek, while the rest of us inspected the summer igloos of the few miserable Chukchi residents. They were the remnants, the poverty-stricken weaklings of the tribe, who were practically supported by the Baron. Tuberculosis and trachoma were in evidence. Inside the canvas wall-tents, of which the ropes were anchored by boulders, was erected a square tent of reindeer hide, about five feet high. On lifting the side curtain we disclosed naked men and women sleeping together on a bed of skins, about six inches thick. Their heads lay on the edge of the bed just where the curtains fell to it, and, to get a breath of fresh air, they poked their faces through under the curtain. They turned up their visages dully curious at us, but did not rise. One of the men offered walrus ropes, seal skins and harpoons to trade. Albrecht bought a coil of rope for twenty-five cents and a spear head in sheath for the same price. A Singer sewing machine stood in the corner of one igloo and an alarm clock hung from the beam.

Elting and I went in the launch with shotguns and got about twenty phalarope, as these little snipe were darting about on the surface of the smooth bay, snapping up insects. Kleinschmidt netted them, while Albrecht steered the boat. Just before returning to the schooner we killed a violet-green cormorant. Kusche returned with a bag full of birds and bugs; Dr. Young with insects and sore feet from his ten-mile tramp in mukluks; Collins and Lovering with reports of no pasturage for game in the mountains back of the village. Several of the Russian officers on the ice-breakers came aboard after dinner, among them Baron von Hoininghen-Huehne, after whom I had inquired on the "Vaigach." He was a tall young midshipman with a budding beard. Lieutenant Helchert stayed until after midnight and partook of our cold supper, and we had a long conversation. He said that the revenue cutter usually patrolling the coast was detailed near Kamchatka and that no Cossacks were on duty south of Kolyma River, which runs into the Arctic Ocean about nine hundred miles west of East Cape.

These two ice-breakers, the "Vaigach" and the "Taimyr," had proceeded from Vladivostok to the point where we met them under orders to sail through Bering Strait into the Arctic Ocean, and attempt to reach St. Petersburg by the Arctic, a feat which had never yet been successfully accomplished, although Nordenskjöld in 1878 had made the passage eastward from Europe to Bering Strait. After we returned from the Arctic to Alaska we learned that our Russian friends had not succeeded in reaching St. Petersburg but had discovered a new group of islands far north in the Arctic, and had returned to St. Michael with this important news.

These two Russian ships rounded Cape Deshnef August 6th, and the "Taimyr" proceeded westward along the coast, while the "Vaigach" was sent north to ascertain the condition of the ice. Through many loose floes she succeeded, on August 12th, in reaching a point within ten miles of Wrangell Island, where the heavy ice prevented closer approach. Thus while we were at Herald Island the "Vaigach" was about one

SIBERIAN HUT OF BOARDS

Photo. A. M. Collins

In constructing this residence the owner had exceeded the bounds of Chukchi extravagance by collecting a great quantity of wood in a country where trees are unknown, and driftwood or wrecks are the main source of supply. The numerous dogs are typical of all native villages.

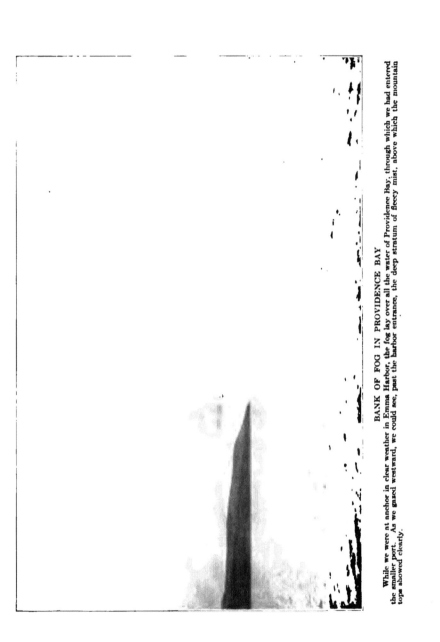

BANK OF FOG IN PROVIDENCE BAY

While we were at anchor in clear weather in Emma Harbor, the fog lay over all the water of Providence Bay, through which we had entered the smaller port. As we gazed westward, we could see, past the harbor entrance, the deep stratum of fleecy mist, above which the mountain tops showed clearly.

hundred miles west of us and nearly as far north. A week later the "Taimyr" found a new small island northeast of New Siberia.

Both vessels were at Cape Chelyuskin, the most northerly projection of Asia, on September 1st, but unbroken ice barred further progress westward. To find a passage they steamed northeast for thirty miles until a new, long, narrow island was sighted. Around the eastern side of this they went and steered northwest. Thirty miles farther north they discovered new, high land containing glaciers. Landing parties surveyed twenty miles of the eastern coast and hoisted the Russian colors on its northern shore at a point 80° 4' north latitude, 90° 12' east longitude. In an effort to find a way around the new island the ice-breakers pushed beyond sight of the land to 81° N., 96° E., but were compelled by very heavy ice to return to Cape Chelyuskin.

Here it was found that the ice-pack, at least forty miles broad and three to four feet thick, was an impassable barrier. Commander Vilkitsky therefore ordered the expedition to return eastward.

They surveyed Bennet Island and recovered the collections of Baron von Toll, who had perished in the Arctic many years before, after rounding Cape Chelyuskin, and started south September 22d. New ice was now occasionally found and the navigation became difficult, but the water was open after 70° N. and 180° E.

Fierce storms obliged even these stout ships to seek shelter at times, but they reached St. Michael October 9th and thence went to Petropavlovsk in Kamchatka.

At 1.30 A.M. the "Abler" weighed anchor and passed out into the dense fog which lay like a layer of wool over all the waters of Providence Bay. The fog remained thick about us until the middle of the afternoon. On leaving Providence Bay at four o'clock in the morning, the captain laid his course to clear Indian Point (Cape Chaplin) by several miles and breakfast time found us running before a heavy wind which had made the schooner behave most uncomfortably during the night. When supposedly abreast of the long, low sandspit making out from Indian Point he changed his course for the Point according to his dead reckoning. We were now rolling heavily in the quartering sea. The fog shut out everything a few hundred yards distant, and the repeated blasts of our fog horn brought no answering echo from the cliffs. At any moment we might suddenly see the surf under the bow, and then it would be a question if the flat, underpowered old "Abler" would be able to scratch away from the lee shore long enough to pass the danger. Most of us spent our time, while waiting to see what would happen, playing dominoes in the cabin.

A serious situation had developed between Kleinschmidt and Ed Born which threatened to prevent our having a chance to hunt in Siberia. Although the two men were friends fifteen years before and had frequently done business together, they had fallen out on this trip before we boarded the vessel in St. Michael, and Born now refused to enter any more ports in Siberia because we had not found an official to clear us at Emma Harbor. Kleinschmidt was angered and it looked as if the bad feeling might jeopardize the rest of our trip. Accordingly when we casually entered the pilot house and found Born and Larsson there it was not a surprise for the former to say, "Well, I guess we will have to put into Nome."

That opened the subject and we talked it over for about an hour.   After it had been emphasized that we had no part in any controversy and that all personal differences should be settled after the voyage was carried out as planned, and should not be allowed to spoil the trip, Born came over handsomely and agreed to coast up Siberia as we desired.   The friendly atmosphere appeared once more to have been restored.

It presently proved that we had overrun our reckoning and gone past Indian Point before we changed our course to pick it up.   We ran through the fog-bank and found ourselves about sixteen miles eastward of our supposed position.   Indian Point lay far on our weather quarter and the snow-streaked mountains of Kayne Island in Seniavine Strait lay dead ahead about fifteen miles away.   We were too far to leeward of the land to hold the course we most desired because of the "Abler's" inability to go against the strong wind. Instead of being able to get in between Ittygran and Kayne Island we were forced to go under the lee of Kayne Island and sail almost around it through Chiyarliun Pass at its north to an anchorage in the shelter north of Ittygran Island opposite Glazenap Harbor.

CHAPTER IV

UNDISCOVERED SHEEP IN ASIA

A T this point Kleinschmidt on his way to Nome, before meeting us, had learned from the Chukchi chief, Tangana, that mountain sheep were supposed to live in the hills somewhere northward. Collins and Elting now went with him in the launch from our anchorage to inquire further about them. Several natives had come out to us in a large skin boat with their wives, children, dogs and skins. Kleinschmidt put the rest of us ashore and towed the skin boat to their village around a point several miles away. Kusche and Dr. Young went off with shotguns to collect birds, and secured a Pacific eider duck, red-throated loon and young ones, a Mongolian plover and young, and some phalarope. Returning in the launch Kleinschmidt and Elting shot two slaty-back gulls, two pigeon guillemot, and a horned puffin.

Lovering and I fired in vain at some eider ducks with a .22 rifle and then climbed over the saddle of the hills at the northwest corner of the island. The hills were covered with sharp loose stones, large and small, blackish from exposure, where not covered with red, green, cream or orange and black lichens. Much of the hillside showed gaudy red tints of iron and Kleinschmidt said he came upon a chunk which was extremely heavy. Between the tumbled heaps of stone the draws were covered with tundra, moist from the undercurrent of running water,

which here and there came to the surface in deliciously
clear and cool springs.   Many brilliant flowers decked
the mossy tundra; yellow, purple, light blue, rose, red,
and white.   Little low creepers resembled cherry trees
and junipers, though hardly protruding above the moss,
but the willow grew several inches tall.

We were all aboard by noon and the schooner got
under way, with two natives from the distant village on
board to guide us to the supposed sheep country.   Not
that they knew anything themselves about it, but others
who herded reindeer in Penkegnei Bay, the northern arm
of Seniavine Strait, had brought three sheep carcasses
to trade earlier in the spring.   The animals were said to
be small and darkish but with the characteristic curling
horns of the wild sheep as found in America.

It was highly interesting to us to hear this, for no
mountain sheep had been discovered as far north and
east as this; their known haunts in Eastern Asia being
confined to the Stanovoi Mountains in Northern Siberia
and the Peninsula of Kamchatka.   Dr. C. Hart Merriam,
of the Biological Survey, told me after our return, however, that he had seen sheep horns some years previously
at Plover Bay.

We were ultimately destined to disappointment in our
quest for sheep at this point, but were finally convinced
that the sheep existed not far from the head of the bay
in which we lay at anchor.   Five days were to be wasted
in a vain attempt to go inland and hunt for them.

Upon arrival we went ashore in the launch and while
Kleinschmidt interviewed the families of the deer men
(Chukchi who herded reindeer for an occupation and
living), Kusche, Lovering and Collins walked up the
marshes to the westward with shotguns while Elting and

5

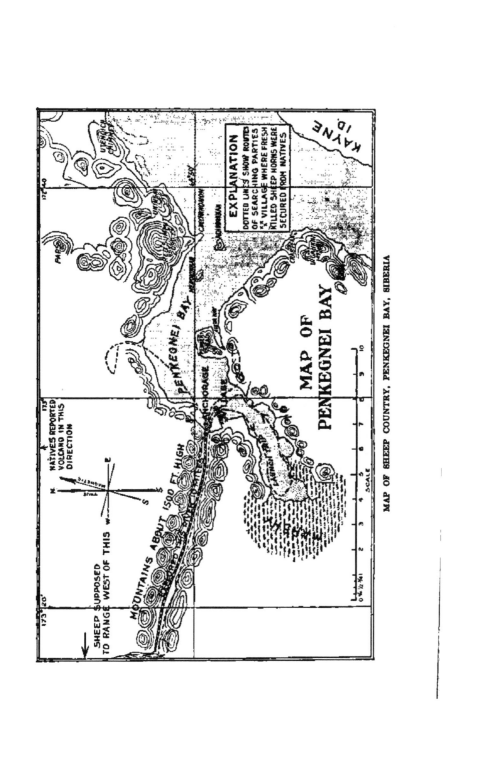

MAP OF SHEEP COUNTRY, PENKEGNEI BAY, SIBERIA

I strolled on the beach without bringing down any game. A female eider duck and her brood swam hurriedly away from the shore, the old bird refusing to rise at our approach and leave her little ones defenceless on the water. A large number of red phalarope busily scurried to and fro on a little sandspit, like so many ants, as they picked for food in the edge of the water.

Kleinschmidt came back from the few huts which marked the Chukchi settlement upon a small bluff at the head of the bay, to inform us that the most of the men of this village were off salmon fishing, and that he had seen in an igloo the skin of a young sheep. We were anxious lest the men would not return in time for us to employ them in hunting.

Later in the evening, however, a skin boat came alongside with three strapping fellows in it. We showed them a photograph of a sheep's head, which they recognized. They explained with many gestures that the like animals lived on the hills about us, indicating a general westerly direction. But, "No more," they said, "all finished." Their long story, interpreted by one of our Ittygran men who knew a little English, and sifted down to a word or two, meant that they had seen three sheep and shot them all about fifteen days ago, and that they had come upon the animals two "sleeps" inland from the village. This might mean that it would be ordinarily two days marching of eight or ten hours per day, or possibly it might be as much as thirty-six hours marching each day, or a total of seventy-two hours, according to the circumstances in which the natives may have found themselves. It was not unusual for them to go long distances without lying down to sleep if lack of food or other emergency necessitated a rapid or prolonged march.

In proof of their statements they pulled out of a sack two
small sheep horns, of an animal evidently freshly killed,
and about two years of age. These horns were secured
from them. We bargained with them to pack for us and
guide us in a quest for more of these animals, but they
would not start in foggy weather. We had been treated
to such most of the day. Accordingly it was decided to
wait and hope that the sun would dispel the mist which
hung about the mountain tops everywhere from three
hundred feet of altitude upward.

But the next day the fog still lay low around the
hills and precluded hunting until it should clear. Our
camping equipment was overhauled and made up into
packs with sufficient clothing and provisions for four men
for seven days, and we waited for the weather to turn
favorable. Our plan was to have two or three local men
take us to a likely place about a day's march inland, leave
us there to hunt for a few days and to return to carry in
our things. We traced maps of the coast to be ready to
take compass bearings, but the day passed in waiting,
and no lightening of the enshrouding mist encouraged us.

In the afternoon I went to the village with a pocketful
of chewing gum and bought several interesting native
utensils: a fire bow and spindle with which the natives
kindle fire upon a piece of dry wood by making the
spindle whirl rapidly with the bow. It was equipped with
a socket to hold the top end of the spindle in the shape of
a knuckle of a reindeer. Among other things I secured
were a bone beater for flogging the frost out of the sleeping
robes, reindeer bits made of horn, the double points of a
walking stick for traveling on the ice, a reindeer whip
with bone goad, a foot brake for a sled, and a bola for
killing birds. This last instrument was very interesting

ABANDONED VILLAGE AT ITTYGRAN ISLAND

Photo. A. M. Collins

Ittygran Island lies in Seniavine Strait at the southeastern corner of the Chukchi Peninsula. As elsewhere on this coast, driftwood is the only supply of timber. Tree trunks and whale jaws, erected as boat racks, here marked the site of a former settlement. The figure of Dr. Eiting affords a scale of comparison.

MOUNTAINS AT PENKEGNEI BAY, SIBERIA

Photo. *Gilpin Lovering*

Five days were spent in vain efforts to hunt sheep at the head of Seniavine Strait. The fog almost constantly concealed the hills and made hunting impossible. Collins is seen searching with his glasses for game, at a moment when the fog drew up from the mountain sides.

and was called by the natives "iplokotok." It consisted of about seven walrus teeth tied to the ends of strings about a yard long, the other end of the strings being knotted together. This weapon was swung by the user and thrown into a flock of ducks as they swept over head. Upon striking a bird the heavy ivory pieces caused the strings to wrap themselves tightly and instantly around the bird's wings and bring it to the ground. All these curiosities cost me nine sticks of chewing gum, a dozen boxes of matches, a half pound of tobacco and twenty-five cents in silver. With other like specimens they were later presented to the Museum of the University of Pennsylvania.

Dominoes, cards, chess and checkers, reading, and writing diaries, filled in the dull hours aboard; and bird shooting and butterfly collecting passed the time ashore when we would otherwise have been idle while waiting for the weather to change. But these indoor pastimes palled when we were eager to try for this unknown wild sheep.

To get up appetites for lunch, the two kayaks were put overboard and amid much amusement we tried to navigate them. Lovering and Collins finally circumvented the "Abler," but Elting and I mainly sat in them to see if we could keep our balance. They were so narrow that it was fatal to let back or arms rest on the gunwale of the circular cockpit, but if one sat perfectly quiet on the floor they would not rock.

It seemed possible to us that the fog might lie in a narrow belt near the coast and as we could not see anything higher than some three hundred feet, it was decided to explore a short way inland from the water's edge. If we could scale the hills and see for a considerable distance, there would be a chance and we could make a camp to hunt from. Collins and Lovering went directly into the hills north of the harbor; Elting and I, westward up the river valley for about five miles. The bed of the valley appeared to be composed of countless sharp stones which had washed down from the steep hills as they disintegrated and shed their loose coating. Over this broken ground a spongy tundra had grown more or less thickly. Recent landslides still lay on the surface and made walking uncomfortable; elsewhere moss and lichens bedded a dozen kinds of beautiful flowers. Occasionally the soil was swampy where clear rivulets watered it. Mostly it was dry and resilient. Here and there a bird rose from cover; we caught in our hands a young eider duck and a young Mongolian plover. Not once, however, did the fog permit us a view of the jagged mountain tops one thousand to fifteen hundred feet above us. Some five miles inland we could see about three miles farther toward the head of the mile-broad valley, which did not seem to differ in character farther up. Then we climbed up into the mist of one of the flanking heights. Nothing was to be seen beyond fifty yards. It was a hopeless proposition for sheep hunting and we returned to the schooner.

Two days more went by fruitlessly while we waited for the fog to lift. Different members of the party scoured the country in every direction for ten miles without discovering signs of sheep, making it evident that to secure this game we should have to march a considerable distance inland, and have favorable weather for searching the country with our field glasses.

On one launch trip to the main arm of the bay Elting and I shot several of the abundant water birds. Among these were a male and female eider duck, the former brilliant in white and green, the latter a modest brown in color. We also secured one crested auklet, a little plump bird, distinguished by an erect tuft of feathers rising just back of the beak. Two gray and white speckled murrlets were unable to dive in time to escape our lead. We chased a merganser for nearly a mile before securing it, as it swam rapidly through the water, but ran into a flock of pintail ducks and brought down six of them. Two white Point Barrow gulls and one glaucous-winged gull were among the handsomest birds in the bag. These birds were destined for museums.

We bought a few more ivory trinkets from the Chukchi, and Elting secured for a pound of tobacco an old bow and arrows in a quiver crudely embroidered with rectangular designs. Since the introduction of firearms by traders, the natives had abandoned their primitive weapons, and good specimens were difficult to secure. Most of those shown us had deteriorated very much for lack of care.

We were getting uneasy, for our time was becoming limited, and the season open in the Arctic is but a short one at the most. Collins and Lovering gave the deciding impetus to move on after returning with a discouraging report from the head of the river valley which Elting and I had partially explored. There had been absolutely no sign of sheep, though they had gone ten miles from the head of the bay, and though the fog had lifted somewhat and given hopes of fine weather. It seemed certain that we would have to march several days inland and take a week or two for a fair chance to secure the game. We did not have so much time at our disposal, for we were bound far north where the

season is uncertain and we had to allow time to take
care of unforeseen delays.

Fog and head winds we had already experienced in
plenty. We were very soon to learn, however, that other
difficulties might be placed in the way of those who
attempted to enter the mysterious and dreaded Arctic
Ocean, and for the success of the main objective in our
trip it was well that we did not tarry further at Penkegnei Bay. Much disappointed, we promptly voted
to start at once.

Our stay had not been entirely valueless. The land
mammals of the Chukchi Peninsula were known certainly
to be: the Arctic and common foxes, wolf, wild reindeer,
land bear, marmot, weasel, otter and three varieties of
lemming. To these we had convinced ourselves that we
must now add a mountain sheep.

The fog had set in thick again. The "Abler" weighed
anchor in the evening, bound for Ittygran, to put ashore
the two natives who had brought us to the reindeer
men, and through the dense fog groped out of the bay.
We sighted only one bit of land, the bold head near its
entrance. All the rugged grandeur of Seniavine Strait
was enveloped and concealed from us by the misty
shroud. Carefully we made our way to the Chukchi
village on Ittygran, and debarked the natives early in
the morning; then proceeded out to the open of Bering
Sea.

By daytime the fog had lifted and we noted the
jutting headlands of easternmost Siberia, Cape Nigchigan,
Novosilski, Nunyagmo and East Cape, which last the
Russians called Deshnef. For some time in the forenoon the trading ship "Belvedere" was visible, hull-
down to the southwest, but before we reached East

Photo, A. M. Collins

DOORWAY OF A CHUKCHI IGLOO

At Welen all the doorways faced the west, and were narrow slits between heavy posts. Dogs as well as the human inmates had free access. In the center of the hut a ring of stones marked the cooking fire-place, and at the back of the dwelling a small square tent of reindeer fur was used as a sleeping place for the entire family.

CHUKCHI IGLOO AND BOAT FRAME

The stones and ropes which keep the hides from being blown off the roofs of the huts are illustrated in this view of a characteristic house at Welen. In the foreground is the skeleton of an umiak, constructed of driftwood, which is covered with a well-fitting skin of sewed walrus hides.

CHUKCHI PUTTING SKINS ON AN IGLOO

The natives of Welen erect a framework of poles, with the roof-beams braced by oblique struts in the interior, and cover it with reindeer, seal and walrus skins. A small narrow doorway and a smoke vent at the peak are the only openings. Ropes of walrus hide are strung over the roof to lash the skins in place.

A CHUKCHI CACHE AND SKIN STRETCHER

Sledges, boats and all articles lashed together with rawhide are placed on platforms above reach of the ravenous dogs. Walrus, seal and reindeer skins are stretched between stout poles to dry. The ends of the timbers in this picture, which was taken at Welen, Siberia, rest on a whale rib and a vertebra.

Cape fog and darkness had again closed in and we lost sight of this extremity of Siberia.   In these auspicious conditions we passed through Bering Strait, and, for the first time in our lives, entered the Arctic Ocean.

It was difficult for those of us who were not sailors to get our bearings in the all-concealing fog, but during the forenoon after the day on which we left Ittygran the anchor went down, the fog horn blew several times, and a quarter of an hour later several walrus-skin boats came alongside.

We were anchored about one-half mile off the beach at Welen, the largest Chukchi village on the Arctic coast, situated just on the north side of East Cape.

CHAPTER V

A LIGHT northwest air was stirring, hardly potent to ripple the water of the Arctic as we lay near the beach at Welen. The anchorage was safe enough if the wind was very gentle, or if it blew from the south; but should it increase even to a moderate breeze we should be obliged to put out to sea, as the open roadstead offered no shelter whatever, and many a ship had been driven ashore at this point.

Departing from here, it was our aim to reach Wrangell Island, about three hundred miles away, in the Arctic Ocean, latitude 71 north, longitude 178 west, to hunt walrus and polar bear.

All the voyaging in the frozen ocean of the north is dependent upon the movements and condition of the ice-packs, which in summer melt and withdraw sufficiently northward to permit of traffic to a considerable extent around the shores of the continents bordering on the Polar Sea. But ice moves also at the caprice of the wind, and offers, in addition to the sudden and violent storms which prevail, hazard to all navigation.

The Arctic ice is generally low-lying, comparatively shallow fields or floes, in no way comparable in thickness with the icebergs detached from great glaciers on Alaskan shores. The polar ice-pack, by which is meant the perennial body of ice surrounding the Pole, never entirely disappears. It is formed primarily by the freezing of the

surface water of the ocean, increased in thickness by
pressure which piles cake upon floe, but on the other
hand decreased by melting and evaporation so that, having once attained a normal thickness, it does not vary
greatly from year to year. From the southern edge of
the polar pack in all directions from the Pole are broken
off countless fragments, a few feet to several miles in
area, and these are in almost constant motion, now
jamming together to form an impenetrable mass, now
drifting apart before the wind, and scattering over a vast
area of water. A strong breeze would send this drift-ice,
as it is called, at the rate of two miles per hour, or nearly
fifty miles in a day. A characteristic feature of its movement is that the smallest pieces drift most quickly before
the wind, while the other masses follow them with a speed
varying according to their smallness, the largest floes
going the most slowly. Thicker ice travels less quickly
than thin floes because it reaches farther down into the
water, and consequently is less affected by the wind.
As the ice thus floats before a breeze it opens up thousands of passages or leads through which vessels are
successfully navigated.

In going through the ice captains are careful not to
let the vessel get pinched between floes which come
together, for the ice meets ice with a resistless momentum
which would crush the stoutest-sided vessel. That the
dangers of travel in the Arctic ice are considerable is
illustrated by the fact that very few vessels can get
adequate insurance against the risk, and if they do, only
at a high premium. Three ships were crushed in the
Arctic ice near the coast of Alaska during and after the
time when we were in the frozen ocean.

Captain Hooper, of the Revenue Cutter "Corwin,"

after reviewing the data as to ice conditions in this part of the world collected from the year 1610 to 1881, sums up in the following words:

"It will be seen by the foregoing that from the earliest date of which we have any account, the ice-pack has remained permanently near the north coast of the Asiatic continent. Generally a narrow lead of navigable water exists along the shore during the month of August and part of September. This lead is partly filled with broken ice, and is liable to close at any time by a wind blowing on shore. . . . Along the American continent we have much the same condition—the navigable channel along the shore and the pack in the offing. . . . The ice-pack is generally found near Icy Cape on the east side of the Arctic Basin, and near Cape North (Irkaipy) on the west side, the southern edge of the pack forming an irregular curve between those places. . . . It must not be supposed, however, that the ice which fills this sea and extends south into Bering Sea during the winter months, is all melted during the short season of warm weather. The ice-pack, which is at all times broken and rent by currents and by changes in temperature, is constantly in motion, and with the temperature above the freezing point, a continued wasting away of the ice occurs, owing to the friction of its parts, aided to a certain extent by the direct rays of the sun and by evaporation.

"As this wasting and melting goes on all through the polar regions, the southern limit of the pack under the influence of the Bering Strait current, the outset from the large rivers and the innumerable small streams formed by the melting snow, which empty into the Arctic Ocean, is pressed to the northward, closing the open spaces in the

ARCTIC DRIFT ICE

Photo, Gilpin Loering

Ice pressure piles cakes upon the floes and wind and water carve them into fantastic shapes. The sharp outlines of the newly broken blocks of winter and spring are softened by melting during the summer. Under water, the floes usually project in a shelving forefoot and at the water-line are deeply eroded.

CHUKCHI OF WELEN, AT CAPE DESHNEF, SIBERIA

Photo. A. M. Collins

These maritime Chukchi lead a life similar to that of the Eskimo, chasing the game of the sea, but also herding reindeer. They are sturdy and resourceful, but starvation and disease have decimated their numbers. Fur shirts or parkas, fur breeches and reindeer-hide boots are their principal garments.

pack, and leaving the lower part of the sea comparatively free of ice. In the latter part of September and October northeast and northwest gales prevail. These force the heavy ice down from the north and on to the shores of each continent, and sometimes entirely through Bering Strait, leaving open leads and water holes to the north. Now, however, these are soon filled with new ice, which holds the pack in the southerly position until the melting and wasting of the following season begins and allows it to retreat to the northward again. . . .

"We know by the accounts of all Arctic navigators, from the earliest dates of which we have any record down to the present time, that the region surrounding the Pole, so far as it has been penetrated, is filled with the heavy ice already described, except in the immediate vicinity of land, and there it is open but a few weeks in the summer. Hence we see that the northern limit of navigation depends upon the northern limit of the land."

The natives who swarmed over our rails when we came to anchor were a sturdy lot of Chukchi. Partly by the chase of the whale, walrus, seal and birds, they had to wring a living from the savage ocean which remained closed to navigation eight months of the year. Yet trading ships frequently visited their town and took away furs, whale products and ivory in exchange for rifles, ammunition, flour, sugar, tea, tobacco and various implements,—not to mention whisky.

These men brought a roll of skins to our deck, but they were not worth troubling about—a small polar bear and a few reindeer. Instead of dealing with them we filled our pockets with chewing gum, tobacco, knives, matches and gum drops, and went ashore in our dory to see if we could bargain with the women in exchange for these delicacies.

On nearing the broad, steep shingle, which was composed wholly of well-worn rounded pebbles, the boat was backed end-on and we jumped ashore, the sailor pulling out again to save the boat from being rubbed by the little breakers. Boys were hurling pebbles here with the same kind of slings as those used by natives in distant lands: a sinew cord fastened to each end of a bit of leather, in which a small hole seated the missile.

A row of about forty igloos, not counting four or five box-like yellow, blue or pink frame cabins, was strung along the turf above the beach and when the fog thinned a bit we could see that a large lagoon lay just over the rise a few hundred yards beyond the ocean shore. At the east end of the settlement the west butt of the high bluff, which makes East Cape a conspicuous landmark twenty-nine hundred feet in altitude, abruptly fixed the limit of the sandspit.

Aside from the round-topped, skin-covered igloos the most striking feature of the town was the great number of whale skulls, vertebræ, ribs and jaw bones strewn about the place. Indeed, the skulls and vertebræ seemed to underlie much of the top-soil. They were laid in rows to form terraces for the huts, built into the walls of caches, and used as weights to hold down the skin covering of the houses. Whale jaws and ribs were set upright in the ground in fours and the boats laid high and dry on cross pieces lashed to them; incidentally also above the fangs of the numerous dogs which would eat the walrus skin covers. Whales' bones and rocks were far more plentiful than wood. Driftwood was the main source of supply of this latter material, for no trees were growing within range of vision.

Naturally we entered many igloos, practically all in

the cluster, and sought for implements and small characteristic objects in trade for our nicknacks. Leaf tobacco put up in half-pound packages and chewing gum were freely accepted in payment, but many demanded money.

The usual formula was, "Do you want to make trade for this?" holding up the article.

"Yes."

"Well, how much do you want?"

Then ensued a long and guttural conference with the squaws, or with any native who happened to be in hearing. At the end of this the word "mauneta" (money).

"Well, how much money?"

The answer would be, "You speak;" or else "One dollar;" or simply "one." A half pound of tobacco generally bought a walking stick or fishing tackle, and if the seller hesitated, a stick of chewing gum or a box of matches turned the balance. The only American coin they knew was the silver dollar and I made a long argument in explaining that two quarters and a half were equal to the larger disk. But their ideas of the values were vague. A five-cent stick of chewing gum (which they chewed with tinfoil, paper and all), was not preferred to a half-cent box of matches.

As we wandered through the village, entering the doorless huts without invitation and without offence, we surprised the women at various domestic tasks: cooking thick, greasy soup, cutting up red raw meat for dogs, sewing mukluks with incredibly close stitches, mixing the red tanning liquor of the willow, twisting shredded sinew into three-ply thread with a rapid roll of the heel of one hand over the other. Most of them had let the warm fur parka fall from one or both shoulders, exposing their pendulous breasts. But this embarrassed them not a bit before us. Some were pretty and affable; others shy; a few older ones averse from a close inspection.

The characteristic sleeping place in each igloo (and it was the summer residences that we saw in use), was placed at the side of the hut opposite the door, which in every house faced the west. A mattress of dry grass was laid on the trodden earth between logs six inches in diameter, placed in a square. On this a large skin was spread, flesh up, and laced over the logs, which thus became pillows. About five feet above the floor a frame of light rods slung to the roof poles supported a canopy of red tanned reindeer skins with the fur inside, tightly sewn together, hanging down to the ground outside and enclosing the logs. All members of the family slept side by side with their heads toward the doorway.

The hut was roughly circular in shape, twenty to thirty feet across, with dome-like roof rising from a vertical wall about five feet high. Posts, four inches in diameter, were driven into the ground to form the latter and connected at the top by lighter stringers. A central pole rose about twelve feet, surmounted by a pair of parallel heads several feet long. About three dozen rods, wrist thickness, were lashed to the wall top and spirally laid together on top of the central pole. The middles were then pushed up by cross pieces braced on slanting struts which were bedded on whales' bones, all near the center of the igloo. This gave the roof its dome. Rawhide skins were then laid over the whole, umbrella-like framework, their edges weighted down against storms with walrus-hide rope, to which large stones or whale vertebræ were fastened at their lower ends, so that the ballast hung close to the ground.

At the apex a flap lifted to let out the smoke from the fire built in a small circle of little stones, with another small stone in the center. Pots swung on a chain over this. Natural wood crooks were used as hooks for vessels which were not in use and other utensils hung around the walls. A number of parcels wedged between skins and timbers proved, when pulled out, to be hunting or fishing gear or other household articles. Nowhere in this village did I see such repulsive filth as I had been led to expect of people living the Eskimo life. The men, women and numerous children looked happy and prosperous. Probably about two hundred of them called this place home.

Scattered over the ridge between the lagoon and the ocean low mounds of sodded whales' bones marked the roofs of underground igloos, entered by a burrow. One such was used as an ice house, another pit, covered with planks under a gibbet, was not a hanging trap, but a walrus-meat storehouse which stank abundantly. Nordenskjöld described these as the abandoned homes of another tribe, called Onkilon, who were driven away by the present Chukchi. Other authorities consider them as evidence of an unsuccessful attempt by the American Eskimo to colonize Asia.

The wrestling plot was partly ringed about with stones and the ground was much trodden up as if wrestling was a favorite sport. One of the blue wooden cottages, when unlocked by the owner, revealed a store stocked with various merchandise: furs of wolverine, reindeer and bear, flour, ammunition, primers for cartridges, a phonograph, whale guns and other articles. Tacked to the wall, pictures of the Tsar and Tsarina of Russia overlooked benevolently the petty trade of this

6

distant outpost of their empire. Outside of this building a high military mast was planted and guyed.

Frank, the rich man of the place, took me to his cache in a small frame house, and offered a good light dog sled for ten dollars—being willing to accept six. When Kleinschmidt engaged him as one of three men to go with us, hunting walrus farther north, and take one of his skin boats for use in the hunting, Frank was much pleased. He cemented the business arrangement by giving Kleinschmidt his Christian name: "Me and you all same Frank."

We shopped industriously among the natives, buying curiosities and trinkets: ingenious fishing tackle, the line made of whalebone, so that it would not freeze, together with the sticks and reel, with which it was pulled out of the water to avoid wetting the hand. A boy's toy sling, a harpoon, a walking stick, snow shoes, some old ivory also fell to our seductive chewing gum and tobacco, and we had to give a keyhole saw for one of the stone lamps in which the natives burn seal oil, using moss as a wick.

There was a very pretty girl, Chewingo, among the young women of the village, who quite won our hearts. But any budding romance was nipped by the cold wind from the northwest which forced us to leave our anchorage suddenly.

The breeze freshened, and as we could no longer lie off the unprotected beach and besides were otherwise ready to make our attempt to reach Wrangell Island, we started and drove all day against the head wind. Three of the natives, Frank, John and Slim, had been taken on board, together with Frank's large skin boat to be used in hunting walrus. When the rising sea began to knock us back as fast as we came the watch set sail on the port tack and stood offshore, stopping the motor to make the vessel ride more easily while we slept. Nevertheless the "Abler" rolled a great deal and was not comfortable during the night.

Early the next morning, July 29th, we came about to the starboard tack and as the fog grew thinner toward noon we sighted land: steep cliffs, nearly a thousand feet high with surges dashing forty feet and more up the sides. Presumably this was Cape Unikin. We came within two miles and stood off again. The wind increased and we tacked inshore in the middle of the afternoon, but when land showed once more through the mist, we had hardly gained any ground. Off we went again, and lay to under short sail all night, stopping the motor at five o'clock in the afternoon. We were just at the Arctic Circle, having already crossed it three times in the "Abler."

There was a hideous night ahead of us. The wind had grown to half a gale and the crested combers bodily blew the flat-bottomed schooner to leeward like a chip. Strangely enough she did not pound, and shipped practically no water. Down in the hold the nine-ton engine was excellent ballast.

Tickling at the back of my head made we search the long foliage with a fine-toothed comb, which Elting bought at St. Michael, and three slender white seam-squirrels were the harvest. Doubtless I had caught them in the igloos.

There was no sleep for me. The gale whistled through the rigging and the seas threw us around in our bunks all night. Three times I went out on deck in pajamas (for I had not yet weaned myself from undressing to go to bed) to see what weather we were making, and the outlook was not reassuring. A dense fog flew by on the wings of the storm, seemingly from an unlimited source. Should we be able to ride out the blow, or would it carry us ashore on the low bleak coast of Cape Prince of Wales on the Alaskan side? The test came soon.

At midnight we heard a repeated knocking, aft. "An old iron oil drum must have broken loose below," I thought at first. But the sound was right at the stern, so I hastily put on some clothes and went out. The Captain, the mate and a sailor were looking over the stern. I went close to the Captain and yelled into his ear, "What's the matter?"

"Our rudder's gone!" shouted the Captain.

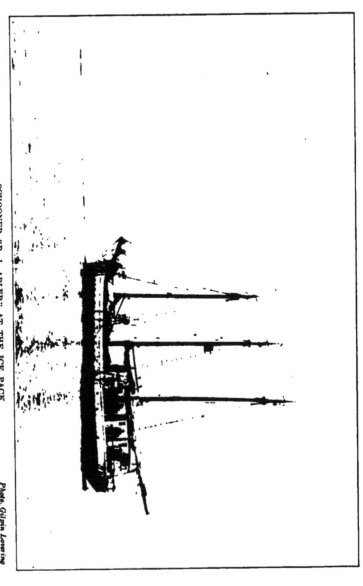

SCHOONER "P. J. ABLER" AT THE ICE PACK

Photo. Gilpin Lovering

The vessel for the Arctic cruise was of 116 tons, 120 feet long, 25 feet wide and of 7 feet draught. She carried sails on three masts and had an auxiliary motor of 85 H. P. which used low-grade gasoline. A large cabin house provided three staterooms, dining room, pilot house and galley. Other rooms were in the hold.

MAKING THE JURY RUDDER GRIP

At her first attempt to reach the Arctic ice the Schooner "Abler" lost her rudder in a storm. Long planks were put over the stern and by pulling these to one side or the other, the vessel was navigated 150 miles into a port where repairs were made. At times some of the crew had to weight the emergency rudder so that it would turn the ship.

CHAPTER VI

"OUR RUDDER'S GONE!"

IT'S good-bye to our Arctic hunting, thought I. Over the stern I could see the broken stock and feel the tiller slap uselessly from side to side.

The wind showed no intention of abating, and we were about forty miles off shore with no means of steering the old craft. The waves were sweeping down on us mast high and it was fortunate that the schooner was lightly laden or she would have had a hard time in the seaway. The saving factor in the situation was that the wind was now blowing in a direction which would carry us through Bering Strait. If we could steer the vessel to leeward we might have a chance to save the ship by getting under the lee of East Cape or, if weather permitted, of running into Port Clarence about one hundred and fifty miles distant on the Alaskan coast. At Port Clarence the small town of Teller offered a chance of repairing the damage. Should we not be successful in this attempt we might be dashed against the precipitous sides of the Diomede Islands in Bering Strait or be cast ashore on the Alaskan coast north of Cape Prince of Wales. "In case we're thrown up on the low sandy beaches near Cape Prince of Wales," remarked Ed Born with a quizzical smile, "we can get ashore without wetting our feet." Then it would be simply a question of walking a few hundred miles to reach means of communication with the outside world. But the vessel would be lost and our Arctic trip ended.

(85)

I went back to bed, but not to sleep. Elting had been in his berth ever since leaving Welen, and was awake, so I told him the trouble and we wedged ourselves firmly into our bunks to await the morning.

By breakfast time the crew had chained two long heavy planks, which we happened by luck to have on board, over the stern so that their ends trailed in the water, and could be steered by the wheel chains which were made fast to tackles running to their outboard ends. The worst of the matter, however, was that the old rudder still held fast at the keel shoe and lashed from side to side, making the slender grip of the emergency planks almost powerless. The old rudder stock had parted just above the rudder and the mate had discovered the accident by noticing that the wheel in the pilot house turned freely, as it naturally would after the strain of the rudder had been broken off. It was the slapping of the tiller against its stop blocks that we had first heard.

All day long we tried to free the old rudder while we were drifting and steering as best we could straight before the wind. We hauled up on the guy ropes, we rigged a tackle to the spanker boom; Lovering even suggested shooting the pintle loose as the stern rose on a wave. But it was useless; the encumbrance now jammed at one side or the other, now followed docilely in the midst of the wake, but off it did not come until six o'clock that evening. Meantime we had picked up land: East Cape looming through the fog a few miles off. The gale still drove us before it on a wobbling course toward the Diomede Islands.

Fortunately the damaged rudder finally freed itself. Just after supper the Captain rushed into the saloon,

calling, "Come out and help us with the rudder!"
There it was, fast by guy ropes and tackle, diving from
side to side like a dolphin or a great skate; plunging out
of sight, swinging itself out of water, sounding for the
propeller like a monster chafing at its bond and bent on
destruction. Soon we had a line on it to pull it forward
on the port side, and an Eskimo lance ready to cut the
starboard guy line at the word of command. The
"Abler" lay to, wallowing in the sea on the port tack,
making leeway so fast that all lines were taut as wire
stays. The cursed thing had managed to wrap its guy
ropes several times around the propeller and now tried
its best to stave in the ship's planking. But the
"Abler" slid off too fast for it to get to her. At last
the Captain sliced the guy rope, and like a hooked tarpon
the rudder ripped the forward line out to windward and
fought it there, hanging broadside to it and running back
and forth deep under water. A bight of this line was
taken to the tackle on the foremast head and hauling on
this brought the rudder up near the surface, but several
fathoms to windward, worrying at the ropes until the
foremast whipped it out of water as the schooner rolled
in the trough. We threw a line around the tackle and
little by little warped the demon in near the ship's side,
then took a fresh bight with the tackle and presently had
it lying lifeless on deck; a cold mass of steel and wood
six feet deep, four and a half feet wide and six inches
thick, weighing seven hundred pounds. It had cost us
three hours of ceaseless work after it broke free, to bring
it in.

The engine turned and chewed the ropes on the
propeller to oakum and once more we straightened out
on our course, holding it fairly well, but obliged to steer

largely by handling the sails, as the jury rudder did not give enough resistance. At times several men had to crawl down the planks close to the water, in order to make it drag enough to turn the vessel. The fog screened all glimpse of land. We were still to windward of the Diomedes, drifting down upon them. Kusche would not go to bed, "till we passed dem dam Diomedes," for they offered only steep rocks and dangerous beaches for landing, and he wanted to be ready to jump. Although attempt ng to make a twenty-mile passage on either side in the night we passed through the channel one and one-half miles wide between the two islands without seeing a sign of either of them in the dense fog.

The morning after this day of trouble and anxiety broke overcast, and with distant fog, but the sun afterwards drove this away and we found ourselves southwest of Cape York, nearly at the entrance to Port Clarence. The desolate mountains were reddish yellow and nude of vegetation. The sea was smooth; the light breeze favorable, and we made into Grantly Harbor, where the mining port Teller lay on a sandspit. The breeze lasted until we had navigated the hundred-foot wide channel and cast anchor in eight feet of water. Then it turned around and blew gently from the opposite direction. Had it not served us favorably to the last we could hardly have come safely into port.

We had been out sixteen days, had entered the Arctic and four times crossed the Arctic Circle, and were now disabled at a point only two days' voyage from St. Michael, whence we had started. The season in which it was possible to stay in the northern ocean was so brief that any delay might be disastrous to success. On entering Teller we held the fond hope that a hustling machine shop would soon put things to rights for us.

But this illusion vanished quickly. Scarcely a score of people dwelt in the village which ten years earlier had boasted two thousand inhabitants. There was no machine shop, there was no blacksmith or mechanic, there was not even a supply of ordinary, necessary tools or materials with which to make the repairs. As for means of welding the old stock to the rudder again—we presently smiled at the idea. No regular steamers called at this decadent hamlet, and even if the rudder could be repaired or made anew at Nome, which was doubtful, it would take a week to get a boat around to fetch it and deliver it, besides a week or two for doing the work at Nome. To put this chance beyond question the wind began to blow stronger from the southwest so that we could not venture out in the "Abler" with our emergency gear. This last the Captain and Ed Born flatly refused to consider, as it would jeopardize the one's commission and the other's insurance. Born, especially, took the whole misfortune with singular calmness, while Kleinschmidt and the rest of us gnawed our lips in helpless anger.

The "Alaska," a forty-seven ton auxiliary schooner, lay partly hauled on the beach. She had just been purchased in Nome by Stefansson for his Arctic expedition, and had managed to reach Teller after they had discovered that her propeller was worthless, her clutch in bad shape and her engine in need of overhauling. She was about sixty feet long, double-ended, high-sided, with two masts and a small rig. The fore and aft decks at the rails, lower midship and tall ugly pilot house over the engine space made her look unusually clumsy. Bunks for three of the crew, two engineers and fifteen men in the cabin, provided for an abundant number. Her cargo, too much for her to take safely on a long voyage, had been placed in a warehouse, and the men were tinkering with her machinery and waiting for a new propeller. Dr. Anderson was in charge.

Also hauled on the beach were the "Kotzebue," a stern wheeler, and the "Dewey," an old scow, which had lain there six years. These vessels all contributed to our help.

The day after our arrival the launch "Wilhelmina" came in from Nome with a bridal couple on board, and took back with her a note from us to the postmaster at that place, asking him to forward mail to us at Teller by the next boat; and if we should have left in the meantime, to bring it back to Nome on its return voyage.

Kleinschmidt, who had been scouring the town, now came on board greatly excited. "I've found an old rudder in the 'Dewey,'" he cried. "It looks as if it might do." Forthwith the Captain went to it and measured it. With a few changes it might serve, but would the material be good enough after six years of rusting to stand the strain of hard service? It was entirely of steel, one-quarter inch plate passing round a stock, and riveted together. Many blows of the hammer to test it brought down huge scales of rust within and without. "It might do," said the Captain. Kleinschmidt bought it for fifty dollars.

An entire day went by while we got the rudder out of the "Dewey." She was so deeply embedded in the sand that a pit had to be dug to let the stock slip down from the sleeve far enough to withdraw its length.

While the crew was at this labor we four passengers started to a large reindeer herd on the tundra back of the village, beyond a small lake. They let us approach

within a few yards and then slowly went away. A few
were white, and some piebald, but most of them dark
gray. Some had begun to rub the velvet off their
horns.

While taking this walk I made a first close acquaintance with the tundra, the characteristic moor of
Arctic coasts. In distant appearance like rolling meads
of firm smooth ground, the surface of this locality on
nearer view was seen to be most uneven: thickly sprin-
kled with niggerheads, clods of turf six or eight inches
high and about as far apart. To walk was galling,
because it required care to place the foot between the
niggerheads and it frequently slipped off when put on
them. This curious formation interested me so much
that I sat down and dissected one of the warts with my
hunting knife; letting the other men ramble on, as they
had no definite object.

The autopsy of the niggerhead, then, revealed several
well-defined strata: (1) long round straight grass blades
like a wiry shock of hair; (2) fine light green feathery
moss; (3) decayed stems of green moss; (4) decayed grass
leaves matted horizontally; (5) live grass root bulbs; (6)
decayed grass roots, through which live grass roots grew
downward; (7) black loam formed by old grass roots; (8)
gray clay.

On top some small lichens and flowers flourished.
The ground between the niggerheads was similar in
formation, but the moss was larger and the grass scarce
or absent.

This ground covered with niggerheads is found in
certain kinds of topography; elsewhere the surface is
less uneven.

The rudder from the "Dewey" had been brought on

a hand cart, about half a mile from where the old scow
lay, to the rear of a meagerly fitted tool shop of which
Kleinschmidt had engaged the use.   It contained a
bench and vise, a few drills and dies.   We borrowed tools
from the "Kotzebue" and the "Alaska" in the shape of
ratchets, cold chisels and hack saws.

Now we naturally expected to see Captain Larsson
lead an onslaught on the job that would finish it up in a
day or two.   But oh, no!   This was Sunday, which
agreeably to ship's laws and in accord with the biblical
injunction must be observed as a day of rest while the
ship was in port, although when on the high seas one
would not have taken the skipper for a deeply religious
man.   Indeed, he addressed himself to the task as if it
were to give occupation for the rest of the summer.   A
good rest, plenty of food and sleep were necessary for
successful mechanical work, and besides a word from Ed
Born, we suspected, had said, "to take his time about it."
We raged among ourselves, but hardly liked to say much
openly because Kleinschmidt was our official spokesman
and he had not been able to hurry things.   As the delay
was costing him about seventy dollars a day, Kleinschmidt was nearly wild.   Larsson, however, pursued his
placid existence, reading and loafing about the ship during the morning, and as he was the mechanical man of
the party it seemed unavoidable to let him take his own
way.   If others had undertaken and done the work in a
way which did not meet his approval, he might have
refused to go to sea.

Jimmie, the cabin boy, took advantage of this acces-
sibility of dry land to have a fight with the cook.
"Cook, he bad man," Jimmie confided to me.   "Me
want to leave ship here."

DOMESTICATED REINDEER AT TELLER, ALASKA

Photo. A. M. Collins

Dr. Sheldon Jackson, a missionary, imported a few reindeer from Siberia to Alaska in 1891, as an experiment in supporting the Eskimo. Besides furnishing meat, leather and milk, the original 1,300 animals have increased to nearly 40,000 head and are a valuable asset of the country.

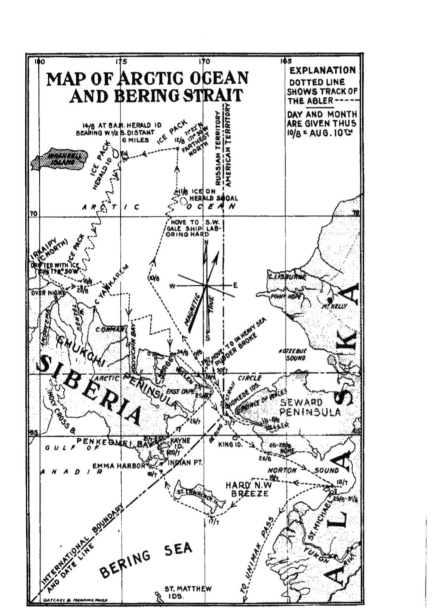

MAP OF THE ARCTIC CRUISE

Ed Born also showed a disinclination to go into the Arctic with us. He was lounging near our open cabin door while the four of us were in the stateroom, and hinted that he wanted to quit the party. "Frank (Kleinschmidt) and I have had it pretty hot at times, all the way up from Seattle," he explained, "and there are some things a fellow can't stand for. Of course I won't leave him in the lurch, but if I can get an engineer, I'll put the engine in good shape and go back to Nome."

At this we blew up and stated concisely what we would think of him if he deserted us. Kleinschmidt, coming at the sound of high voices, inquired, "What's the trouble?"

"No trouble, Frank," said Born quietly. "We are just having a talk and you don't need to butt into it." We explained to Kleinschmidt, however, what the matter was, and left the two men, telling them it was foolish to quarrel after a friendship of fifteen years' standing.

The basic reason for the rupture between Born and Kleinschmidt was Born's fear that on her return to Seattle the "Abler" might be libeled for wages if Kleinschmidt could not pay them. The latter had set aside three thousand, five hundred dollars for this purpose, but carried one thousand dollars of it in a letter of credit for emergencies. A secondary reason for disagreement was the fact that both of them had joined in buying about thirteen hundred dollars' worth of trading goods with which to turn a profit during the trip, by buying furs from the natives, and so far they had not been able to dispose of any amount of it. Thus, as we guessed, it would not be disagreeable to Born to delay in Teller to try to sell things to the natives, while Kleinschmidt, though due to profit by this, was certain of a far greater loss to himself of money and reputation if the voyage dragged out too long or failed of its purpose. He had chartered the schooner from Born, and was responsible for all the running expenses. While the latter was aboard officially as engineer, yet as owner he had great influence over Captain Larsson and could raise objections of legality or formality in the most unexpected ways.

The result of this talk was apparently a truce.

We also grasped another slight opportunity of furthering our objects. During the morning a launch passed us from the Revenue Cutter "Bear." It was anchored at the Reindeer station in the bay seven miles from Teller. "Tools and possibly some other help," flashed through our minds. Kleinschmidt took to the suggestion and the launch was made ready. Elting had just gone ashore for a walk. We headed him off, for he had a letter of introduction to Captain Ballinger of the "Bear," and we also picked up Larsson who came along the beach at that moment. Frank Born ran the launch. Elting thought that Ed Born wanted to get Captain Ballinger, who had the proper authority, to appoint Larsson chief engineer as well as captain of the "Abler." With Frank as assistant engineer we would be technically entitled to go to sea and in this way Ed could leave us, go to Nome and await the return of the "Abler" from the Arctic. "I had no business to come up here at all this summer," said Ed. "I didn't have to do it, but I thought I would have a nice trip, and I am sorry I started."

An hour's run in the launch brought us to the "Bear," a steam brig built in the seventies for Arctic exploration and still serviceable. Captain Ballinger was a medium-sized, well-built man with the look of an eagle. Bishop

Rowe, the much-respected head of the Episcopal Church in Alaska, was among those we met on board. "We'll lend you anything we have, excepting what we need ourselves," was Ballinger's reply to our request for tools, and Larsson went below to see the machinist. The rest of us were entertained pleasantly in the ward room.

On the way back we suggested working two shifts of men on the rudder, as our officers insisted on an eight-hour day, and we offered to take the night shift. "If you'll do that," Larsson answered, "we'll make twice the time," and accordingly we were detailed to work from supper until eleven o'clock each evening until the job was done. Larsson had found a few drills, a little tool steel and a few nuts on the "Bear," but nothing else that was of any use to us.

Other defections cropped out. Kusche talked of staying at Nome until we returned from the Arctic. Albrecht and Kleinschmidt had a quarrel. Jimmie quit his job and went ashore. "Now you will have to work twice as hard," said I to the Japanese cook. But he grinned. "Cabin boy, no cabin boy—all same to me; but only two meals a day," he answered. It began to look indeed as if our expedition to the Arctic might be broken up, even if we succeeded in repairing the rudder in time to get there.

There was nothing to do, however, but watch every move in the game that threatened to defeat us, and block it if possible, while putting our efforts in whatever they would count. We had apparently dissuaded Ed Born from leaving, and to make this more certain Elting had Ballinger's promise that we would not sanction it. We hoped now to speed up the fitting of the new rudder if we possibly could.

At a seemly hour after breakfast the captain, mate and Chukchi sailors started work. Most of the morning was spent in placing it on trestles and rigging shears and tackle for turning it over. The day shift also chipped off a strip along the lower part of the steel plate so that the stock would project down deep enough to fashion into a pintle. Aside from this the captain spent much of the day in making cold chisels from steel obtained on the "Bear," but they proved too brittle and broke against the extremely tough metal of the rudder. None of them proved serviceable.

During that afternoon we made the acquaintance of an old man, J. H. Wood, the United States Commissioner, who formerly lived in New York State and now kept the principal store in this village. He had recently lost his wife and was lonely. As I came out of the store Kleinschmidt casually asked me if he could raise five hundred dollars among the four of us. But it happened that we did not have that amount of cash altogether. I heard no more of this and presumably Kleinschmidt had to break into his letter of credit in order to replenish the provisions for our journey into the Arctic.

After supper the night shift went to its job in high spirits, directed by Larsson.

It was remarkable how nearly the picked-up rudder fitted the "Abler." The steel stock, three and a half inches thick, was exactly the right size, but about three feet too long at the top; the lower end, which fitted into a hole in the skeg, had to be trimmed down to a two-inch diameter for about three inches of its length, and a strip must be sheared off the plate across the bottom of the whole rudder about four feet distance (which was done by the day shift on the first day). Then a square head must be made on the stock to take the tiller and drilled for a set bolt. The whole rudder must be encased in wood, for which a score of holes had to be bored through the steel plates, each of these plates being a scant quarter inch thick. By eleven o'clock the first night we had bored all the holes in the plates, using hand ratchets and "old men" (wooden frames to support the upper end of the drill) and had sawed the lower end of the rudder stock around at the new shoulder to a depth of five-eighths inch. After doing all this we heartily cursed Ed Born, for this was the job he should have done and yet he said he was busy overhauling the "Abler's" engine.

While the night shift took an eighteen-mile tramp into the hills and lunched on broiled ptarmigan, the second day of work on the rudder produced little visible results of the day shift's labors. Useless chisels were again the principal output.

Events took an interesting turn at noon. On coming out of Judge Wood's store the men were leaving shore in the launch and were unable to hear my hail. So I walked_down the beach to the "Kotzebue" to find a boat to take me out. Here a tall spectacled man inquired for Kleinschmidt and we rowed out in a skiff borrowed from the "Kotzebue."

"Are you the man he bought the rudder from?"

"No, I am the marshal," he answered.

"What's up?"

"Well, just a social visit." He seemed to hesitate. "They've been trading with the natives without a license and I have come out to warn them that it is against the law."

Once on board, the marshal, John Riordan, lunched

7

with us, excusing the unpleasant nature of his mission, and a good feeling seemed to reign. Born maintained that he had a right to trade if not on shore, or if the ship were not made fast to the shore by ropes. The marshal did not, however, yield his ground. Born made light of the matter after he had gone.

The night shift made twenty-three bolts of five-eighths-inch steel with a thread turned on each end and tapped out forty-six old nuts to the proper size, besides chewing at the rudder pintle with a hack-saw and the one cold chisel that would stand the work. It had become plain before this that the rudder was made of excellent tough steel and had not been injured by its long exposure to the weather. Indeed, the greatest difficulty we found was to cut it at all with the few tools we had. These consisted of two hack saws and a half dozen blades, one good cold chisel, two ratchets and four three-quarter-inch drills. It was sheer drudgery that the other men of the day shift seemed to avoid as much as possible. The biggest job they did was to saw the head of the rudder stock off at the proper place, leaving to us the fashioning of it for the tiller. Even with working at night each detail of the work required such a long time to carry out that we became more than anxious to push it as fast as our limited means permitted. At its commencement the captain had set Friday night for its completion. On Wednesday morning we now started in to work in the day time as well, to try to save half a day if possible, for we were accomplishing considerably more than the crew in the same length of time. Elting and I sawed away at the head of the rudder stock, cutting slabs off four sides to square it for the hole in the tiller. We took shifts at it with two saws, each scraping hard for a few minutes at a time in order not to overheat and break the fragile blades. Just three hours elapsed before the first slab came off and we pushed the slit about one-third into another side by noon.

Elting and a Chukchi hacked off this one and half of a third during the afternoon. That night Kleinschmidt and I finished this part of the work after it had required practically twelve hours of steady sawing.

By ten o'clock we had broken all the hack-saw blades which were sharp enough to make an impression on the hard material, and progress became so discouraging that we evidently would not get through by morning if we worked all night. As a last effort, therefore, I went to the "Alaska" and said to the engineer, "I'll give you a dollar for the use of another hack-saw blade." Out it came and he would not take any money.

The mate kept his bed all day, complaining of his head, in which he felt a pain attributed to an old stab wound. Larsson busied himself still making useless chisels and running off now and then "to get something," which he never obtained, but Born made up for his previous indifference by fitting much of the planking which was to encase the metal plates of the rudder, and for which we had turned out the bolts. His interest may have been quickened by a desire to leave the scene of impending disagreement with the authorities. The hand of the law was, however, too swift for him.

During the day's work an accident to Lovering caused us a great deal of anxiety. It came after several warnings. In chipping down the rudder stock pintle, Collins held the chisel in tongs and Lovering swung a heavy hammer hard against the tool. Small bits of metal flew off like bullets. One gashed Born's cheek, another brought blood on Chukchi Frank's brow, others cut Lovering in the cheek and chin and then one struck him in the left eye, between the nose and the pupil. He was blinded for a few minutes and the blood suffused the white of his eye, but presently he continued the work. Elting examined the wounded eye and said that it was impossible to see if the particle of steel had stayed in the cut or had bounded out. If it had come out again Lovering would be none the worse, but if it remained he would infallibly lose the eye. To probe would only aggravate the matter. Only a powerful magnet could remove the foreign body, and one was not available short of Seattle or San Francisco. It was futile to try to rush Lovering to either of these places, for two days would settle the question and we could not reach either city at the quickest in less than two or three weeks. We took pains to conceal our feelings from Lovering, who had not been told all this, but it depressed us greatly. Fortunately he recovered completely.

Born was caught in the toils of the law. We heard all about it from the authority, Judge Wood, after our night work was over. When I walked to the "Alaska" to borrow the final hack-saw blade, the judge came out of his store to tell me that the other fellows were up in his living apartments above the trading room. So after Kleinschmidt and I had finished our stunt, we went there.

In a cosy, warm room the old gentleman set out whisky and cigars and welcomed Kleinschmidt with us. After general talk Kleinschmidt said he understood Born was liable for trouble.

"I had not intended to say anything about that matter in the present circumstances," replied the Judge,

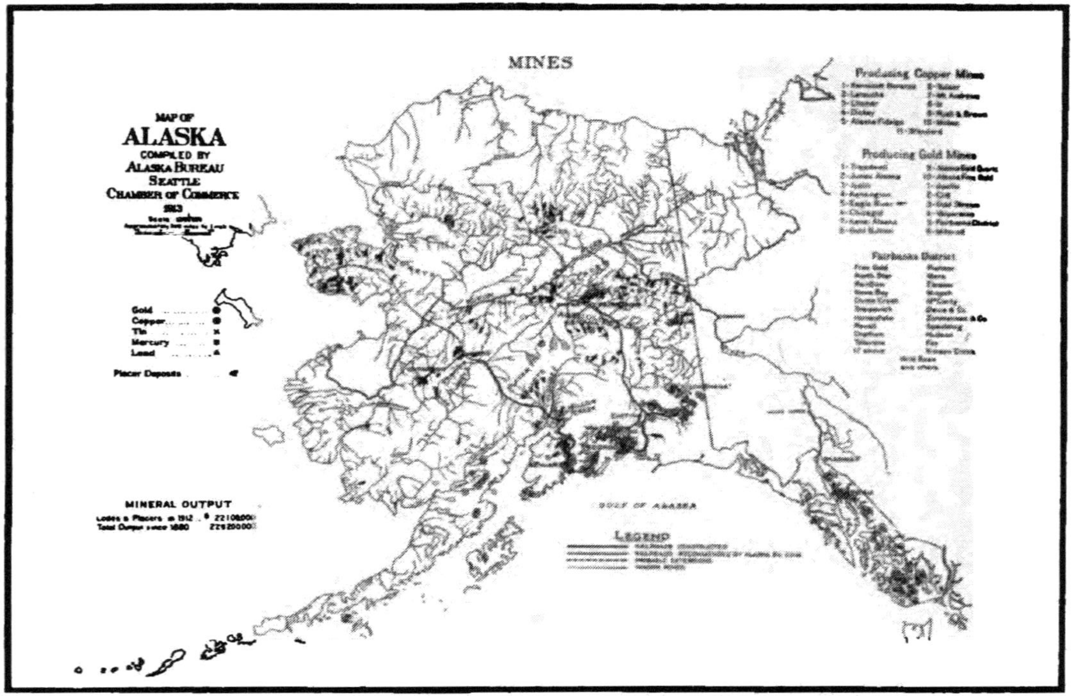
MINES
MAP OF
ALASKA
COMPILED BY
ALASKA BUREAU
SEATTLE
CHAMBER OF COMMERCE
1913
Gold
Copper
Tin
Mercury
Lead
Placer Deposits
MINERAL OUTPUT
Producing Copper Mines
Producing Gold Mines
Fairbanks District
GULF OF ALASKA
LEGEND

Courtesy of Alaska Bureau, Seattle Chamber of Commerce

MAP SHOWING LOCATIONS OF MINES IN ALASKA

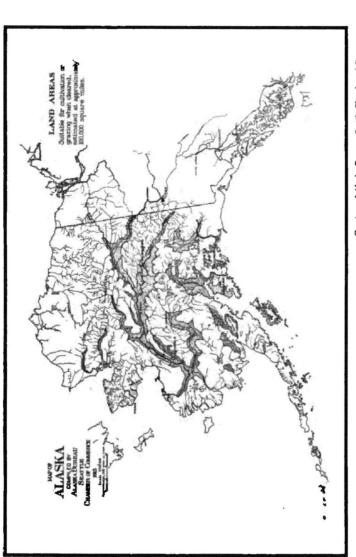

Courtesy of Alaska Bureau, Seattle Chamber of Commerce

MAP OF ALASKA SHOWING AREAS SUITABLE FOR GRAZING OR AGRICULTURE "but since you have opened the subject I may tell you that Born has been found by the marshal to have traded with the natives on three separate days, and some of it since his warning. A fine is the penalty for the first two offences; for a third breach, imprisonment for sixty days to six months. The law states that trading on three separate days constitutes three separate offences. I have sent the marshal for Born, and expect him here now. It will not hold your vessel or detain the rest of you if Born is put in jail here."

This was rather a facer for Kleinschmidt, who was actually Born's partner in the deal; but he affected ignorance that any trading had been done since the warning.

"I don't want to inconvenience these gentlemen," said the Judge, indicating us, "whom I have met and like, and that is the only consideration that would deter me from inflicting the full penalty for his defiance of the authorities. It will not cause you any delay, gentlemen," he added.

"We are bound for the Arctic and it would deprive us of our chief engineer," some one remarked, "just when we are most in need of both of them to relieve each other."

The Judge considered this matter for a few moments. "Well, then, I will let him off," he decided. It was a very generous action on his part. Not only the law had been broken, but his personal pride hurt and his business robbed of trade which would normally have come to it. "I wish to make it clear," he concluded, "that I will do this solely out of consideration for these gentlemen."

We thanked him heartily and word coming up at that moment that Born was downstairs, the Judge left us.

In a few words we unbosomed ourselves to Klein-schmidt and explained that the rest of our journey together was to be a hunting trip and nothing else. Then we all went to the schooner, except Kleinschmidt, who stayed to see Born through.

A minor change had taken place in the personnel on board. Jimmie had come and gone, taking with him a bulging suitcase. When he first came aboard legend said that the bag was nearly empty. A few trifles began to be missing about this time. In place of Jimmie, the great hulk of Slim, the Chukchi from Welen, was dressed up in a suit of Kleinschmidt's and was ready to serve us as cabin boy. He had had experience on some of the whaling ships.

Larsson, Born and Kleinschmidt went to work on the rudder after breakfast on the last day, and we watched them get at it, as there was not enough more work to keep all hands fully occupied. We had undertaken at the beginning to do only night work on the job, and in spite of this fact, Larsson showed some impatience with us for leaving him early in the morning to carry it to completion. Before coming off the "Abler" our master mechanic had gauged the socket in the skeg more exactly by thrusting a tapered pole into it. According to this measurement the pintle, which we had shaped on the lower part of the rudder stock, proved a little too large, but Born's mightly blows reduced it, and by noon the entire work was finished. It remained only to take it out to the "Abler" and see if it would go into place. We had hustled into three days and a half, work that the captain had estimated would need at least five.

The great mass, weighing a third of a ton, was now put on a light hand cart and trundled to the water's edge, where we had brought up a large flat scow on which to take the rudder to the schooner. The little hand cart collapsed under the weight just as we reached the shore, but a dozen stout men carried the rudder on the scow. We towed the scow to our ship, ropes were made fast and the rudder pried overboard with levers, so that it hung under water at the "Abler's" stern. A thin, strong wire rope led down through the rudder port and was made fast to the head of the rudder stock so that with a tackle it could be pulled up through the hole until the head of the stock showed above deck. If now there were play enough in the sleeve to let the rudder be drawn up at one side of the heavy iron strap which projected out from the keel and formed the lower socket, we could drop the rudder straight down again so that the pintle, in the lower end of the stock, would fit into the hole in the skeg. The only question remaining now was whether we could do this. At first, the lower end of the rudder jammed against the skeg, and the upper end of the stock was pressed into the soft lead lining of the rudder port. But several hours' hewing at the latter enlarged the opening enough, and finally the monster settled itself properly in all respects. The rest was easy—putting on the tiller, rigging the chains and setting a heavy collar so that the rudder could not slip up again. By supper time the "Abler" was once more seaworthy.

We returned all borrowed tools to the generous men of the "Alaska" who had given freely what they were taking for a desperate three years in the Arctic, replaced the few which we had used from the "Kotzebue's" shop and left for Captain Ballinger of the "Bear" what we had not used of the stores obtained from him. Now we were all ready to start north again.

Not quite, however. For the cook reported that we had no fresh meat on board. Although there had been plenty of time to get several reindeer from the herd which had been in the neighborhood of the village during our stay, this necessary provisioning had been put off until now the reindeer had been driven to market at Nome. Consequently, Kleinschmidt had to send Frank Born and Dr. Young in the launch about fifteen miles up the river to get a couple of carcasses from another herd. They returned at breakfast time the next day, after an all-night trip, with two fat deer, weighing one hundred and sixty and one hundred and seventy pounds, cleaned, but not skinned. One had a fine set of antlers which was saved for Kusche. Much to our regret the "Professor" had decided to go to Nome to collect beetles, birds and small mammals while we were in the Arctic, and had been therefore set ashore with his baggage to be picked up at Nome on our return.

FORMS OF THE ARCTIC DRIFT ICE

The upper view shows a floe-berg of more than average thickness. The lower scene gives
an idea of the appearance from a vessel's deck of the expanse of sea filled with loose cakes and
floes through which ships push their way slowly and cautiously.

DESHNEF, OR EAST CAPE, THE MOST EASTERN POINT OF ASIA

The rocky mass of East Cape, 2,900 feet high, is visible for many miles and is an unmistakable landmark. This view, taken from the beach at Post Deshnef, looks northward through Bering Strait into the Arctic Ocean. In the foreground Chukchi men are drawing a skin boat out of the water.

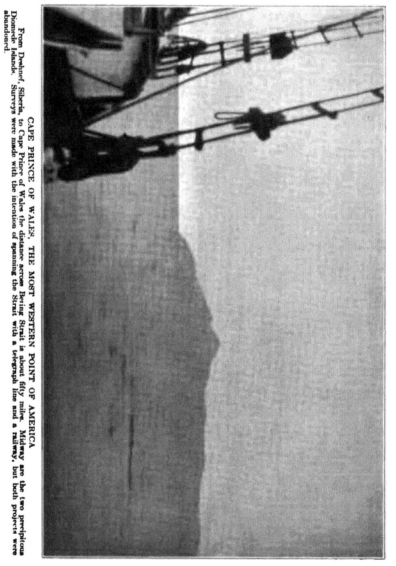

CAPE PRINCE OF WALES, THE MOST WESTERN POINT OF AMERICA

From Deshnef, Siberia, to Cape Prince of Wales the distance across Bering Strait is about fifty miles. Midway are the two precipitous Diomede Islands. Surveys were made with the intention of spanning the Strait with a telegraph line and a railway, but both projects were abandoned.

A YOUNG HUMPBACK WHALE

Photo. A. M. Collins

This young whale, about 30 feet long, was found dead, floating on its back north of Bering Strait. The span of its extended flippers was as much as its length. Decomposition had greatly inflated the black and white body and it swam high in the water.

CHAPTER VII

AT last we turned our prow again toward the Arctic. On the morning of August 8th we weighed anchor and passed out into Port Clarence Bay under a cloudy sky in a slight drizzle with a light northwest air stirring. Later the sky cleared and Cape Prince of Wales, the most westerly point of continental America, stood out bold and stately against a red and golden sunset in the northwest. Two faint dark spots on the horizon of a calm sea marked the Diomede Islands. In the swift current which set northward through Bering Strait we plowed our way into the Arctic for the second time. Once it had thrown us out crippled; we could not know what adventures now awaited us in this defiance of its powers.

We were aroused early next morning to look at a young humpback whale which lay dead, floating on its back. Its enormous fore-flippers extended far to each side of its black, fluted body, which was swollen with the gases of decomposition.

East Cape lay on the port quarter, Cape Unikin abeam. At noon we were three hundred miles from Wrangell Island, going well with the aid of foresail and spanker and motor, the good breeze astern, the weather sunny and delightful. For the fifth time on this voyage we crossed the Arctic Circle.

Bright sunshine continued to temper the increasing

coolness as we steadily forged northwestward, but the
wind freshened and the barometer fell rapidly on the
third day out from Teller.   As only enough fuel for
eighteen days' continuous running of the motor remained,
it was shut off during the afternoon.   A flurry of rain
seemed at first to account for the falling glass, but
presently the wind hauled to the westward and then
ahead, forcing us to stand inshore to gain by the northward drift.   By evening the wind had shifted again, this
time to the southwest, and we lay to all night on the port
tack, making leeway northward in a heavy and growing
sea.   A gorgeous red and orange sunset belied the inten-
tions of old Boreas, for by morning the wind was whist-
ling at forty miles an hour.

Only an hour's sleep was given me that night, for the
damp chill penetrated my night clothes, which consisted of heavy underwear, flannel shirt, sweater, breeches
and two pairs of heavy stockings, and over me four
blankets and a winter ulster.   The wind did not abate,
but flecked the black-blue, angry sea with frothy white
scud.   Wave after wave combed against the vessel, sending her like a match box, and once in a while the crests
dashed up her sides and over the cabin house.   We made
good weather of it nevertheless, but lay off and on and
logged no progress except that of our drift.   The endless
rolling and pitching were exceedingly tiresome.   Dr.
Young lay in his bunk reading a book with another under
his head.   Albrecht moped in the saloon, his head down
on his hands.   A little whirl of snow passed over.   A
dead walrus floated by with a half dozen gulls riding in
its lee.   Probably it had been killed or wounded by the
"Kit," a Norwegian vessel, which we heard was hunting
these beasts for skins and ivory.   The tawny mass

bulked large at two hundred yards distance and stank from afar. Off to leeward the Captain showed us the meeting place of two opposing winds, indicated aloft by mare's tails aiming toward each other at their upper ends.

"There," said he, pointing out a differently colored patch of sky near the water between the mare's tails, "is a flat calm, where the air currents meet."

By adding a cap, buttoned over my ears, to the duffle worn the night before, and throwing a fur parka on the blankets in addition to the overcoat, I slept snug and warm. The gale was moderating, but we were still one hundred and twenty miles from Wrangell.

"Ice ahead!"

This cry from the crow's nest, a barrel lashed to the rigging of the main mast, brought all hands on deck. Nothing was visible from below, but less than an hour raised the gleaming horizon of white on all sides but that from which we had come. It was about noon, and after dinner I climbed aloft to enjoy the great spectacle. The morning had broken clear and sunny with a moderate breeze W. by S. and we were steering N. by W. Now, however, a light fog, accompanied by snow flakes, shut out an extensive view, but revealed a majestic frame of low-lying ice floes far and near.

The Arctic ice-pack north of Siberia and Alaska is characteristically low because almost entirely formed on the level sea surface, and where we saw it the base was from two to ten feet above water. About one-seventh or one-eighth of the bulk swam above the sea; the underbody reached far down into the depths. But its surface was very rough and in places great blocks stood on end or were laid layer above layer where the grinding of the pack had tossed up fragments in the break-up of the floes, to freeze fast where they happened to fall.

Seen from aloft, the coloring was very beautiful. Many spots and hummocks were soiled a yellowish brown apparently by contact with land or the bottom or dirt-strewn by the wind. At this late period of the summer the constant lapping of waves had eroded the water line of the cakes so that the snowy upper crust overhung the water often for many yards, and would treacherously crumble if one stepped on it. The wide forefoot of the ice under water, which naturally did not cave away after erosion of the top, shimmered a delicate green through the sea, in contrast to the deep blue of the ocean, and many fantastically carved caves in the surface ice glowed with a wonderful ultramarine blue against the pure white of the untarnished covering.

But if the sun's rays failed to penetrate a gloomy mist overhead, the whole aspect changed. It lost the brightness and beauty, and put on a most sinister face. Gray and dull white prevailed; the green became cold and lifeless, the blue turned to grayish black; then the exquisite grottoes gave forth no luster; they were simply dark spots in the ice. The leaden sky pitilessly seemed to hang over and to forbid us.

So quickly as the sun, beaming through or sulking behind his mantle of fog, could change in an instant the whole meaning of the ice, so rapid were the leaps of all our human spirits, as chance laid one incident or another before us. Little things, too, raised and depressed us, for many little things were fatal in so short a season as we had for our ambitions.

The first bright day out from St. Michael was blotted by the gale forcing us south of St. Lawrence Island.

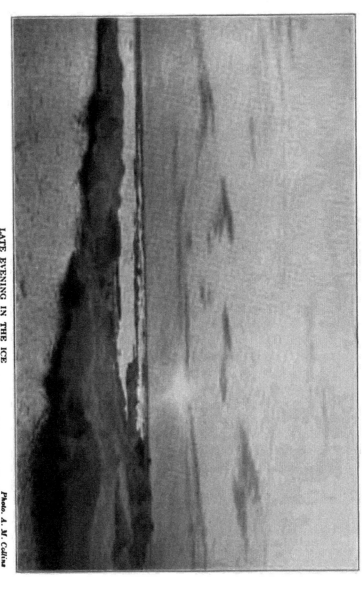

LATE EVENING IN THE ICE

Photo. A. M. Collins

The descending sun cast shadows and rosy and purple tints upon the ice which enhanced its natural beauty. This photograph was taken about 10 P. M. when the level rays had brought into relief the inequalities of the floes.

Photos. A. M. Collins and Gilpin Lovering

POLAR BEAR IN THE WATER

The polar bear is a strong swimmer and crosses wide leads from floe to floe without hesitation. These photographs are of a she-bear which swam out from the ice field to investigate the schooner. She dived when the ship came too close. The lower picture was taken after one of these dives when the bear was just rising again to the surface.

Our expectation of Siberian hunting was dashed by the absence of Baron von Kleist. Hopeless fog prevented us hunting the sheep at Penkegnei Bay after we had taken advice of the Russian officers and proved they were there. We entered the Arctic successfully in spite of the dismal weather. Our fears of shipwreck there, when we lost the rudder, were lightened by finding that we could navigate with a jury rudder. Congratulations succeeded tense anxiety when we moored in Teller Harbor. Then our hopes of a speedy repair were broken by the poverty of the place as we found it. Coming upon a providential rudder nearly made to hand, was almost offset by the loss of a precious week in getting to sea again. Born's threatened defection barely preceded the events which formed his desire to get away from Teller in any way he could. A quick run for two days up from Teller was averaged down by adverse weather. Sun and fog, fair and foul wind, a little gain and a little loss,—and our feelings were constantly alternating between hope and despair.

But hardly had we come up with the ice, when the greatest event of the voyage threw us to the height of excitement; for, surveying with eye and glass the marvelous panorama spread beneath the crow's nest, I spied a tiny chunk of ice in the water, and noticed that a black speck on it shifted from side to side. It needed but a glance through the binoculars to recognize it as a polar bear, swimming toward the boat. Shouting, "Bear!" I came out of the rigging like a monkey and everybody on the ship turned out instanter.

Kleinschmidt brought up his moving-picture cameras. The "Abler" changed her course and maneuvered to cut the beast off repeatedly from the ice floes a quarter mile distant. Each time as we were about to run her down the bear dived and swam under water for a few yards. We could see the great body at a considerable depth, showing light green through the water. After we had taken all the pictures we wanted a bullet broke the bear's neck at the base and then with considerable difficulty we got a rope around the body and hoisted it on board. It was a female, seven feet five inches from nose to tail. The fur was loose in places and was stained yellow and brown with grease secreted from the body, probably also from rolling in dirty ice, and perhaps from seals on which she had fed. It was thoroughly scrubbed with water and soap to clean it as much as possible and then salted. The carcass was swung up and kept for food.

This unexpectedly early encounter with big game put us all in the best of humor. All the disappointments of the past month vanished like mist before the sun, and we eagerly looked forward to more encouragement. Nor were we long deferred.

At this point we were some seventy-two miles east of Herald Island, in latitude 71.20 N., longitude 171.30 W. We were in the latitude of Point Barrow, the northernmost cape of Alaska, and of the northern side of Wrangell Island. This was the most northerly point that we reached on the cruise. The storm had greatly taken us out of our course.

The "Abler" was put toward Herald Island and threaded the leads among the broken ice floes until evening. Just after supper a black lump on a pan developed into a sleeping walrus, and we could see long ivory as he fitfully tossed his head. We kept our wind from him, and Kleinschmidt and Elting in the two kayaks, lashed together to make them steadier, paddled off to stalk the game. From deck and rigging we watched the whole affair. Both men had slipped white cotton parkas over their furs to harmonize with the general scenery. They paddled surely toward their victim, freezing into ice as he occasionally raised his head, and when screened by the ridge of the hummock on which he was lying with his tail in the water, they tied the kayaks and stalked over the little hill to a range of about thirty yards. The walrus was not once aware of danger and, when the slender steel bullet of the .280 Ross rifle went into the back of his head, simply relaxed without moving his position. Then the hunters raced back to their raft, for the floe to which it was fastened had begun to drift apart from the other. We rounded to the scene in the schooner and found a very large specimen dead on the ice.

The Pacific walrus is well known to be a greater animal than the Atlantic variety, but we were really surprised to see how monstrous this one actually appeared. Unfortunately he was not measured in the haste to get off with him, and this same haste was largely responsible for an exasperating calamity. The head, with the scalp on it, was soon cut off and Kleinschmidt called for a rope. The end of an old one was tossed over the rail and he made it fast to a slit in the hide.

"Haul away!" he cried.

"Are you sure that's secure?" asked Elting anxiously, as the trophy slid over the ice.

"Oh, sure," answered our mentor, and up the ship's side it slowly crawled. Three men were hauling. The weight, about 200 pounds, was hard to raise in that way. Suddenly the rope parted and down went the whole thing into five hundred feet of water. Kleinschmidt stamped

around and Elting said little but looked very sick.   In
fact my roommate took it so hard that he did not sleep
that night.   It was a very unfortunate occurrence which
might have been avoided if we had carefully examined
the rope, for after the accident the line was found to be
rotten.   Ever after that we took no more chances, but
first of all made a well-tested rope fast to the walrus's
head and if possible through his mouth in such a way
that there was little danger of losing it.   There was no
repairing this loss of Elting's, so we hoisted aboard the
hide with the flippers and some blubber.

This affair completely nullified all the cheering effect
of our first polar bear that morning;   yet our first day
in the ice was at least eventful.

The "Abler" in her further course pushed aside ice
pans nearly as large as herself.   Awakened at two in the
morning by the repeated shocks of ice cakes against the
schooner, I turned out and found Larsson on watch, ram-
ming through heavy drift ice at top speed.   This seemed
to be a habit with him.

"Where are we heading, Cap?" I asked.

"Straight for Herald Island," he replied.

"Why not turn out to the thinner ice and see if we
don't make better time?" I suggested.

He did so and soon got too far out into a heavy
southwest sea which drove him back to cover, as it was
unpleasant to see great masses of ice hurtling on all sides
of the boat, threatening to stave in her sides.   Elting
and I watched from four o'clock until breakfast.   Small
patches of dirty snow continually misled us into thinking
we were again upon walrus or bear, for the resemblance
of color was perfect.   The mate got stuck in a jam for
several hours in a fog where we could not see three hun-

dred yards and then, turning a corner, made fast to a heavy floe. Soon the mist lifted and revealed the steep crags of Herald Island some twenty miles to the west.

Herald Island is a granite formation about six miles long, two miles broad and some 1,200 feet high. It was discovered by Kellett in 1849 and named for his ship. Polar bears, white foxes, gulls, murres, auks, guillemots and other birds live on it, amid a scanty vegetation of poppies, grasses, moss, lichens, sedges and dwarf willows. This rocky upthrust of soil into the bleak Arctic Ocean acts as a pivot or anchorage for vast fields of ice. So well as we could see, the pack to which we were moored extended solid to the islet.

Several hours we lay idle, and then made off. A lead took us east for a short distance and after supper the cook spied a great bear staring at us from the top of a hummock at the edge of the floe not two hundred yards away. Two cubs immediately showed themselves beside her, and Collins, Lovering and Kleinschmidt put out at once in the kayaks. But the quarry did not wait. They turned and walked leisurely into the ice-pack, and from the crow's nest one could see them moving across the frozen field toward the north end of the island. The mate sighted four others which were moving in the same direction from a point not far distant; all were much beyond reach before the hunters had landed. The men followed the bear tracks a few hundred yards and stood, puzzled, their vision limited by the innumerable hummocks. We, aloft, could make out still another bear quite near them, but had no means of signaling our friends and the great animal slowly moved away without hurry, pausing frequently to gaze at the apparition of our masts which jutted into his view.

8

It was very slow and difficult going on the surface of the floe. Seen from above the whole sheet was pitted with countless pools of water, canals and lakes; some only a few feet deep, many punctured in the center clear through the deep ice. Most of them were too deep to wade; the banks of all were steep and slippery. A detour three or four times as long as the air line was generally the only way of reaching any point. In and out of these basins the bears, on the other hand, made their way regardless of the water and their slowest walk could beat any man's quickest run.

So our three companions came back to the "Abler" and we pursued the lead. A dirty snow patch several times attracted our eyes, but we had actually passed it before it clearly resolved itself into a bear asleep on a snowy hillside a hundred yards in from the bank of the lead. Collins and Kleinschmidt were off in the kayaks while the "Abler" rounded to. Still the animal dozed on. The men landed and crawled up. Suddenly the beast awoke at the rumble of our engine and stared at the ship. It was quite beyond his understanding. He ran a few steps to the top of a hill and stood, magnificent, trying to make us out. Then the rifle puffed, a hind leg thrust out and he rolled off the hillock away and out of sight. The 45-70 Winchester had knocked him bodily over and he lay dead where he fell. It was a splendid male bear. His head and claws were immense and he was especially thick set, measuring from nose to tail eight feet, one inch. The lower canine teeth were worn and broken down half to the gums. We dragged him with difficulty to the nearest water slew, towed him by a rope nearer the lead, and skinned him in the rain. The hide, like that of the first bear, was much discolored and the long hairs were loose.

The captain and mate had taken observations with an artificial horizon of molasses in a saucer and reckoned out our position within a few miles of its exact one as shown by the fog revealing the island clearly six miles away. A beautiful golden sunset promised more fog for the morrow and the southeast wind seemed to confirm this probability.

"We'll lie moored to this floe till the wind shifts," announced the captain. "If it comes out of the northwest we'll have to move or be bottled up."

Promptly at midnight the air current switched to that quarter and we cast loose. At first we laid a direct course for Wrangell Island and ran into a blind pocket. Another and another lead gave the same result. Then the fog shut us in totally and we lay moored from noon to 3.30 P. M. waiting impatiently for the sky to clear. All this while cake after cake of ice, up to an acre in area, drifted in to nestle near us, gradually filling the bight in which we lay. About the time we were crowded out anyway the curtain drew up enough for us to see about two miles. From the masthead nothing was visible but broken fields of ice. Leads appeared to open in various directions, but we tried them for two hours in a general southerly course, hoping to break through the barrier and get directly out. But all in vain. It was evident that the ice lay packed against Herald Island and considerably east of it, except for the passage north of the barrier, through which we had penetrated to six miles from the lonely spot of land. Captain Larsson threw up his arms and said, "I give it up."

There was nothing left to do but try to back-track to go out as we had come in. The question was, would we be able to make it, or would the ice have been driven in hard enough by the recent southeast winds to block the way?

The mate went on duty. First, then, he steered northeast to more open water, east and southeast, and at last southerly, led on by the sky sign of blue and white bands of clouds near the horizon, indicating clear water. Steadily we made our way, now through fairly open places, now crowding denser pans out of our track, till at length the welcome groundswell lifted our forefoot a little as the subdued semblance of a wave wriggled to us under the ice, and by 9 P. M. we were in open water again. We had nearly been caught in the ice, and no one could tell when, if ever, we should have been released again. It was near this position that the "Jeannette" was beset in 1879 to drift for twenty months and finally be crushed. I felt relieved. My hunting companions did not seem to think seriously of the matter at all. They apparently assumed all the time that it was a matter of course that wherever we got in we could get out. But the lateness of the season, so near the usual time of freezing up, made me rather anxious.

Elting went on deck early to find the captain on watch, bucking crowded broken ice in a calm sea covered with frozen slush an inch deep.

"I'm headin' for Wrangell Island as straight as a bee," was his answer to our now usual greeting.

We never knew an hour at a time what way we were bound, in these days. When the mate took charge at 4 A. M. he headed southeast at once, for fear of the sea freezing and tying up the boat; as he said that this "mush" immediately preceded the freeze-up. The thermometer stood at 29°, about the freezing point of the sea, and the wind was a mere northwest whisper. By six we

DRAGGING A BEAR TO THE SHIP   *Photo. A. M. Collins*

It required the strength of several men to haul a good-sized female bear over the ice, while a half dozen could hardly move the largest specimen—a male. Wherever possible all meat obtained by the hunters was saved and eaten.

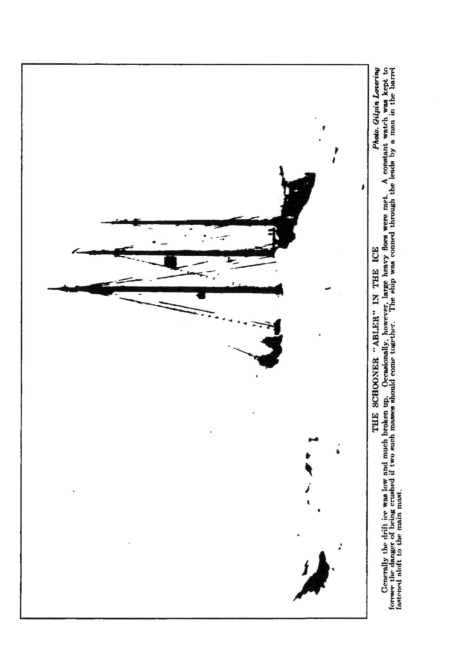

THE SCHOONER "ABLER" IN THE ICE

Photo. Gilpin Lovering

Generally the drift ice was low and much broken up. Occasionally, however, large heavy floes were met. A constant watch was kept to foresee the danger of being crushed if two such masses should come together. The ship was conned through the leads by a man in the barrel fastened aloft to the main mast.

had reached open water and presently turned northwest once more, for Wrangell. Two or three walrus rolled off their pans as we passed through broken ice which gradually increased in density. Murres scurried through the ripples, seeming to emerge from underneath every cake. Soon we had to steer off again southward and at noon a rather vague dead reckoning placed us only fifteen miles southeast of our position of twenty-four hours previously. But we were outside the pack, instead of inside, and in small ice.

The floes increased in size; fog precluded any range of vision and the wind had dropped. At 10 P. M. we tried to moor to a pan, but the ice was so rotten that the Eskimo sailors refused to set food on it, so we let the ship drift in the light south air among the scattered ice. A little thermometer stood at 28° when I turned in, but the extreme dampness made the chill felt clear through the body. Putting on my parka with the fur inside failed to give me a wink of sleep in the whole night, so I got up at four in the morning and drank three or four cups of coffee from the Thermos bottle which the cook had filled for early morning use. In passing round the deck I noticed that several basins containing photographic negatives had frozen. All the rigging and the dark wood glistened with rime.

Ice began to hem us in and the propeller bit hard at one piece before we had started. Once on our way the ice was more open, the wind light from the south. We ran to and fro all day. Now we steered some hours westerly till we found ourselves in pockets, the ice growing tighter and tighter till we could no longer push through it; then we had to come out again and feel our way, bend south and make to the westward when it seemed feasible. But all this was in the dense fog. It was a blind man's groping. When this sort of thing first began it was uncanny, but by now we were quite accustomed to it. Every one cordially cursed the weather.

For an hour we tied up to a big, hilly floe which was doubtless grounded. The mate found on it a beach pebble as big as a pigeon's egg. For what fabulous tale this was to be the basis I know not. Kleinschmidt took motion pictures of us climbing the highest peak, perhaps thirty feet above the water, and slipping down again, while Born made some repairs to the dynamo. This important part of the engine, by the way, was frequently in trouble all summer.

Through many a twist and turn into the bights of the ice-pack, we made a generally south by west direction, which would bring us to the Siberian coast somewhat west of Cape Vankarem if the trend of the pack kept this course as it had done hitherto. In crossing some of these large pieces of open water the "Abler" rolled and pitched a great deal during the night as she sped before the heavy north wind. When morning came this shifted to a few points west of north and lightened very much, so that the pack sheltered us and gave smooth water. It was clear and sunny much of the day, and someone of us watched for game from the cabin house roof all the time. Nothing appeared in the morning. Except by unusual accident we did not expect to see bears among the small ice cakes. One might of course be surprised in the water as he made his way from one floe to another, but as a rule we found they ranged over the larger fields. These we examined carefully with our glasses. The bears appeared to lie up mostly in the hollows, beside a seal blow-hole, waiting a chance for food. If they remained there we might readily sail by and miss them. Probably on this account we passed unknowingly many more than we saw. Unless in motion they were very difficult to make out, for the fur was the exact coloring of many a patch of soiled ice. The black nose was a fairly convincing mark for distinguishing them.

The polar bear is found everywhere near land north of Asia and America, principally on the coasts and islands which are surrounded by drift ice, and even on ice-fields far out at sea, where he enjoys his best hunting.

Cagni found a bear 120 miles from land and Nansen, during his long drift in the "Fram" and his sledge journey, reported bears at great distances. Several were seen upwards of 100 miles from the islands of New Siberia, one 150 miles north of Spitzbergen, one 200 miles northwest of Franz Josef Land, one 230 miles northwest of Franz Josef Land and 210 miles north of Spitzbergen. A solitary wanderer was found 270 miles north of Cape Chelyuskin, the nearest land then known, but new islands were discovered in 1913 stretching northward from this point, which greatly reduce the actual distance of that bear from his home on solid ground. Nansen also saw fresh fox tracks 200 miles northwest of Franz Josef Land.

A male and female, sometimes accompanied by one or two large cubs, make extended excursions together, but larger bands are not often seen. Their principal food is seal and young walrus and it is thought that they also consume large quantities of seaweed, grass and lichens.

One explorer writes:

"We saw a bear hunting a seal; the bear followed the edge of the ice-field, hiding itself as much as possible, so as to be able to spring on the seal and seize it when it came near enough."

It may be that the polar bear hibernates if food is hard to obtain, for dens have been found, occasionally with bears in them, but this does not appear to be a regular habit, as they are frequently met at large during the winter. They are, however, lean at this time of year and a dead carcass sinks in the water, while the reverse is true during the open months when food is more easily caught and they become very fat. Females pregnant, or with very young cubs, are rarely come upon, for they lie up during this period.

The time of year when cubs are born seems to be more extended than is the case with some other mammals. Thus the Duke of the Abruzzi writes on April 2d:

"While walking near the level summit of the cape (Fligely, Franz Josef Land), Hans sinks into a den inhabited by a she-bear. The den is hollowed out of the snow and communicates with the exterior only by a small opening, through which Hans, taking up a good position, fires, and kills the beast. We then come up, and enlarging the opening of the den, drag out the bear, and two little cubs, hardly larger than cats." And the same party, on April 9th, came upon "two little cubs, bigger than those found at Cape Fligely."

F. G. Jackson, exploring the same country five years previously, found on February 3d a female bear and newly born cub, hardly larger than a big cat, in a den which he describes as follows:

"The lair was situated on the steep, sloping edge of the plateau at the front of the rocks, where it runs down to the frozen sea below. It was deeply covered with a hard compact snow-drift, the thickness of the snow

LARGE FEMALE POLAR BEAR   *Photo. A. M. Collins*

The first bear was hoisted aboard by a rope slung around the body. It measured 7 feet
5 inches from nose to tail and was estimated to weigh about 800 pounds.

BLACK, BROWN AND GRIZZLY BEARS

1. Common black bear. (*Ursus americanus*.) Maine (Wilson Potter). Length of skin, 5 feet 10 inches; width, 5 feet 9 inches.

2. Alaskan brown bear. (*Ursus kenaiensis*.) Kenai, 1912 (Wilson Potter). Length of skin, 7 feet 11½ inches; width, 7 feet 11 inches.

3. Grizzly bear. (*Ursus horribilis*.) White River, Yukon T., 1910 (Wilson Potter). Length of skin, 7 feet; width, 6 feet 2 inches.

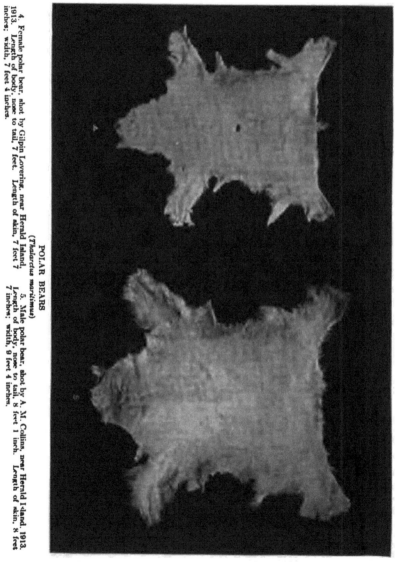

POLAR BEARS
(Thalarctus maritimus)

4. Female polar bear, shot by Gilpin Lovering, near Herald Island, 1913. Length of body, nose to tail, 7 feet. Length of skin, 7 feet 7 inches; width, 7 feet 4 inches.

5. Male polar bear, shot by A. M. Collins, near Herald Island, 1913. Length of body, nose to tail, 8 feet 1 inch. Length of skin, 8 feet 7 inches; width, 9 feet 4 inches.

Photo. A. M. Collins

BRINGING IN A YOUNG POLAR BEAR
Kleinschmidt, Elting and Lovering retrieving a cub in the two kayaks, with which the hunters stalked polar bear and walrus.

above the lair being about four feet. The lair had evidently been there for a very considerable period. . . . Polar bears do not, strictly speaking, hibernate at all, . . . only the females lay up for a very considerable time to bring forth their young."

Nansen shot a she-bear on June 23d, with milk in her breasts but no embryo and no trace of young, and on July 6th killed two cubs with their mother, commenting:

"It is remarkable how large these cubs are. I could hardly imagine that they were born this year, and should without hesitation have put them down as a year old if the she-bear had not been in milk, and it is hardly to be supposed that the cubs would suck for a year and a half. Those we shot by the 'Fram' on November 4th last year were hardly half the size of these. It would seem as if the polar bear produces its young at different times of the year. In the paunches of the cubs were pieces of skin from a seal." Probably the cubs continued to suckle after the time actually necessary for doing so.

In spite of his great size and strength, for the polar bear is among the largest of his kind, he is not difficult to kill and usually takes to flight when wounded. When he sees a man on the ice, the bear will stalk him, frequently climbing hummocks to spy and sniff. He can thus generally be shot at close quarters. An unarmed man may frighten off a bear by loud cries or rapid movement of the arms, but if he runs the bear will pursue.

"Bear-hunting is very easy," says the Duke of the Abruzzi. "A bear sees and smells a camp long before man is aware of his presence, and hunger generally compels him to approach. It is not, therefore, necessary to look for him. Our dogs, which were so many, and

wandered about freely all day, pursued every bear they
saw. The larger he-bears were able to escape if they had
only eight or ten dogs at their heels, but if they were
attacked by a pack of thirty or forty, they were obliged
to stop, and climb up on a hummock, or to range themselves against a block of ice by way of defence. We
thus had time to come up and shoot them from a distance of a few feet. None could escape us. The dogs
were sometimes wounded in the hunt, almost always by
the he-bears, and rarely by the she-bears. They were
so nimble in avoiding the bears' blows that their
wounds were never serious, and the doctor's assistance
was only required three or four times to sew them up,
even later on, when they became more daring in their
attacks.

"We killed many she-bears, often accompanied by
two cubs, which from their equal growth seemed to be
twins. During the summer we mostly killed she-bears,
and later on, during the winter and spring, only males;
some of these were of considerable size, measuring up to
nine feet five inches along the back. We had very often
bears' flesh to eat; the best parts were the heart, the
kidneys, and the tongue; the rest was not equally pal-
atable.

"A bullet from a rifle of .303 caliber aimed at the
shoulder, or at the forehead, was quite enough to kill a
bear; but if they were running away, several shots were
required. We never found that the bear attacked us;
we always saw them make off in the opposite direction to
that from which the shot had been fired."

Female bears with cubs are bolder than others and
more determined in their efforts to secure food. One
stalked Johansen, Nansen's companion, knocked him

down and was about to kill him with a bite in the head when Nansen shot her. Then the two cubs peeped over a hummock to see what the prospects for a meal were.

Various travelers have remarked that the meat is good if not too well grown. My own appreciation of the fat, oily flesh of summer was perhaps not sufficiently whetted by starvation to join in this chorus of praise. But at least it tasted better than walrus.

In the afternoon, about three o'clock, when Collins was watching, he sighted a female and cub on a good-sized floe about a mile square. But they did not wait for Lovering, Elting and Kleinschmidt to reach them in the kayaks. They traveled at a tremendous pace, straight across the floe away from us, never stopping. The mother went first and the cub followed her without lagging a bit behind.

The hunters came back and we went around the ice field as fast as possible in the schooner. We had followed them by eye to the farther water's edge and when we got around the floe it was a close question if they had crossed the lead there and gotten away among the hummocks of the next field beyond, for they could not be seen. At last Frank, the sailor, made them out very near the far edge of the water, swimming fast. After them we put the ship and overhauled them. Lovering and Elting stood in the bow. As the big one climbed out of the water less than one hundred yards away Lovering creased her on the back. She snapped at the scratch. His second and third went into the rump and loins, and down she went. The cub hesitated and then went off and into the water beyond the narrow pan. Elting shot it through the head with his Ross, and the soft bullet did not much hurt the skin, though it wrecked the skull. It also was a female.

We hauled them aboard and went on all afternoon through thick and thin as before. After dinner another big bear was seen perched on a hummock a few hundred yards in from the lead. She squatted there unaccountably unconcerned, till Elting, Kleinschmidt and I got ashore in the kayaks. We stole up behind a good-sized hill and the bear became restive. She was just ready to move off, for she was suspiciously watching the schooner by this time. Seeing this, Elting fired and I let go as if at a three hundred yard target. Evidently the distance was not less than a quarter mile, however, for she went off unhit, pursued by another ball from Elting. We ran fast across the floe, about a half mile, jumping deep slews and wading shallow ones, while the "Abler" went around the field. The game had made it much faster and was well out across the open water when we got to the place it had left the ice. We hailed the schooner, but as she passed close by, Collins shouted that the bear would get away unless they followed it immediately, so they went on and left us on the floe for a half hour while Collins shot the bear and got it aboard. They were a mile away and we could hear the animal yell as the several bullets struck her. She measured six feet, ten inches, and had a fine white pelt. A good deal of hot talk passed between Born and Kleinschmidt and we had to hold them apart as a result of the chagrin which the latter felt at being left on the floe.

THE FIRST WALRUS OF THE HUNT

Photo. Gilpin Lovering

Dr. Elting stalked and killed the first walrus which was sighted. Behind the hunter appear the kayaks which were used to pursue the game. These arctic canoes are narrow, light and seaworthy and are used when there is much ice in the sea. They are completely covered, except for a small cockpit, with skins.

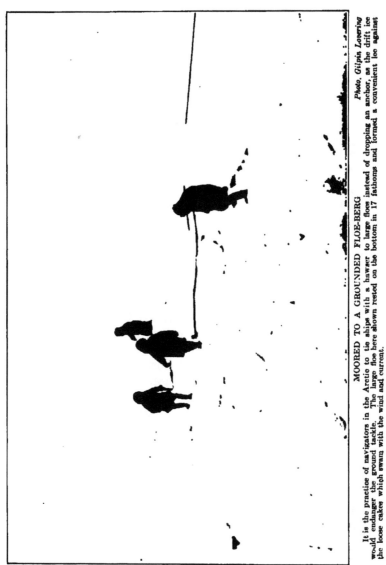

MOORED TO A GROUNDED FLOE-BERG

Photo, Gilpin Lowering

It is the practice of navigators in the Arctic to tie ships with a hawser to large floes instead of dropping an anchor, as the drift ice would endanger the ground tackle. The large floe here shown rested on the bottom in 17 fathoms and formed a convenient lee against the loose cakes which swam with the wind and current.

CHAPTER VIII

AMONG THE WALRUS HERDS

DURING the night we came south in a heavy following wind that kicked up a big sea and rolled the old barge about a lot. We ran through points of loose ice making out eastward from the main body and between them across pieces of rough open water.

The U. S. Revenue Cutter "Corwin," striving to reach Wrangell Island in 1881, found at first exactly the same ice conditions as we did thirty-two years later. The vessel was somewhat south of the island with no leads visible by which it could be approached. "The solid appearance of the ice," reported Captain Hooper, "and the fact that there was no material change in the depth of the water, convinced me that there was no possibility of reaching the land from this direction until a decided change should take place. So we determined to follow the ice to the westward. . . . Accordingly after getting out of the lead, we followed the edge of the western pack towards the southwest, keeping close alongside of the ice. On account of the thick weather, and in our anxiety to find the pack trending westward, we kept running into leads in that direction, only to find ourselves disappointed and forced to turn back. Instead of trending westward, as I had hoped, it gradually took a more southerly direction, until it ran nearly north and south, and presented an almost unbroken front, and in this condition it extended to the Siberian coast at Cape North. Apparently the entire sea north of the Siberian Coast and west of Wrangell Island was filled with heavy pack-ice."

By morning we had found an opening into a bight of the ice, fairly clear but with many broken fragments inside the barrier, to windward of which we had sounded twenty fathoms. Round and round this we cruised, looking for walrus, all morning, without success. Then one of the sailors saw a large herd climbing up on a floe about one and a half miles away. With our glasses we could see their numbers steadily increasing and the dark patch they formed spreading over the floe. New candidates for positions on the ice swam up to the edge looking for a foothold, and before giving up would make the circuit of the pan. Others floated near by. Still more rose and dived continually. Down the wind came to us the chorus of grunts as the walrus squabbled among themselves for comfortable postures.

Elting, Lovering and Kleinschmidt pushed off in the two kayaks lashed together, but mistook the direction and made a very wide detour, having to climb several ice hills before finding the herd. Finally they reached the floe and after repeated attempts to get to close range succeeded in arriving within seventy-three yards. Elting knocked down and, to all appearances, killed one walrus, which fell over and made no move. He wounded another, which slipped off the floe and immediately climbed back again. In spite of Elting's attempt to hit him once more he got off, and then to our surprise the dead one suddenly rolled over and was lost, followed by a bullet from the gun. Lovering did not fire.

The latter sighted another herd after dinner, but it

was a long distance away and in trying to near it the mate in the crow's nest lost the exact location and we went past.   Then it seemed as if it had been an illusion, for all dark patches were only shadow and dirty snow; but on returning along our track we found the walrus again.   Lovering, whose turn it was to shoot (for we had arranged a rotation of chances), invited me to go with him and Collins in the kayaks.   The man who had the shot had always the first choice of when and what to shoot, as well as direction of the stalk and the right to fire exclusively or to permit the others to shoot.

We paddled nearly a mile from the "Abler"—the afternoon had well slipped by—and reached a small ice-pan, about one hundred square yards in area, one hundred and fifty yards to leeward of the larger piece on which the walrus lay.   To get there we had to pass and not disturb a dozen of the huge beasts which were sleeping and idling in the water to our right.   Some floated upright, their heads out to the ears, their tusks dipped below the surface so that they could look about.   Others slept awash, their heads under water and the round of their rumps and great shoulders showing a few inches above the ripples.   For at least a half hour they would remain in this position, and doubtless could do so much longer, though we never timed any exactly to learn how long they could comfortably stay under.   Some lazily turned their faces towards us, but I doubt if their vision was good enough to see us at the distance, about seventy-five yards, or they would have indulged their notorious curiosity to see what we were.   In any case we resembled a cake of ice as much as we could dress the part; over our fur parkas we had pulled white cotton ones that concealed every dark part of our clothing while

we were seated or crouching, and the low hulls of the
kayaks were difficult to distinguish from the shadow
which lurked under the overhanging edge of nearly every
piece of ice. As we were to pass any of these brutes in
the water we bent over and paddled hard with a low
sweep of the lower arm to make as little movement as
we could. In this fashion the two kayaks poked their
noses into a little cove in the ice block we were aiming
for, and we crawled out and tied to a rough corner.
Carrying our rifles carefully to keep snow out of the muz-
zles, we made our way to the side facing the walrus herd
on the larger pan.

In the water just at our left front five monsters sank
and rose, blowing spray from their nostrils, as they
stood upright, with a noise like an engine exhausting
steam. They were not more than fifteen yards away.
A lone bull rose almost under our peering faces and
ducked instantly in surprise. He came up again a little
farther off and then, curiosity conquering fear, drew close
again in a series of dives and breaks, till he had inspected
us several times within a few yards, from three sides. It
almost looked as if he were about to hitch up on the ice
and lie down beside us. This lucky whim did not decide
him, however, and soon he went off. About thirty-five
were counted in the water.

Two presented a comical sight as they lay on their
sides on a very small piece of ice between us and the
larger troop. They snuggled close together, face to
face, their tusks occasionally getting in each other's way,
and patting each other now and then with their fore
flippers. If one shifted a trifle farther off, the other,
wriggled close up to him again. Both were bulls, keeping together for warmth or comfort. All of the walrus

we hunted were males. The females at this season were
segregated for the purpose of nursing their young, which
are born in the spring.

But our chief attention was centered on the large
gathering of animals crowded upon the ice pan to windward of us. They were at least forty in number, for we
counted that many that we could see, and were packed
together to the very edge of the ice. Many, lucky
enough to have arrived early and secured places in the
middle of the floe, were forced to sit up by the pushing
of later comers, and expressed their discontent by frequent grunts and ill-natured tusk jabs at their neighbors.
Some hung to the edge of the dry ice by their fore-
flippers, their bodies resting on the under-water shelf,
awaiting a chance to force a way up on a newly vacated
spot. Some bodies lay over the others, and when one,
annoyed at being too insistently squeezed or lain upon,
sat up and brandished his formidable teeth in the air,
several more generally were inconvenienced enough to
rear up too and argue out the point with him by voice
and ivory. Their squabbles lasted only a minute, began
with a couple of sharp pecks at the flank or shoulder of
the offending animal, caused a sudden shift out of the
way or a few clashes of tusks, and ended by both creatures falling back to sleep with a long sigh of resignation
at the petty bothers in having to live with others.
Large tuskers seemed to be the tyrants of the rookery
and the others often imitated their example; in a small
herd they even prepared to lie down again after a bullet
had brained the leader and laid him motionless on the
snow. Around the edges of the pan walrus were "milling" all the time, rising to blow and sinking at once;
some rose high out of water looking for a vantage ground

9

on the ice.   In their persistence they frequently went round the herd several times before giving it up to join the other disappointed fellows at a little distance.

No attempt to picture the walrus herd would be faithful did it not attempt to show the uncanny impression which such a sky-line made upon the eye.   Out of a tangled darkness of bodies, projected here and there a vast bulk tapering to a relatively small head, which, stretched upward in the same line, waved its two teeth aloft for a moment and then fell back again into the mass.   The fat lips were wider than the head at the eyes, and, as the back of the skull merged into the trunk, increasing in diameter to the middle of the body, the outline looked more than anything else like a giant worm with huge antennæ.   At other spots a pair of points marked where one lay on the flat of his back.

They were grotesque caricatures of human beings with big toothpicks in their mouths; hulking idiots quarreling all the time and yet unwilling to live alone.

We were drifting on our small floe faster than the walrus and widening the distance.   Lovering had found the front sight broken off his rifle, but he fired, nevertheless, and naturally missed.

At that the walrus rose and tumbled into the water. A twist of the body rolled off those at the edge of the pan, two rolls saved the next, and those caught inside hobbled on their flippers as fast as they could and plunged in.   The whole party then stood up in the sea, milling till the air was full of spray, facing the bare, dirty ice floe and showing every sign of anger and wonder at their disturbance.   They spouted, grunted and blew, rising and falling like the valves of a compound engine, trying to find out what had happened to them.   Some raised themselves on the edge to look over the brown stained surface and dropped back still mystified.

In this way they tramped the water around to the farther side of the pan, and when they were there we made ready to get away, for angry walrus in the water often attack boats, and our fragile raft would not have lasted a second if they had come for us. Outlying walrus had also hurried to join the demonstration, so the coast was fairly clear.

An amusing detail was the action of several sea gulls which we had noticed perched on near-by ice as if by accident. But so soon as the last walrus had left the rookery these alighted and began to pick up food: probably stray clams and ordure.

Darkness had fallen, for by this season the sun was setting fairly early, and a snow squall was rapidly approaching. The "Abler" cast loose and began to move off, growing fainter and fainter, dissolving into nothing for a few minutes as the snow fell. I was alarmed, thinking that they had lost sight of us and in trying to come up were getting farther away. We jumped into the kayaks and were about to push off when a huge walrus broke water near us and Lovering was for waiting on the floe. The prospect of waiting or paddling was equally unpleasant if the schooner had mistaken our direction, for the ice field swallowed up small objects like men at a mile distance, and the whole pack was drifting nearly two miles an hour. On the other hand we might break our hearts with paddling before we could catch the ship if she continued to move. It did not take us long to decide for the second alternative, so we fired several signals, started and bent hard on the paddles. After a half hour of stiff labor we met the vessel coming back and they relieved us by saying that they had not lost us, but had gone to an open place to turn around.

Painstaking observations of the sun by captain and mate indicated that we were just off Cape Vankarem, on the Siberian coast. When, however, the land presently came into sight it proved that our chronometer was quite out. We were, in fact, fifty-two miles farther west than the observations placed us

Collins asked me to go with Kleinschmidt and him on the next stalk. As the schooner cruised through the fairly open ice field in a glassy, calm sea, with bright sunshine warming the keen edge off the ice-breath, we came close to a small group of our game, the walrus, huddled upon a very small cake. Kleinschmidt directed our movements. The very faint air that was stirring we feared would be enough to give the quarry our scent and no ice large enough to lie on was nearer than fifty yards on the lee side. A tall cliff rose ten feet high just beside the rookery, and an expectant gull sat upon it, but we dared not risk making it, for the walrus sat up and looked around frequently. There were four of them and the two that had good ivory lay badly for our position on the leeward floe.

The best shot is to have the back of the head presented, for the heavy forepart of the skull stops or turns even a high-power bullet, and the side view gives but a very small area into which the lead must go to reach the brain. This spot lies fifteen inches from the muzzle and three inches below the top of the head, just back of the tiny hole marking the ears. It is extremely hard to reach the brain and many a one would be missed by the best shots; even if wounded severely they are able

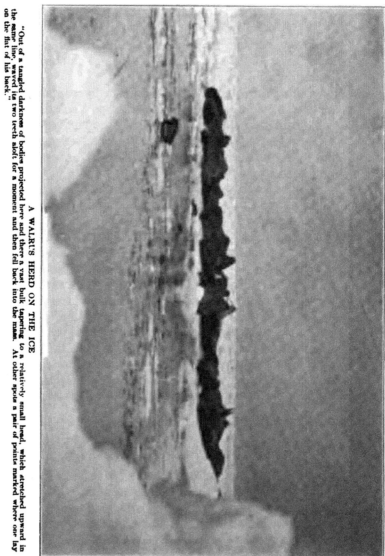

A WALRUS HERD ON THE ICE

"Out of a tangled darkness of bodies projected here and there a vast bulk tapering to a relatively small head, which stretched upward in the same line, waved its two teeth aloft for a moment and then fell back into the mass. At other spots a pair of points marked where one lay on the flat of his back."

Upper Photo. Gilpin Lovering

WALRUS HERD AND A LARGE TUSKER

Above: Walrus on an ice-pan, seen from a neighboring floe.
Below: Lovering seated on a carcass. The neck and shoulders of the walrus are heavily
marked with swellings in the skin.

with one twist to gain the water.   The bodies sink instantly and do not rise again for several days, after decomposition has inflated them.   We never hoped to recover any if they left the ice.   If instantaneously killed by a brain shot the enormous, flabby hulk fell limply on the ice.   If, however, it lay on a slope, or part of it overhung the edge, it was pretty sure to slip off and be lost.

At this lot Collins, I and Kleinschmidt fired in rapid succession and all the walrus disappeared.   Collins was totally baffled, for he said he had a dead sure aim.

Kleinschmidt then took Elting to another small group with the same lack of success.

From very early times the ivory tusks of walrus have been an article of trade with Europe, and nearly a thousand years ago men were trying to describe this animal, which they had never seen.   The mediæval nature-fakers added detail to detail until an extraordinary legend had grown up about this uncouth monster.

Nordenskjöld, for example, quotes Albertus Magnus, who, in the year 1280 described a walrus hunt as follows: "The walrus, while the sleeping animal hangs by its large tusks to a cleft of the rock, is taken by the hunter cutting out a piece of its skin and fastening to it a strong rope whose other end is tied to trees, posts, or large rings fixed to rocks.   The walrus is then wakened by throwing large stones at its head.   In its attempts to escape it leaves its hide behind.   It perishes soon after, or is thrown up half dead on the beach."

The walrus is a relative of the seals.   Like them it has developed the fore and rear legs into flippers for swimming, while retaining the toe nails on each digit. The body is largest at the shoulders and tapers off gradually to the tailless extremity, the form being perfectly adapted to rapid motion through the water.   In the walrus the upper canine teeth grow downward to a great length and serve as tools for digging out of the mud the clams and other shell-fish on which the animal lives.   We found walrus in water twenty to thirty fathoms deep, undoubtedly just over the areas where suitable food was most abundant.   Evidently the beast dives to this great depth and, while standing head downward in the water, grubs up the bivalves from the bottom, feeling them with the stiff bristles of its upper lip and sucking them into its mouth.   The great molars crush and eliminate as much of the shells as possible and swallow the rest.   We found quantities of broken shells in their stomachs, and occasionally live clams hanging to the higher bristles of the muzzle, whence the long tongue could not lick them off. Seaweed is also found in the stomach, whether swallowed incidentally or by design.   Nansen saw one walrus 150 miles from land in water more than 12,000 feet deep, evidently far astray.

To get a sufficient meal the walrus must be able to stay under water for a considerable time.   We watched them for at least a half hour, sleeping at the surface, as is their habit, the lungs inflated, head under, only the round of the back showing above the ripples.

That they make air holes through thin ice is attested by F. G. Jackson, who watched one lying on its back under the surface enlarging a small hole which it had drilled with its tusks.

The young are born in the spring, and immediately after occurs the brief mating season.   At other times the sexes keep apart.   One or two, and sometimes three, young are born, apparently every three years, tenderly

nursed by their mothers and savagely defended against
all comers.   An eye-witness says that he once saw a
polar bear stalk a young walrus and imprudently spring
within reach of the maternal guardian.   One drop of her
mighty head buried the long tusks in his body and a few
more blows ended the combat before his teeth or claws
could seriously damage her thick hide.   Various evidence
seems to show that the adult walrus has no fear of bears
and is generally respected by them.

The skin of old walrus showed numerous scars of
wounds received in combat or from the sharp ice, while a
multitude of large swellings covered the thickest parts of
the hide, from the neck to the loins, possibly caused by
some skin disease.   We found every fold of the carcass
infested with little brown-red ticks, similar in size and
shape to the common wood tick.

Curiosity and gregariousness are striking characteristics of the walrus.   A boat or any unusual object will
draw a herd of astonished monsters around it and sometimes cause great danger to hunters.   Kleinschmidt had
a kayak ripped open by a female walrus two years before,
and had to swim for his life to a near-by cake of ice.

Nansen had several interesting episodes while crossing
leads in his kayak.   One of these he describes vividly:

"Suddenly the walrus shot up beside me, threw itself
onto the edge of the kayak, took hold farther over the
deck with one fore-flipper, and as it tried to upset me
aimed a blow at the kayak with its tusks.   I held on as
tightly as possible, so as not to be upset into the water,
and struck at the animal's head with the paddle as hard
as I could.   It took hold of the kayak once more, and
tilted me up, so that the deck was almost under water,
then let go, and raised itself right up.   I seized my gun,

but at the same moment it turned round and disappeared
as quickly as it had come." It had, however, ripped a
large hole in his canoe.

Another occasion was not so serious:

"Up they (the walrus) came again immediately
around the boat. . . . They stood up in the water,
bellowed and roared till the air trembled, threw themselves forward towards us, then rose up again, and new
bellowings filled the air. . . . The water foamed and
boiled for yards around. . . . Any moment we might
expect to have a walrus tusk or two through the boat,
or to be heaved up and capsized. But the hurly-burly
went on and nothing came of it."

Henry G. Bryant, when with Peary, was attacked by
a large herd of walrus and succeeded in repelling their
persistent efforts to capsize the boat only by the use of
rifles and axes at arm's length.

It has often been remarked that walrus herds keep
lookouts posted, while the majority sleep, to warn them
of danger. We could not confirm this. It seemed to us,
from our repeated observations at very close range, that
the supposed sentinels were merely animals who had been
disturbed by their fellows and had reared up to look
about for a comfortable place to lie down in. Their eye-
sight is evidently very poor and their hearing dulled by
the constant noise of the ice. Several times, also, we
gave our wind to them without disturbing them in the
least, though their scent was doubtless keener than any
other sense except that of touch.

Another detail wherein our observation differed
from the books prompts a contradiction of the statement
that the walrus is a hairless animal, and in this respect
to be grouped with the whale, porpoise and hippopotamus.

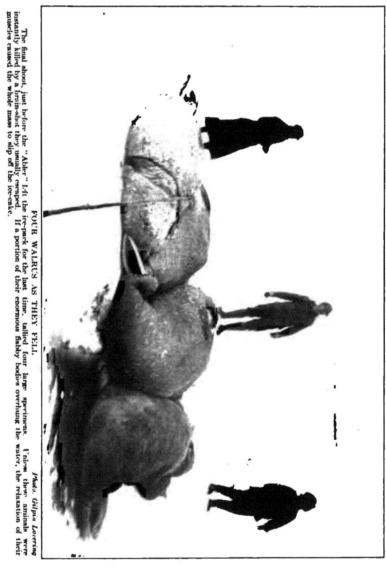

FOUR WALRUS AS THEY FELL.

Photo. Gilpin Lovering

The final shoot, just before the "Abler" left the ice-pack for the last time, tallied four large specimens. Unless these animals were instantly killed by a brain-shot they usually escaped. If a portion of their enormous flabby bodies overhung the water, the relaxation of their muscles caused the whole mass to slip off the ice-cake.

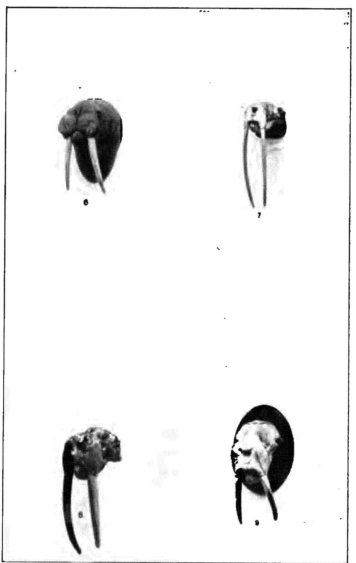

ATLANTIC WALRUS (Nos. 6, 7, 9)
(Odobaenus rosmarus)

6. Small male, Smith Sound, 1907. National collection (John R. Bradley). Tusks from gum, 16; circ., 6¾.

8. Pacific walrus (small) for comparison with Atlantic variety.

7. Female. National collection (E. P. Larned). Length, 26; circ., 4¼.

9. Male. National collection (Harry Whitney). Length, 24½; circ., 7½.

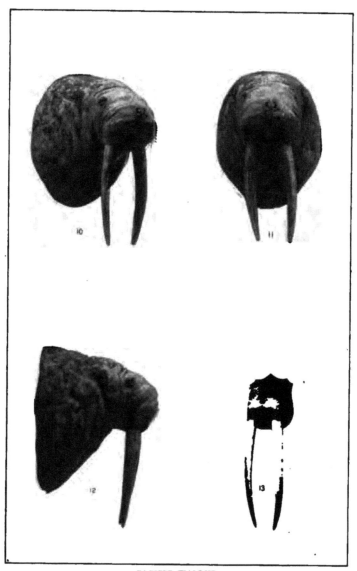

PACIFIC WALRUS
(Odobaenus obesus)

10, 11, 12. Male Pacific walrus, Irkaipy, Siberia, 1913 (F. M. Scull). Length, 34 1-16;
circ., 11½; weight of tusks, 23 pounds 7 ounces.
13. Male Pacific walrus, Point Barrow, Alaska, 1910. National collection (Henry A.
Caesar). Length, 36½; circ., 9⅛. (Record for length.)

STARTING ON A WALRUS STALK

Photo. Gilpin Lovering

Two kayaks, lashed together, were put overboard, the hunters donned white cotton parkas and paddled off toward the game, keeping ice blocks between them and the quarry. In this way a herd of walrus could be approached to within 30 yards or less.

Mention should be made of the fact that every specimen we secured, even the oldest, was covered with a
sparse brown fur nearly one inch long.

It was now Lovering's turn again, for I had shot
second to Collins.   He and Kleinschmidt stalked a herd
and while the latter was getting his motion-picture
cameras out of the kayaks Lovering shot four walrus
dead with four rapid shots.   The photographer got his
feet wet and on the long paddle home suffered greatly
from the cold.   Lovering urged all the way that Kleinschmidt do nothing until he had helped recover the four
dead walrus, as the wind and current were setting them
rapidly westward into the thick pack.   Nevertheless,
Kleinschmidt would change his gear and sent Lovering
off in the dory with Albrecht and two Eskimos, promising
to follow him at once in the umiak, while Collins and
I started in the kayaks.

Collins and I had a long journey before we got to any
goal.   First we headed for the sea barrier where we had
earlier seen several herds and found ourselves in a heavy
groundswell among great heaving blocks of ice that
threatened any moment to crush our tiny vessel.   As
they rose and fell, grinding against each other or pounding their overhanging edges on the water, the surf broke
in spray high above their windward sides and the green
and white water swirled through the crevices between
them.   The only fact which made it possible for us to
navigate among them was that they moved almost at
one speed and kept their distances from each other for
a long time.   The lighter, smaller ice always drifts
faster because affected more by the swifter surface current, but it would take time for all intervals to be closed
up.   The kayaks also were swept by wind and wave still

more rapidly than the ice. We had principally to guard against being caught under the edges of a tossing floe, which was not easy when Collins mounted some of these to look about for walrus. Not happening upon any for the first hour of our search, we went on with the current, now and then catching a glimpse of the dory, which had taken a course farther inside, to leeward.

At last we sighted some animals lying on a very small pan where the cakes were packing tightly together. It was easy to approach, almost to windward, and gain a piece of ice hardly twenty yards away. For some time the best tusker lay badly and the other three interposed when he raised his head. Then all were still. They would not rear up. Collins was ready to shoot. I was still in the kayaks, keeping them in a safe position. The sky was threatening snow; time was shortening. So I threw a few small pieces of ice on the lazy brutes. Each time they were thus tickled the walrus sat up angrily and quarreled with each other over the annoyance. But the big fellow lay down so quickly that a sure shot was hard to get in. Then I hit him full on the back and he got up and stayed there till Collins had put a bullet into his brain. Down he fell as if asleep, and the others, mildly surprised at the rifle report, but accustomed to the sharp noises of the ice, made no haste to get away. Indeed, they snuggled down again beside their dead mate, although a tiny jet of his blood was steadily pouring out on one of them. At Collins' invitation I then climbed up and shot two of the others, but they slipped into the water and were lost.

Lovering had heard the shots and now came to the rescue, for it would have been a long, tedious task to hack the head off with our small knives and carry it all the way back to the "Abler" in our little kayaks, and night would have long fallen. When we started to skin him the walrus tried to rise and Collins shot him again. With knives and axe we got the head off and into the dory. We had a stiff row home, towing the kayaks; the ice was packing so fast that it was nice work to pick our way among the slush and small bits.

Lovering had been unable to find his trophies and was trying to control his anger. Half way to the schooner, from which we had drifted some three miles, we came up with the umiak (which Kleinschmidt had put out after we got away), drawn upon a floe while its crew was skinning two walrus. Elting had secured his first specimen and then invited Young and Kleinschmidt to have a shot at the next herd. Kleinschmidt bagged his and as they broke for water, the little doctor hit one in the head and brought it down,—a regular "wingshot." As we approached Kleinschmidt asked,

"Did you get them?"

"No," answered Lovering shortly.

We pushed off and reached the schooner at six-thirty, tired with the rowing.

From the rigging we could then see Kleinschmidt on top of a high hummock at a great distance, looking for the missing carcasses. An hour or so afterwards, he came back with the news that he had located them just beyond the floe where Collins had shot his.

Although the mate thought we would find the lost walrus next morning, it seemed to me futile to look for them; and so it proved.

We started at five o'clock of the morning and cruised for a couple of hours in the vain attempt to find Lovering's game. They had vanished into the pack, if, indeed they had not been jolted off into the water.   Four sleeping animals did for a few minutes revive our hopes, but as they got our wind they betook themselves to life and safety.   We now left the field on the east side of the pack and pushed westward through the narrow barrier into a great sweep, several miles across, where the ice blocks were more loosely scattered.   Sixteen herds of walrus were here visible at one time, and the aggregate within sight at one time must have been many hundreds. We sent at least one hundred of them into the water, as we made a final effort to locate Lovering's lost ones, and then tied up to a floe to hunt afresh.

Up to this time I had not had the first shot at any walrus, though I had fired at two lots after the gunner had selected his head.   Collins and Elting each had one to his credit, so Lovering and I put off in the kayaks to try our luck.   Two good-sized bunches lay to windward and first we made for the leeward lot, while the umiak with Collins, Elting, Kleinschmidt et al went after another collection a half mile farther to leeward.   These jumped into the water, when I fired at the lot we were after, just as our friends were about to stalk them.

Not to fill out an empty paragraph, I missed my shot because, foolishly leaving on a heavy glove, the finger caught and made the barrel shift, and the whole herd escaped.   We lay motionless on our ridge ten feet wide and perhaps fifty long, within thirty-five yards of the infuriated creatures as they milled around their yellow resting place, for we wanted to go on and, had they discovered us, the walrus might have kept us marooned for several hours.   Presently the band dispersed, part of it making for the other neighboring troop, which, a half mile to our right, had not been at all alarmed by the shooting.

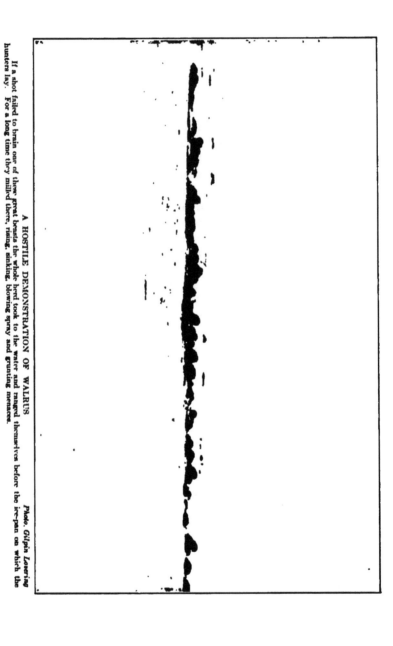

A HOSTILE DEMONSTRATION OF WALRUS

Photo. Gilpin Lowering

If a shot failed to brain one of these great beasts the whole herd took to the water and ranged themselves before the ice-pan on which the hunters lay. For a long time they milled there, rising, sinking, blowing spray and grunting menaces.

HOISTING A WALRUS ABOARD THE SHIP

By a tackle through the tendons of the tail flippers, the great mass, estimated to weigh 3,500 pounds, was hauled on deck with the donkey engine. Large males measured 13 feet from nose to flippers. The "Abler" carried seven carcasses to the Siberian coast as winter food for the natives.

It was now almost a flat calm. We had given the walrus a half-hour to forget their assault, and this seemed ample for their stupid brains. Then we set out on the most interesting of our stalks: interesting because the water between us and our prey was alive with members of the herd that we had just provoked and we could not tell what their temper might be if we ventured among them. A number were swimming around the occupied ice-pan seeking a roost, as was their habit; others were arriving and leaving, above and under water.

Prudently making dashes from one straggling cake to the next, we got within two hundred yards. Just as we pushed out from the refuge at this point, a huge walrus rose right in front of us and dived with a snort of surprise. Not less startled than he, we retreated to the other side of the berg, which was about six feet high, and lay for a few minutes in a little cove of the floe. Then we fared forth again and made a dash to the next cover. Fifty yards to the right of this a group of walrus stood in the water and turned their fishy eyes at us, but we passed them unmolested and waited for some time at the third floe, until the several individuals on both sides of it had gone their ways. It was now a longer stretch to the most likely position we could see for a shot. Once safely there we got up to the top, five or six feet above water, and looked across to the densely crowded rookery seventy yards away. At one corner of this a wounded animal from the other troop was staining the ice red as he tried to climb to a resting place, but he did not succeed in finding asylum and went back again to the others in the water.

"I'll take a shot from here," announced Lovering, rather dubious at the distance, which was somewhat too

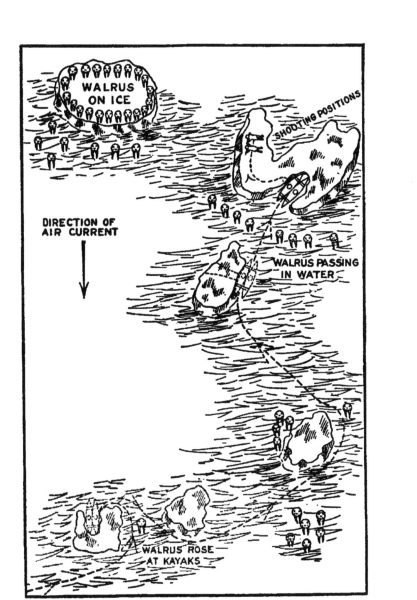

PLAN OF LOVERING'S WALRUS STALK

great for certainty. We had well learned that the small brain was extraordinarily elusive, even when one had an apparently perfect aim.

But another cake, irregular in shape, lay very close to the herd, so close in fact that it was doubtful if we could reach it undiscovered. By this time, however, we had some contempt for the enemy's organs of sight and hearing. The only consideration remaining was the frequent passage of walrus between it and us.

"You might kill from here," said I, "but you ought to have the best chance; so let's get to that other floe."

"I think that's better, too," said he, "but I didn't like to propose it to you on account of the loose walrus around here."

We took our opportunity and nothing came at us, pulled the kayaks into a crack in the ice, made them fast with a seal hook, crawled over the crest of the pan, slid on our bellies to the shelter of the ridge, which ran at right angles to the side where we had landed, barely screening us as we crawled into position only thirty-five yards from the nearest walrus on the ice. It was sure death for some of them, with the firearm in my companion's hands and he laid out two and nearly got a third. Curiously, the one he picked for second best had the bigger tusks. All the others gained the water immediately. None of them ventured back upon the floe, so we waved our caps to the "Abler" and she came up and took the heads and bodies on board. The latter were to supply with winter's meat the three natives we had brought from Welen.

The umiak came in while we were at dinner, with one head shot by Elting. They had stalked four herds and killed thirteen walrus, recovering only one of that number.

"Do we have to get out?" asked Kleinschmidt excitedly as he stepped on board.

"No; why?" answered the mate, who was on watch.

"We heard you blow the whistle and had a dickens of a time to push through the ice." (A whistle was the recall signal for boats if it became too dangerous for the ship in the ice.)

"No, we didn't whistle."

What all of them in the skin boat had heard was never found out.

Two black serrated spots a few miles westward were marked from the masthead and after dinner the "Abler" tied up to an ice block within a half mile of them. From the rigging I could see the flash of large tusks among the smaller lot of walrus, so Lovering and I paddled the kayaks round several flat cakes, bending very low to escape detection, and emerged on a pan hardly thirty yards away. I put a fatal shot in the back of the big fellow's head and flattened out two more, then told Lovering to shoot, as he so far had only two. The rest were moving fast by this time and he got only one small one. There had been seven or eight on the ice. Our four shots, within thirty minutes after leaving the ship, had each told a fatality, but we could see the animals apparently still breathing, though they lay perfectly quiet and to every appearance dead; so we hurried across and shot them all over again to make sure. It took four hours to skin the scalps, cut off the heads and hoist these and the enormous bodies on board. The largest measured eleven feet, one inch from the end of his nose along the back to the end of the body, to which length the flippers added two feet, and bore heavy tusks protruding twenty-six inches from the gums. The total length of the tusks was thirty-four inches, girth eleven and one-eighth inches, weight twenty-four pounds the pair, as measured six months after the killing. These were the biggest specimens secured on our voyage. The second was a good trophy, but the third and fourth were rather small.

Both Collins and Elting had fired from the umiak and missed, so they now took the kayaks while we were skinning our trophies and dyeing the ice a deep red for yards. They got back while we were at supper and guided the "Abler" to the cake where Collins had killed a very light-colored walrus. We had seven whole carcasses on board and they filled the port side of the deck with a flabby mass of flesh which we sensed would soon waft an evil odor through the ship.

In view of our finding walrus numerous at this locality it is interesting to compare the following notes of Nordenskjöld, writing his diary in 1878, of this same portion of the coast. "The walrus now appears to be very rare in the sea north of Bering's Straits, but formerly it must have been found there in large numbers and made the region a veritable paradise for every hunting tribe. While we, during our long stay there, saw only a few walrus, Cook, in 1778, saw an enormous number." While in winter quarters at Kolyuchin Bay, near here, he wrote: "Only two sea mammals have been seen in this region in the course of the winter, viz: the rough or bristled seal and the polar bear."

At noon we had drifted in a northwest direction twenty miles from our position of two days before, and the ice had come with us. We tied up for the night to a big berg grounded in seventeen fathoms that sheered off the many smaller pieces of drift ice. These scraped the

10

"Abler's" sides all night long and closed in behind us. A moderate southeast wind sprang up and the glass began to fall. It looked like a blow for several days. We were in the ice no one could tell how far. It was full time to think of getting out, for we were just a trifle east of Irkaipy (Cape North), or three hundred miles west of Bering Strait, with a head wind, the time of freezing for winter not many days off, and not two weeks' engine fuel aboard. Our provisions and coal were running low. The only preparation we could boast against the dread Arctic winter was a deck-load of walrus meat. An ever-present anxiety was the danger of ice coming against the rudder or propeller, and many times in the night the watch had to fend off threatening ice cakes, which swung as they drifted past us. Had one of these been set against us, or had we backed into any in our maneuvering, a slight touch of their mighty force would have carried away our rudder and propeller. If the ice packed together so thickly that we could not force it aside to get out, we were caught. Many a small piece passed underneath the vessel, as she went through the fields, and clanged ominously among the whirling propeller blades. Any of these might break or loosen the screw. Should we be frozen in the pack the north-westerly drift could take us out to the unknown and unreachable, with a fair chance of breaking up the ship on the way. Even if we did not drift far and tried to winter through, the next break-ups might not release the ice so far as it had done this season. There were thus several kinds of disasters which might easily happen, each nearly as fatal as another.

CHAPTER IX

CLEAR weather at any rate partly offset the difficult nature of our situation. Nearly all day the sun flashed brilliantly upon the ruffling water and the exquisite crystals of the ice. Some miles to our south we could see the low, dark, undulating line of the dreary coast tundra a little above the dazzling fields of ice. Twenty or thirty miles farther inland a desolate range of mountains with snow-streaked summits was piled several thousand feet in the air. Not a tree or bush was visible, for the plant life of the Arctic shore is fitted to cling tenaciously to the ground against the terrific winds of the long winter night. Driftwood, however, was plentiful on the north coast of Siberia, wherever the bold, rocky headlands gave place to steep, shingly beaches.

An interesting picture of Arctic land conditions is drawn by Haacke:

"The North Polar regions coincide in general with that portion of the far north where tundra covers the ground almost exclusively, beyond the last outpost of stunted timber. Their natural southern boundary, viz: the northern edge of the timber line, lies south of the Arctic Circle in America, but in Europe and Asia north of it, and reaches farthest north in certain parts of Siberia. The character of the landscape and vegetation of the tundra owe their chief features to the Polar climate with its long, cold winter and its short, cool but amply lighted summer. The chief characteristics of the Arctic winter are the searching winds, which sweep many parts of the tundra clear of the light snow-fall and heap it together in deep drifts elsewhere, and also the dryness of the atmosphere. So great is the ruling dryness of the air under the clear but sunless heaven of winter that the breath does not condense even in the greatest cold, and tobacco disintegrates into dust. Winter continues far into the spring months of the year, bringing its coldest weather as late as March or April. Warmth quickly follows in May, ushering in a moist summer, hottest in July and beginning again to retire in August. In the highest north the sun does not set during the greater part of June, July and August. While its continued presence melts enormous quantities of ice and snow, the air does not become comparatively hot. The heat of summer is, however, very unequal in this part of the Polar regions and at least on the coast and at sea the air is generally of a refreshing coolness. Some towns in northern Siberia, indeed, bear the undesirable distinction of being the hottest in summer and the coldest in winter of any places on earth. The extreme variation of temperature at one city is from ninety-three degrees above zero to ninety-four degrees below zero, or a total range of one hundred and eighty-seven degrees Fahrenheit. Frequent, light rains are the consequence of these conditions. Fog is uncommonly abundant, occasionally almost continuous, and so thick that sometimes it is impossible to see a few paces distant. The fog is also damp, cold and penetrating, often wetting everything like rain, and indeed, many times can scarcely be distinguished from a drizzle. It is evident that a short and misty duration of

A YOUNG NATIVE OF SIBERIA
Photographed at Cape Serge. This boy was well dressed in furs and wore a small bell, evidently to prevent his loss in foggy weather. The Chukchi children were numerous and happy, playing merrily with each other or helping their elders in their work.

HOME OF A SIBERIAN SQUAWMAN

A white man, Wall, had built himself a pretentious house of boards at Cape Serge, on the Arctic shore of Siberia, and lived here with his native wife. For his personal quarters he had made a separate room, which he used also as a storehouse for his more valuable property: ivory, ammunition, cloth, furs and groceries.

the warmth of summer would make no deep impression on the frozen land. Repeated examinations have shown that within the Arctic Circle at a depth below twelve to eighteen inches from the surface the soil is perpetually frozen. Mastodons, mammoths and other prehistoric animals which have become buried in the soil before human history began are excavated in a wonderful state of preservation. The meat and the hair still adhere to the bones, so well preserved that the dogs feed upon their remains.

"Despite the continually frozen ground, a covering of plant life extends over the ice-free portions of the tundra, consisting mostly of lichens and a few species of precarious plants. Only in the southerly portions of the tundra do meadows and little patches of willows appear at the edges of streams and in the fiords, together with stunted clusters of evergreen shrubs, which grow among the lichens and moss of the tundra. But where the severest climate reigns the verdure consists only of small patches widely separated from each other by bare stony ground, and this is called 'rock tundra.' Oases of moisture exist where the melted waters collect in shallow depressions of the tundra. There the soil becomes a muddy swamp with a shallow layer of turf supporting a struggling growth of moss and small blooming plants. Among these are many warm oases where the vertical rays of the long summer sun melt so much ice and heat the water so warm as to produce brilliantly colored gardens of plants in profusion and variety. Only about two months does the swift passing of summer allow for the relatively rich and brilliant flowering.

"The Arctic flora does not possess features peculiar to itself, and represents only a degenerated picture of the

flora of the northern temperate zone. Over similarly
formed expanses the landscape offers a most dismal
monotony. There is no variety, no shadow, no night.
There is nothing to hinder wind or light; over all rages
the wind, and otherwise there is an uncanny stillness.
All summer the single, endlessly long summer day is
illumined by the pale light of a mist-veiled sun.

"But he who transfers his gaze from the distance to
an examination of the foreground, sees here and there
little spots of bloom of the delicate heather, water berries
or the clustering dryas. Here and there the white coral-
like reindeer moss bedecks the ground and now and then
a half-buried dwarf willow and other low, close-clinging
plants. Occasionally also are seen brilliant poppies,
mostly in the neighborhood of places where water trickles
in the early summer. At such localities a luxuriant
growth of grass takes the upper hand. The tussocks
increase in size to a diameter of about three feet and a
height of some eighteen inches, similar to the common
niggerhead of our swamps. Otherwise the bright green
coloring of the grass in more temperate climates is
replaced by brown and yellow which do not relieve the
dreariness of the landscape."

Irkaipy, just east of which we now were, was the
farthest point reached by the celebrated Captain James
Cook on his last voyage of discovery in 1778 and called
by him Cape North. It has no other right to this dis-
tinctive title and is better known by the native name.

We turned south and wound a tortuous way through
the closing pack toward the shore, where a lead of clear
water a few fathoms deep separated the land from the
heavy grounded ice. All day long we threaded this
passage, thanks to the "Abler's" shoal draft of only

seven feet, with the pack a mile seaward of us. We passed three igloos on a high beach at the mouth of a river.

But this good going ended, for we came to the mouth of the Amguyema River, flanked by lagoons in the tundra, and against the easterly point formed by silt from the stream the southeast wind had jammed the ice even up to the shore. The water was so shallow that a line of small separate chunks of ice had grounded, and we bumped the bottom when we tried to cross this bar. After successfully getting over it at another place the Captain could find no means of making further headway, and we decided to tie up for the night. Larsson was for anchoring—a very unusual thing to do in the ice—and some one asked the mate, as he was putting on his parka, instead of turning in,

"Isn't it your watch off?"

He replied, "Yes, but I'm going to see we get into a good place, so I can sleep."

There was much joviality at supper in discussing the advantages of spending the winter here, though some held out for a tramp of several hundred miles along the beach to East Cape and others for attempting the voyage in our small boats. Chukchi Frank said it was a month's journey by sledge.

Ed Born showed, at the next breakfast, the only anxiety he had so far manifested on the trip.

"You can either take the launch and try to find a lead between the point and the shore, or you can go back and pick a way through the pack," he said; "you cannot lie here."

This was his ultimatum as owner of the vessel and the first time he had delivered a command. The situation was in fact grave. It was hopeless to expect that the southeast wind would clear the point of ice and we might lie there several days before a southwest breeze loosened it. Meantime any on-shore wind would set the ice in and we should be done for. During the night many small pieces had sifted around us, for the water had risen a foot or so and freed some of the grounded blocks. It looked dubious even for getting very far except as we had come, and that would not better our position. The floe to which we were moored broke in two and we had nice work to clear the ship. Kleinschmidt asked each of us formally if we were satisfied with our hunting in the Arctic and each replied that he was not. When pressed to name the bag desired each then set the mark at two bears and four walrus. Our leader had probably expected that we would be glad to quit and wished to get us on record with some such expressions. Truth to tell, we were disappointed at the short time the elements had allotted to us, particularly in respect to the bear hunting. Collins had two of these splendid animals, Lovering and I each one and Elting a cub. Lovering and I each had three walrus; Collins and Elting each two. But the immediate question was to get the ship out to safety.

Mate Hansen took to the crow's nest and searched the horizon in all directions with his glasses. Slowly the "Abler" extricated herself and turned back for a little while, then entered the pack and was surrounded on all sides by immensely heavy floes of shore ice. It was so crowded that she continually bumped against blocks on each side, now pushing two cakes apart to pass between them, now bearing against one to turn short enough to make another narrow crevice. There were no open leads at all: we had to go wherever the ice was not jammed so close as to make passage an impossibility. Nor did these conditions improve during the morning. No clearer water could be seen from aloft; only we were headed toward the northeast, where a slim, bluish streak of clouds above the ice seemed to indicate the presence of the open sea. It looked a long way off; ten miles or fifty.

Wind and current were setting the ice at the rate of about three miles an hour, and, with our slow speed and frequent turnings we lost rather than gained anything over the ground. The mountains receded as we made out from the shore, but the next promontory ahead grew dimmer and not clearer as we fought our way through the pack.

Kleinschmidt ran down the rigging at noon and shouted:

"Open water ahead!"

The mate yielded his watch to Larsson and as he warmed up by the galley stove, said in his quiet way:

"By golly, that was the worst time I've ever had in the ice. We had to keep on and I could never see how we were going to do it."

The good news soon made itself evident. We could see a rim of blue water over the deadly white boundary of the floes; more open spaces in the ice appeared, and at last we felt the low ground-swell, its angry crests rubbed off by the outer barrier of ice. Then we came up to the fringe itself; not a collection of cakes with wide channels between, but a grinding, heaving breakwater with few openings, and these largely choked with loose ice. Against the seaward side the waves spent their force in pressing the ranks together, as the weight of a wall bears upon the stones of an arch.   Captain Larsson recklessly attempted to put the schooner through one of these openings and nearly smashed her rudder and propeller against a floe in the seaway.   The sharp ice ripped long gashes in the planking.   He had to back in again with great difficulty and good luck.   At this part of the pack the clear water to windward gave no easy transition from the ice to the sea.   Farther south, inshore, the offing was filled with scattered cakes from the rest of the shore ice to the eastward, and though our part of the field seemed not less dense in that direction, there was a better chance of forcing an exit in the stiller water where the loose drift ice broke up the sea.   In this way we got out later in the afternoon.

But eight walrus on an ice pan came into view.   The mate went to Collins and Lovering and said, "You might as well get these walrus; we appear to be at the edge of the ice."

But Kleinschmidt objected, "You'll get plenty more chances; we're not done with the ice yet.   If I go to Larsson and ask him to wait while you shoot these he'll raise a fuss."

They persuaded him to do so, however, and the kayaks were put overboard.   Collins then asked Elting and me if we would like to go for the game, but we declined.   Collins and Lovering set out at once and in three-quarters of an hour each had killed two good specimens out of the lot.   The tusks of one walrus came in contact at the point.   By five o'clock we had the heads on board and were on our way through the ice to open water.

We lay offshore in a moderate sea with sails up to make progress against the head wind and, when we tacked and fetched in, about midnight, we ran into the edge of the ice again and I was roused by pieces flying through the propeller. Off and on we lay till morning, and daylight showed only open sea; no land, no ice were in sight. We had left the pack for the last time.

The morning broke fair, with the wind still southeast, that is, exactly against the course we wanted to make; so we headed in for shore, a little west of south. Then the breeze lightened and hauled to south. I took advantage of this lull in the bad weather to salt my walrus heads and put them in barrels of pickle, composed of one part alum, two parts salt, dissolved in sea water till the mixture would float a raw potato. Two heads went into one barrel, and the third, on which the skin had been cut very far back, nearly filled a barrel by itself. It was intended that this process should preserve the hides and start tanning.

Collins and Lovering laid their scalps in salt in a large leaky hogshead to drain off the liquor.

The whole party was embroiled by this time in so many feuds that a detached observer (of Arctic experience) might have found nothing to compare it to so apt as a herd of bull walrus squabbling upon an ice floe hardly large enough to hold all. Kleinschmidt and Born kept an armed truce, Albrecht and Kleinschmidt were held together only by the impossibility of separation, Kleinschmidt and the others were impatient at Larsson's sloth, Dr. Young injected himself into every conversation, Ed Born raised annoying objections at various places. The mate was generally voted competent and attentive to his own business. Frank Born talked much but stepped on nobody's toes. Kusche had probably foreseen all this and quietly dodged a monthful of it.

In such case we sped through the grim Arctic Ocean on a beautiful afternoon. The wind was now a mere mermaid's breath, while in the southwest the dark clouds had been swept up high above the horizon, leaving a burnished place from which the next shift of wind was to come.

Seven of the morning found us in the small bight, a mile across, on the west side of Cape Serge Kamen. The United States chart outlines this headland as a hook curved to the northwest, half-sheltering a bay about five miles broad. In reality the bights on each side are but little indentations in the coastline, of no value for refuge when the wind is onshore from any quarter. We dropped the mud hook opposite the village Tappan and went ashore. Kleinschmidt and Young wandered off to photograph and shoot birds, while we entered the half-dozen igloos to trade for small objects. These huts were similar to those at Welen. I bought a blubber spoon carved out of wood and a snow shovel for taking ice chips out of fishing holes. Then in the large wooden igloo belonging to Wall, a squawman, I purchased three tusks, weighing ten pounds, for four dollars, from Wall's father-in-law. The proprietor was off on an expedition elsewhere. Lovering paid seven dollars for eighteen pounds, including some beautiful old ivory, darkened and discolored as if fossilized.

At noon we got clear in an increasing west wind, which hauled to northwest and blew to a gale before nightfall. We raced by Welen, having made the seventy-two miles in nine hours, and by heaven's grace were able to see the vast bulk of East Cape in the light mist, else we should not have been able to turn round it before going far past. Then we could not have made

CHUKCHI BOATS ON THEIR RACKS

Photo. A. M. Collins

In order to keep the rawhide coverings of their boats safe from injury the natives erect racks of driftwood or whale bones and place the craft, bottom up, nearly two yards above the ground. The larger photograph was taken at Welen, Siberia. The small vignette, taken at Emma Harbor, shows inflated sealskins which are used as buoys and floats for walrus lines.

POST DESHNEF, OR EAST CAPE STATION, SIBERIA

This view southward from the small village shows the characteristic location chosen by the maritime Chukchi for their settlements. Usually they pick out a strip of beach between the sea and a lagoon. Over this, thousands of ducks pass, and are captured by the natives with their bolas.

our way back against the howling storm and heavy sea.
As it was, we crawled around the steep mountain, wallowing in the billows, and battled for two hours with the
wind in an effort to get up to the village on the southern
side of the cape.   But now the wind was against us, and
even in the comparatively smooth water we could not
make headway.

At midnight the mate said, "It's no use," and turned
back to spend the night hugging the steep face of East
Cape, where the violence of the storm could not touch
us with its full fury.   Back and forth we cruised in a
small space till morning, just holding ourselves from
being blown across the strait, whence it might have
taken days to return.   For we had to unload the walrus
and the three men whom we had brought a month ago
from Welen, before we could run over to Nome and call
our Arctic voyage ended.

As soon as the wind eased up a bit in the early morning we put her again to the test and drove her at top
speed into the furious blast.   Inch by inch she gained
ground and by breakfast time we had anchored a quarter
mile from the beach at Peek, or East Cape Station,
where the Russian post "Deshnef" stood.   A dozen
igloos, sodded up to the top of the wall, overlooked from
a fifty-foot bluff the rambling frame building of the
Russian post and the huts of the squawman Charley
Carbondale.   Chukchi Frank went ashore at once and
walked the six miles across the neck of land to Welen to
bring dog-teams for the work of getting the walrus meat
ashore.   Here we lost the service of our three Welen
natives: Terinkáu (Slim), cabin boy; Humkúi (Frank);
Hwatáwin (John).   They were all intelligent and resourceful men.

It did not take a great while to hoist the seven walrus overboard, all made fast to a long line of Carbondale's. Then the men from the whole village tallied on and hauled the mass gradually in to the beach. Even a little boy joined in the labor. Great excitement and rejoicing attended the arrival of so much valuable meat, for Carbondale said they were often on the edge of starvation and ten walrus would keep this village over a winter. Often he had to stake needy neighbors out of his store and do what he could for the sick. When food ran out they would borrow from the Chukchi at Welen and the Eskimo at East Cape (Nuotan). All events for years to come would date "from the day when the ship brought the seven walrus." Elting gave him medicine for his woman and for a neighbor who had severe rheumatism, as well as a small stock for future emergencies, and won his deep gratitude, for he seemed to sympathize keenly with the natives among whom he had cast his fortune.

"It must be a fine place to live in," I ventured.

"Oh, God! I'd get out if I could," he answered. "I've been here eleven years, only going out once, to Japan and Kamchatka, and I'm not the man I was when I came. Then I weighed one hundred and ninety pounds, now one hundred and sixty. The winters are fearful; the wind seems never to stop blowing, and though it's only about 30° F. below zero the cold is terrific. I've seen eighteen days in succession when you could not make the hundred yards from my house to the beach."

While I bargained for a skin vest, a model igloo and umiak, one of the two Russians who lived in the post asked me to look at a machine which was out of order. Collins and Lovering came too. It was a lathe, made of an old sewing machine, for turning ivory. We suggested repairs by means of drawings and they served tea and presented us with ivory cigarette mouthpieces. Elting got some prizes of carved ivory and fur embroidery. Kleinschmidt spent the day with his motion-picture apparatus.

Frank and the Welen men arrived with dog-teams hitched to iron-shod sleds and made sure of the meat. We said good-bye, gave small presents to the boys and set sail about seven in the evening for Nome.

The northwest wind blew strong and true, sending us across the one hundred and fifty miles of Bering Sea in twenty hours. At noon we passed Sledge Island and anchored in front of the former great mining camp of Nome at 3 P. M. of August 27th. Our venturesome voyage in the Arctic was over. It had been marked from the first by conflict with the elements and it had been an unceasing struggle to wring from it the few precious trophies we brought back with us.

We gorged ourselves with fresh meat, eggs and fruit, and slept ashore in hotels.

CHAPTER X

LETTER reading, the soothing touch of the barber, and the first bath since July 10th at Fairbanks refreshed us wonderfully. We purchased photographs, cigars, a few fancy groceries for use on board, and empty whisky barrels for our skins. The wind was steady northwest all day, but we dared not wander out of town lest it should change and make it necessary for the "Abler" to pull off. The fresh food was more welcome than it seemed possible it could be, and we slept again on shore, as the "Abler" danced a good deal in the open roadstead. I had a little chat with Governor Strong and learned that protests were made against such slaughter of walrus as the "Kit" with her cargo of nine hundred and sixty skins had wreaked.

Recruiting the crew had detained us two days at Nome. George, the white sailor, and Ikede, the Japanese cook, left us. Kleinschmidt got three new white sailors and another who wanted to work his way to St. Michael, a cook and a steward. The last two were gray-haired little men. The cook wore a white chef's cap and the steward brought on board a large mongrel St. Bernard dog which bit the cook in the hand promptly as the engine started and frightened him.

The boatmen charged outrageous prices for taking passengers and freight between the ship and the beach. When we first landed, two launches came out; one, called "Defiance," bringing the quarantine and customs officers. The other, the "Defender," was looking for business. My partners made a bargain with the latter to go ashore at fifty cents a head. Kleinschmidt and Young were in the "Defiance" and her skipper invited me to come with him. No payments were made on the beach. On entering the post office just before boarding the "Abler" to sail away, the skipper came up and said,

"Well, I'll collect about two dollars from you."

"What for?" I replied, innocently.

"For passage ashore," he explained.

"I thought that was free."

"Do you think I do that for my health?" he inquired, in no weak-chested tones.

"Evidently not, but it's an extortionate price. The government paid you for the trip anyhow."

"It's the standard rate, and has been ever since the camp was started."

"Well, prices have come down a lot since those days," I argued, for in fact Nome was the cheapest town I had seen in Alaska. "I'll not pay you two dollars, but I'll split the difference between what you thought and what I thought it was going to be." With which words I handed him a dollar.

We had reached the main street by this time.

"I won't break the price," he said, declining the coin.

"I won't pay more."

"Well, I'll give you the ride free."

"And I won't take it." So saying I thrust the dollar into his pocket.

He pulled it out, threw it in the street, turned on his heel and walked off. I did the same. An Eskimo ivory-seller wandered by, spied the bright money and picked it

11

up.   He stowed it away and began carefully searching the wooden roadway for more.

Kusche rejoined us with many boxes of specimens.

We got on board by means of the launch "Wilhelmina" for one dollar apiece.   Martin, one of our sailors, was very drunk on shore and it required the marshal to put him on the "Abler" with his two reserve bottles intact.   We weighed anchor at 3.30 P. M. after a pleasant stay in Nome, now restocked with meat and provisions, and in the fair northwest wind laid our course for St. Mike, as the Nome newspapers familiarly called St. Michael.

The wind held fair till night and we made good time. Collins and Lovering improved the opportunity by packing their walrus scalps in barrels of pickle.

By morning the wind had drawn to southwest and this kept us from arriving till about 2 P. M.   Collins and Lovering boxed their walrus skulls, but could ship nothing for lack of a permit from the Customs office in Nome, where we had entered the things on arriving from Siberia, so we had to write for the necessary papers to be sent to us at Seward.

Through steady work, cheered on by the mate with the lubrication of half a demijohn of whisky, the crew loaded aboard sixty-seven iron gasoline drums, some full and some empty, and made all ready for an early start the next day.   The light gasoline floated even the full drums as they were rolled into the water beside the ship.   Kleinschmidt owned a new parka given him by Ed Born.   They had disposed of the rest of their trading goods and had evidently partaken of a love-feast.

We started as soon as breakfast was over, in a light southeast air, and steered for the Yukon Flats off the delta of the great river.

The wind shifted to the northeast, still light, leaving the sea smooth, but with a slight ground-swell from the southwest.   Collins and Lovering took advantage of the fair weather to put their bear skins in barrels for shipment.   I examined my walrus, found them in good condition, and spent the rest of the day reading Barnum's "Grammar of the Innuit Language," which Dr. George B. Gordon, of the University of Pennsylvania Museum, had sent to me at Nome.

All sail was hoisted as the wind hauled northwest and freshened.   Cape Mohican, the western point of Nunivak Island, was passed within a few miles.

We were making good progress with a free wind and the weather held promising.   All hands were in the best spirits; even the cook, Louis Meyer, had shaken off some of his sea-terror and told us of his adventures.   He was over seventy years of age, and called himself an old soldier; not without right, for he had been through four wars: the American Civil War, the Franco-Prussian war, the Spanish-American war, and the Boxer Uprising.

"When I was a young fellow in Germany," he related, "my father heard that soldiers in America on the northern side was getting a dollar a day for fighting, and he says to me, 'Louis, you better go over there and earn that dollar a day,' so I went.   I was all through it to Gettysburg.   Then I got into the French war and was at the battle of Gravelotte.   That was worse than Gettysburg.   I'm drawing a pension for that fighting, under my old name of Louis Metz.   You see, my father was no good and my mother married again, a man named Meyer, and I took his name afterwards.

"After I had seen something of the war in Cuba the trouble broke out in China, and I helped loot the inner city of Pekin.

"I was broke in Cairo, Egypt, for a while once and had to live on hand-outs and what I could get from tourists. I would size up a man and go speak to him in his own language and tell a sad story and get his coin—then fake one on the next guy that looked easy. I got pretty good at picking Frenchmen and Germans and English or Americans.

"But the 'Titanic' disaster finished me. It took all my nerve away. I was working in the galley there, washing dishes and so on.

"My God, it was awful. I got into one lifeboat and they threw me out. They threw me out of another and at the third one they hit me on the head with a belaying pin and when I woke up I was on deck and all the boats had left. There was a couple more of us, so we threw a hatch cover overboard and got to it and stayed on it till we was picked up.

"They had me down in Washington when they was investigating the whole thing, and I told them the whole story. But the lawyer that was looking out for the main guy wouldn't let me talk. He wanted me to answer just 'yes' or 'no' to his questions, and every time I started to say anything more the Judge rapped on his table and told me to stop.

" 'I'm here to tell the whole truth,' I yelled out. The Judge pounded with his hammer (I remember thinking what a good hammer it would be for pounding a beefsteak to make it tender) and says, 'You're fined twenty-five dollars for contempt of court.'

" 'All right,' says I, and I says some more about that guy. 'I'll make your fine fifty dollars,' says the Judge, hammering away.

" 'All right,' says I, for I was pretty mad and I told

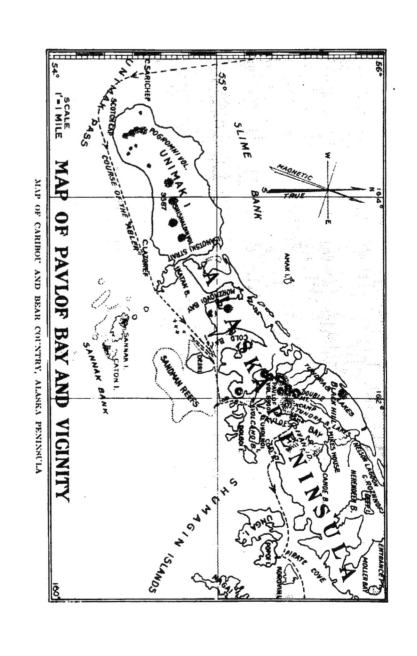

MAP OF CARIBOU AND BEAR COUNTRY, ALASKA PENINSULA

PAVLOF VOLCANO FROM THE HARBOR OF IVAN ISLAND

Ivan Island is evidently an old crater, now partly submerged in Pavlof Bay. It is about a mile long and through two narrow entrances offers an excellent harbor for small vessels. The bottom is of volcanic ash and though we were well protected from heavy seas, the wind sometimes blew so hard that the "Abler" dragged her heavy anchor, some more. Well, he fined me seventy-five dollars altogether, and when I was done he says, 'Now, you'll have to pay that or go to jail.'

" 'Well', I says, 'you'll have to get it from that guy there,' pointing at the fellow, 'he's got my two hundred and ten dollars at the bottom of the sea.' So they was taking me to jail when someone in the crowd saw I was a Grand Army man and there was a lot of 'em in the courtroom. They took up a collection of three hundred dollars and gave it to me."

The steward, who had hair as gray as the cook, whispered in my ear: "That old fellow says he's been cooking for fifty years. Ain't it a wonder he can't cook any better than he does?"

The wind still blew fair and strong. We were churning along with all sail set. Many birds passed us and Kleinschmidt stood in the bow with a repeating shotgun and a scoop net, trying to shoot them over the bow and pick them up with the net. Altogether he secured only one petrel and one red-legged kittiwake. I split a strip of tanned walrus hide to make a gun sling, shaved it thin and curried it with engine oil.

We were going better than we might have expected, almost ten miles an hour, and the long run of seven hundred miles from St. Michael to Unimak Pass, at the western end of the Alaska Peninsula was nearly over.

The captain had corrected the chronometer at St. Michael and had thereby accurately laid his course from the last point of departure, Nunivak Island, so that we raised the western cape of Unimak Island at sunrise as expected and drove through the Pass before a hard west breeze. Another sail rounded far astern and a cannery tender, the "St. Helens," overtook us—the only vessels we had seen on this run.

As the day drew to its close the captain decided to lay the "Abler" to during the night on account of the numerous rocks and reefs among the small islands off the southern end of the Alaska Peninsula. Accordingly we pitched and rolled all night, tacking to and fro across the mouth of Cold Bay, and somehow we lost our position and early morning found us among a lot of angry breaking reefs.

The mate pulled us out of these by a combination of luck and judgment and we went all day among small, rocky islands that rose steeply from the water, and on account of a head wind anchored early for another night in Volcano Bay, a cove just west of the entrance to Pavlof Bay, whither we were bound to hunt caribou.

In the hope of finding some of this game here, so near to its known range, we went ashore, having several hours before sunset, but saw no trace of them. It was evident that the high mountains shut them off from Volcano Bay. Plenty of ptarmigan rewarded Elting, however, and Lovering saw a black fox.

The stream which flowed into the head of the bay was choked with dead dog salmon and also many live ones, which struggled feebly to climb the riffles or contented themselves with holding their own in a pool of fresh running water. Although a large number seemed strong and full of life, it was no trouble to seize them by the small part of the tail and land them. At the creek's mouth, where the fresh water mingled with the salt, numerous salmon swam to and fro, making no attempt to ascend the stream and yet unwilling to leave it. Now and then a small shark snapped at one and sent him panic-stricken, shooting out of water in a succession of long leaps.

This great mystery of the salmon run impressed me there on that little nameless river. The salmon eggs are hatched in a stream and the fish grow to maturity in salt water. Just where they migrate to has never been discovered. But four years after their beginning of life, an imperious command bids them return to the very source from which they sprang, to lay their eggs there and die. In vast schools they come, crowding the narrow channels of fresh flowing water, flinging themselves up shoal rifts and cataracts, tasting no food until they have reached the safe, suitable spawning grounds. There they leave their eggs. Then, exhausted, thin, crippled by the struggle, they die. The imperative process of regeneration has been fulfilled.

It may not be that the physical agony of it alone ends their lives. Some must fail to reach the headwaters of their native stream. Many, such as I saw, were not battered by the rocks nor tired by great effort. It is true that I did not find any still unspawned, but perhaps some were sterile. It seemed as if they were all predestined now to die. They had lived their time, well or ill, and when the call came they went home, instinctively, irresistibly, some to battle through to the ultimate fulfillment of their law, others to fail and expire bathing in the sweet water they had been preordained to crave.

As we turned into Pavlof Bay on the seventh of September the twin peaks of Pavlof Volcano on the left-hand side rose with graceful sweep from the water's edge into dazzling white, perfect cones nearly nine thousand feet high. They dominated the landscape from every point of view. A tiny wreath of smoke, scarcely distinguishable from a bit of fleecy cloud, floated ever at one of the pinnacles. Half way down the broadening bases the snow grew thin and bare rock appeared.   Lower still was nothing but arid volcanic ash on which no vegetation flourished.   Only at a distance, where the mossy tundra had grown for centuries unburied by fresh eruptions, was there a loam that nourished alders and willows.   Not a tree was visible; not a single tree had we seen for two months on the coasts of Alaska or Siberia. · Everywhere was the undulating tundra with its timorous, close-clinging growth, feeding nothing taller than the characteristic alders.

Even the bottom of the bay was composed of the same volcanic ash, through which a vessel's anchor would drag in a hard wind.   To have a safe anchorage we beat against the wind half way up the large bay to a little island, less than a mile long, lying about three miles from the western shore.   Its precipitous cliffs, the nesting place of eagles and gulls, showed no crevice that would indicate a harbor until we drew abreast of it.   Then an entrance, so shallow and so narrow that we barely squeezed through, let us into the perfect, landlocked shelter of Ivan Island.   It had two mouths, being in fact formed by two islands, much as if one should break two little pieces out of a cruller.   Probably the formation was a long-extinct crater.   In this we cast anchor and put the launch overboard.

Kleinschmidt and Ed Born took Lovering and Collins, who had long since bundled up a camping outfit, in the launch and put them ashore to spend ten days hunting caribou.   Elting and I wanted to engage a guide, if possible, and Kleinschmidt was to go some seven miles up the bay and bring back Mike Utecht, who had lived there for sixteen years.   On gaining the cliffs of the island later in the afternoon we could see the launch party shooting birds and caribou on the shore where they had left our friends.   Meanwhile I was trying to secure an eagle with a shotgun, but, though I brought one down as he was flying overhead, he caught his balance just before striking the ground and flapped triumphantly away, none the worse.   Another rose from the rocks overhanging the bay, and at close range I knocked him into the water.   There he pulled himself together and rested on the surface.   Then, to my astonishment, he swam against the breeze by beating his wings into the water, until he clambered out and preened himself on a low-lying rock.   I got within seventy yards and fired as he rose.   Surely some of the big pellets must have struck him, but with long laboring strokes he saved himself from tumbling, gained strength as he flew and was soon out of sight.

The launch had not come back by early morning. Captain Larsson was somewhat worried, as a fresh breeze had blown all night, but waited through the morning while we took on water.   The crew dammed a rivulet flowing from a spring among the alders, fixed a pipe in the dam and thus, with buckets, filled two barrels in the dory.   When full these made the boat very unsteady and had to be emptied carefully by buckets over the ship's side.

The launch arrived at 2.30, laden with a caribou (the Grant variety, which is confined to the Alaska Peninsula), many of the beautiful and rare emperor geese, and hundreds of snipe and other birds.   Mike, too, was in it, ready to help us.   He was a tall, spare man, like a Russian in feature, though he said he had been born in Germany, and quietly confident that he could find some bear for us.

We had ten days at our disposal. As to our plans, Kleinschmidt suggested: "You might spend a few days at Mike's house and hunt the country there for caribou. Meantime I can make a camp inland about seven miles, at a point just north of the volcanoes, and have it all ready for you to hunt bears from there."

"How long will that take you?" we inquired.

"About four days."

So it was agreed. We took our blankets and rifles and Born and the mate landed us at Mike's home.   It was a picturesque cluster of little houses on the dunes just above the beach, on which Mike's three pretty little light-haired girls welcomed us.   The house was low, with hollow wooden walls, nearly two feet thick, filled with turf. Sods were also banked against the sides as high as the windows. A small store stood a few yards off, and other outbuildings, a smoke house and several Aleut huts.   Inside, the house proper consisted of a living room and two bedrooms.   In one of these Mike and his wife and four children slept, and we were given the other. Mike's wife was a very pretty half-breed, about twenty-three years old. He was twice that age.

We were off across the tundra just after sunrise. More than twenty miles it rolled to Bering Sea without a considerable height of land. Small hills, little more than two hundred feet above the bottoms, provided good lookouts, however, and from one of these I counted ninety-nine lakes lying in the hollows on all sides. Nearly all of them were shallow, some depressed a man's height beneath the plain and fringed with alders, others bordered by marshes. Swan, ptarmigan, teal and sandhill cranes, red fox, ground squirrels, porcupines and caribou we saw alive. There were some old land-otter trails.

All the caribou here were still in velvet, and that beautiful fine fur covering of their horns deluded us as to the size of the antlers. The best animal which I shot there proved but a small head.

Elting and Mike made a wide sweep of the country; I packed the caribou home, steering through the baffling swamps by the bearing of a mountain across the bay and felt footsore after a first day's walk of about twenty-two miles. The other men came in after sundown, having done at least thirty miles. They had covered the territory we had laid out for the next day's hunting and found nothing worth while. It was therefore decided to go at once to the camp near the mountains, where Mike said the caribou were likely to be better.

The two Aleuts living next to Mike (and largely supported by him) were to help Kleinschmidt pack up to our camp, and Mike had their solemn promises to be sober. Nevertheless they were both drunk on their *hooch*, made of fermented sugar and flour, and it took Mike's wife to get them started. She treated us to fresh eggs from her two chickens, dogs having killed the other fourteen, and set before us a haunch of caribou, which she had herself shot, dressed and carried home. This, besides looking after a baby and three little girls and doing the usual housework, had taken up a good deal of her day.

It was a beautiful, clear, cold night. The moon swam brilliantly over a bank of black clouds across the bay and cast a broad pathway of light on the rippling surface.

CHAPTER XI

CARIBOU AND BROWN BEAR

HAVING once decided that we should be unlikely to secure good specimens of caribou in the neighborhood of Mike's house, we lost no time in moving to the camp nearer the volcanoes, where Kleinschmidt was awaiting us. By noon the next day we had rowed Mike's dory seven miles down the bay to a point on the shore opposite the island where the "Abler" was moored. At this point a little stream ran into Pavlof Bay where the end of a sand bar, about two miles long, protected a small slew. Mike had built a shack here to occupy in his winter trapping. The dory, belonging to Mike's Aleut neighbors, lay tied to the bank beside Ed Born's red skiff, showing that the men had already packed our camp equipment inland.

It was about seven miles from this shack up to the camp. We started just before noon, lunching on the way in a hollow of the tundra, and arrived about five o'clock at the camp, which Kleinschmidt had pitched among large alders at the foot of a broad flat-top hill some six hundred feet above the table land. Kleinschmidt had brought one 8 x 10 canvas tent, Ossip, the Aleut, had his striped awning-like tent, while Elting and I were to sleep in a little 7 x 7 miner's tent which weighed only five and one-half pounds. Kleinschmidt and Dr. Young had arrived there at noon and had gone off for another hunt after killing two caribou. We spent the rest of the day arranging things for the night.

A CAMP IN THE CARIBOU COUNTRY

Photo, Gilpin Loaring

Small, light tents were found adequate and convenient for ten days at Pavlof Bay, even during hard rainstorms: Alders furnished a scanty supply of firewood, but water was abundant. No insects annoyed us during the early part of September.

GRANT'S CARIBOU IN THE VELVET

Photo. Gilpin Lovering

During early September the caribou at Pavlof Bay had not yet begun to rut. The largest antlers were generally clean of their d<licate fur, while the smaller had not been stripped. Behind Collins and the riders are here seen the twin peaks of the snow-clad Pavlof Volcano, of which the right-hand summit was smoking.

Elting and I started the next morning at five-thirty with Mike, and hardly had we gone a mile from camp when five caribou appeared and ran off to our right down to lower ground, Elting in close pursuit. Within an hour he had killed the best caribou that any of our party secured at Pavlof Bay. It had beautiful antlers 41½ inches wide, 50 inches long, with thirty-eight points. We cut off the head, hung the liver on one of the spikes to dry and left it there to be called for later in the day.

The Grant caribou, which variety is found only on the Alaska Peninsula, is smaller in body than its nearest neighbors, the Kenai and Osborne types. The horns are very long but not greatly palmated. It is similar to the other barren ground varieties.

Our course now led us across a considerable river which flowed out of the foot of Pavlof Volcano and after a northerly direction emptied into Bering Sea. Through the icy water we waded and on the farther bank stopped to wring out our stockings and put them on again more or less dry. Over hills and valleys from ridge to ridge we went, scanning all points with our glasses. All the caribou, however, seemed to have small horns. Finally, as we lay on one of the higher elevations behind a little knob, two or three points of horns just projecting to the sky-line above the stony hillside in front of us, caught our eyes. Closer inspection showed that two of the antlers were clean of the velvet and one was still covered with it. The best animals were lying down. We stalked over the brow of the hill carefully and when I had crawled within one hundred yards they stood up. As they looked at me the gun sounded and they all ran down the slope away from us. But a few yards and the leader fell, shot through the shoulder. It was a handsome head,

53 inches long, with 37½ inches spread, carrying thirty-five points. It was nearly symmetrical, which is not often the case with caribou; the corresponding prongs on each side had almost exactly the same number of points. Leaving this trophy too, we went farther on, as it lacked an hour and a half of noon. But at the middle of the day we settled to lunch on the shore of a little lake.

Our noonday lunches, while hunting here at Pavlof Bay, were a most delightful feature of the sport, and we afterward looked back on them with the greatest pleasure. First we chose a sheltered spot under the overhanging bank of a lake, gathered armfuls of dead alder stems and soon had a cheerful fire going. Mike fitted a handle of green wood to a tin can he brought with him and we boiled lake water to make bouillon and several cups of tea for each of us. Mike produced from his bag slices of bread and balls of force-meat which his wife had made from caribou steak. While tea was brewing we took off our shoes and stockings to dry them and covered our feet with the warm sand. Then for a half hour we smoked our pipes and talked, and when the footgear was ready to put on again we were off for the rest of the afternoon.

As we had covered some ten miles in the morning and were now seven miles distant from camp in a straight line, we made our way leisurely back toward home, picking up my caribou head on the way, and heading for a hill about two miles from camp on the bank of the river, where Mike was accustomed to sit and look for game in his own hunting. But we were destined not to reach home so directly as we had thought, for when we gained Mike's lookout it offered a splendid panorama of the valley between camp and a double hill north of Pavlof Volcano and we sat there for about an hour studying the landscape through our glasses.

At last Mike said, "There's old Bruin!   I would have been disappointed if we had not seen a brown bear."

There was no mistaking the great animal.   Across the valley about a mile from us she was walking slowly along a bear-trail at the foot of the Double Mountain and just below a band of alders which encircled the lower part of the hill.   Occasionally she stopped and plucked at the ground, not hurrying nor yet showing an inclination to rest.   We left the caribou head on the river bank at the foot of our lookout and lost no time in taking after the bear.   Over the undulations of the tundra we traveled as fast as we could, but the animal had a mile start of us, and as we drew close she would stop and turn around to see if anyone was following her.   On the instant Mike would halt and we, behind him, would freeze into whatever attitudes we had at the moment.   In this way we had nearly caught up to our game within two miles from starting.   But the trail which led the bear around the foot of the Double Mountain took her over a little spur on which the alders grew thickly in patches.   Over this ridge she went and we after her.   Cautiously we followed in case she might have stopped among the bushes, but when we had gone half way down the farther slope we caught a glimpse of the animal still going her quiet gait.

A quick dash under cover of the bush and Elting was within a hundred yards.   He knelt down, careless of noise.   The bear swung her head slowly to look at him and the nine-millimeter bullet struck her in the left shoulder, going through heart and lungs.

Instantly the great brute dashed off down the slope to a creek at the foot of it and up the other side of the steep hill.   Just as she was disappearing in the alders here a snap-shot brought her rolling down again to the gully at the foot. She lay on her back in the little trench, breathing hard, and Elting put another bullet through her heart. She was a large female, measuring six feet seven inches from nose to tip of tail. We pulled her by the thick hair out to level ground, cut her open and left her for the next day. It was after dark when we got back to camp, tired but satisfied with a full day's sport.

With this auspicious beginning we naturally thought that the rest of our stay at Pavlof Bay would be very productive of trophies. We did not dream that we were not again to bring in a single head.

Kleinschmidt and Young were, however, excited to the highest degree by our success and the next morning were up at four o'clock, hurried through their breakfast and got off, the missionary swearing a Presbyterian oath that he would bring in as fine a caribou as Elting, on this his sixty-sixth birthday. The mush-pot got burned in the scramble so that we could get nothing to eat for another hour. It did not particularly matter, however, because Elting and Mike were going to skin the bear and I intended to prepare my caribou head for sending down to the shore, and also to carry Elting's into camp. Dr. Young and Kleinschmidt arrived about three o'clock; the little sky-pilot carrying on his shoulders the head of a good caribou which he had brought four miles, wading the icy river on the way. Elting and Mike came in before sundown with the bear skin, which had taken them four hours to get off. Elting's hands were blistered painfully by the long use of the knife.

Our next tramp was the longest and hardest of this trip. The caribou had become wary, for among us we had been scouring the country rather thoroughly and the game had moved off to a considerable distance. Thirteen

miles from camp we went before we saw any animals
with horns that were satisfactory, but we failed to get
them.   The return march was wearisome.   The most
direct route lay across the lava-beds at the foot of the
volcano. A few "deer," as Mike called them, were to be
seen on the flat expanses of volcanic ash, but the rutting
season had not yet begun and we could not approach
the animals in the perfectly open country. A few shallow
creek beds ran through the lava, but generally did not
lead in the right direction for getting up to the animals.

After fording a half dozen rivers and climbing the
steep hills between them we arrived at the crest of the
flat mountain, on the farther side of which our camp lay.
There was not a blade of grass or moss in this wide expanse
of volcanic dust and broken stone.   The sun set while
we were still traveling here and fog and rain shut out all
landmarks.   Elting's feet were badly bruised and cut
through the mukluks which he had worn all day.   We
had to bring the pocket compass into use to reassure our
direction, but even this was not very certain.   Once,
however, the fog lifted enough to show Mike a draw in the
side of the hill which he recognized. A mile more we
traveled and came to the edge of the steep flat mountain.
We looked over the precipice and saw our tents six hundred
feet below.   A long slide down through the sand and
broken stone and we were in camp, tired and hungry.
We had walked more than thirty miles and had nothing
to show for it.

Nor had Kleinschmidt and Young any better luck
with the gun, though the former secured some excellent
moving pictures of caribou, as a reward for his long tramp.
Dr. Young, however, soon paid the penalty for his temerity
in trying to be a young fellow like the rest of us and wade

12

the rivers, for he was soon stretched on his back groaning in the agony of lumbago.

Kleinschmidt went back to the shore with his camera after a day or so and "Papa" lay moaning in camp while the rest of us tried in vain to bring more caribou to bag.

We had another good run after a brown bear on one of these days and Elting, who sat on top of a hill and watched the chase, described it as very interesting.

We were on a lookout near to the one from which we had seen Elting's bear, watching a little brown cub play in the open space among the alders below us. The little fellow romped about until he caught wind of us and dashed to cover. While Elting and I were enjoying this sight Mike was gazing through his glasses at the opposite valley.

"Here's a bear!" he exclaimed; and in fact a two-thirds grown brown bear was following the same trail as that which Elting had shot some days previously. After assuring ourselves that it was big enough to shoot, Mike and I laid off coats and everything that we did not need and ran for it. We jumped into the water and waded the river without stopping to remove our stockings, and ran and walked for a mile. Then coming upon a little height we saw the bear leisurely going close below the alders along the slope of the Double Mountain, just as the doctor's victim had done. But this one never turned and saw us. We followed him fast and carefully. Over the same ridge he went with us hot upon his tracks; then we came up and saw him among the alder patches. But the swift chase had been too much for me, although I had not felt any exhaustion or lack of breath. This betrayed itself when I raised the rifle. For the left forearm wavered and bullet after bullet went wild.

The bear turned as I fired, reared and looked at us, then trotted to the left toward the slope of the hill which he had been going around, as I missed him with the last shell.

All other cartridges were in my coat two miles in the rear. Mike and I sat down on the bank. The bear went up the hill path a little distance, turned and glared at us. The empty gun lay across my knees. Mike shook his fist at the great brute, cursed him passionately and shouted, "I'll come up and club you to death." But Bruin slowly turned and walked out of sight.

"Well," said Elting, when he heard the result of the chase which he had watched almost to the last from his lookout, "you had all the fun of hunting the bear without the trouble of packing him home."

Even if the latter part of our stay in this little camp was dulled by frequent rain, the evenings were enlivened by the stories of two of the sailors who had packed for us. One of these men, Ed Taylor, a tall, lanky young fellow, spent the summer going down the Yukon in search of his fortune, and was stranded on the beach at Nome when Kleinschmidt picked him up.

"I never had such a miserable time in my life," he said. "I am a graduate of an agricultural college and was working on my father's fruit farm in the State of Washington when the idea came into my head to find a gold mine in Alaska. My father was opposed to the notion, because he wanted to make an agriculturist of me. But I thought I was a geologist. A bunch of us went over the White Pass on our own feet and drifted down to Dawson. There was nothing doing there, so we went on down the river and finally landed at Fort Gibbon at the mouth of the Tanana River. Pardon me, Dr. Young, but Fort Gibbon is the worst hole in Alaska.

"For ten days we lay in Fort Gibbon waiting for a steamer to come along. We had hardly anything to eat and naturally no money to pay for steamship fares. Finally, however, we managed to work our way down as far as Kaltag. Here they threw us off. After we had tried uselessly to get down on the river to St. Michael we mushed across overland to Unaliklik, about ninety miles of the worst roads you could find because the tundra was all soft in summer. There were a half dozen of us. We found some Eskimos who had a boat and promised to take us to Nome if we would work our way for them. They treated us badly and did not give us enough to eat. We were blown around by the wind for several weeks, but at last we got there and I spent a month on the beach at Nome. Nome was as bad as Fort Gibbon and there was no job that could be had."

Fritz, the other sailor, broke in here: "Why didn't you eat dried salmon and the other good things that you can find on the beach at Nome?"

"I have no taste for that," replied Ed. "Our first thought was to break into a bank, but we could not find one that looked easy enough. I expect my father has disinherited me by this time," he concluded gloomily.

"Well," said Fritz, when Ed had finished his sad story, "I never was so down on my luck and black in the face about it as you were, you lazy bum. I ran away from my home in Bremerhafen, Germany, when I was twelve years old, because my father apprenticed me to a farmer who treated me badly. I just stuck a sandwich in my pocket and went off and got on a ship belonging to some Danish sailors and cruised around England for a few years, finally landing in Sweden. I have always had great faith in sandwiches.

"When the time came for me to begin serving in either the army or the navy I said to myself, 'Fritz, you are the youngest of eighteen boys in your family and no one of them has ever served Billy the Kaiser and you are not going to break the family record.' But they caught me all the same and put me on one of the warships. One day I cursed one of the officers and he hit me in the face. They put me in irons for a month, and after that they gave me hard jobs around the deck and long hours. But I met some Danish fishermen and I said to them: 'You get your boat about one thousand yards away from ours and at one o'clock in the night show a light aboard of it, and I'll be there.' So at one o'clock that night I saw the light as arranged; I brought a belaying pin down on the head of the watchman and with a sandwich in my pocket, overboard I went and swam to the fisherman. I have had no desire to go to Germany since.

"From there I reached the coast of Chile in South America and worked with a lumber gang, but I could not get along with the boss any better than I could with any other boss, so I finally went to New York and learned the shipbuilding trade. Now I have been in Alaska for seven years and Alaska is good enough for me.

"I don't need to take any orders from anybody here in Alaska and I can punch a man's face if I don't like it. I have never been arrested since I came to Alaska except for stealing food and for fighting. Before I got here I was arrested about seventy-eight times."

This Fritz was a hard character, but he was a good packer and delighted in his power of carrying heavy loads. When it was time to strike camp and move back to the "Abler" Fritz came to our little tent and looked at it carefully. It contained Elting's bed and mine, together with our extra ammunition, clothing and sundry articles. "I'll carry the whole thing down to the shore," announced Fritz. We made two bundles of the lot, slung one upon his back and the other on his breast, and, with the load weighing about one hundred and ten pounds, Fritz got to the shore in three hours.

Dr. Young, though still suffering acutely from lumbago, was put upon his feet, staves were cut and given him, and with these aids he walked the seven miles without sitting down.

We met the launch the same afternoon and got off to the "Abler" without delay. But the next day it was blowing and raining hard and the sea was entirely too rough for the launch to make the shore to bring back Collins and Lovering.

Ed also was marooned at the little shack two miles from Lovering's and Collins' camp, for he had been sent up to the flat mountain to bring back some pots and pans which the rest had been unable to carry down.

While we had been scouring the country for caribou, Collins and Lovering had boarded the "Abler" with six heads, several of which were excellent specimens, and had returned to their camp to make an effort to secure brown bear. Kleinschmidt finally brought them out without any additional trophy, and we were ready to leave for the Kenai Peninsula.

After paying Mike one hundred dollars for his ten days' services, which was a windfall for the struggling fellow, we pressed on him a number of articles, such as boots and clothing, which we did not greatly need and which were most useful to him.

"I cannot thank you enough," said Mike gratefully. "You can understand that it takes about all I make in the year to keep the wife and children, and very little remains for me to get things with for myself."

Lovering's account of his experience while hunting with Collins in this country is as follows:

"On September 7th Collins and I found ourselves encamped a mile from Pavlof Bay among the alder bushes, and within a few feet of a fast-running brook, whose source was the melting snows that cover the greater portion of Mt. Pavlof the year round.

"Towards the south for three or four miles the country was comparatively level and covered with abundant grass; here and there several small streams wound their way down to Pavlof Bay. For the next four or five miles the country was nothing but a barren lava bed with occasional patches of alders growing shoulder high. At this point a ridge ran down to the bay and shut off our view.

"The country directly between us and Mt. Pavlof was very similar to that on the south, but on the north it was much more broken by low, rolling hills and cut by numerous small streams, until, some five or six miles beyond, it assumed the character of the tundra, with a great number of little lakes that could be seen as far as the eye ranged. Stretching out from the northerly side of Mt. Pavlof a long narrow ridge extended for some three or four miles, and ended abruptly in a bold point.

"It had been agreed before leaving the ship that we were to have for our hunting grounds that section of the country south of this ridge, and an imaginary line drawn from it in an easterly direction to Pavlof Bay, and that Scull and Elting were to have to themselves everything to the north and west of the long ridge.

"Nearly all the streams that we saw in this vicinity still had a few live salmon in them, the last stragglers of the run, but there was plenty of evidence to show that a little earlier in the season great quantities of these fish had come up the creeks to spawn and die, or be eaten by the great brown bear. At this season the bear were not feeding upon the salmon and had entirely disappeared from the low country in which we were hunting, although, if we read aright the signs that they left, they had not long since moved up to the higher ground.

"There were numerous caribou, however, running in small bunches of from two to six head, and very easy to approach with ordinary caution. The caribou were just in the stage of shedding the velvet from their horns, and I should say about half the heads we saw were still in the velvet, while the other half had entirely or only partially rubbed it off.

"One of the most interesting things we saw while in this country we stumbled on by accident. We were on the top of a small hill one day and spied a fox some distance below us in such a position that it looked possible to get up for a closer shot. We wound our way through the alders in the direction of the fox, and were about approaching the opening from which we hoped to see him when we were arrested by a great slashing of antlers against the alders, which at this point were probably ten feet high. Forgetting the fox we approached the noise, and finally got up to within about twenty yards of a fine caribou scraping the velvet off his horns with the aid of the alders. We stood concealed and watched him for some minutes. At first we saw nothing peculiar in the action, but in a little while we noticed that he would rub his head against the bushes for a moment,

CARIBOU HEAD, PAVLOF BAY

Photo. Gilpin Lovering

Lovering, showing the easiest method of packing a caribou head. The beams of the antlers rest on flaps of the skin to ease the shoulders and the rifle is laid on the horns to equalize the weight of the head. Pavlof Volcano appears in the distance and the tundra with its alders in the foreground.

WESTERN CARIBOU

14. Reindeer. (*Rangifer tarandus.*) N. Europe and Asia. National collection. Length, 48½; spread, 32; circ., 5½; points, 22 +18.

16. Kenai caribou. (*R. stonei.*) Kenai. National collection. Length, 58½; spread, 39½; circ., 8½; points, 24 +16.

15. Grant's caribou. (*R. granti.*) Pavlof B., 1913 (E. M. Scull). Length, 53; spread, 37½; circ., 5½; points, 18 +17.

17. Yukon caribou. (*R. osborni.*) White River (Wilson Potter). Length, 56; spread, 46½; circ., 7½; points, 24 +22.

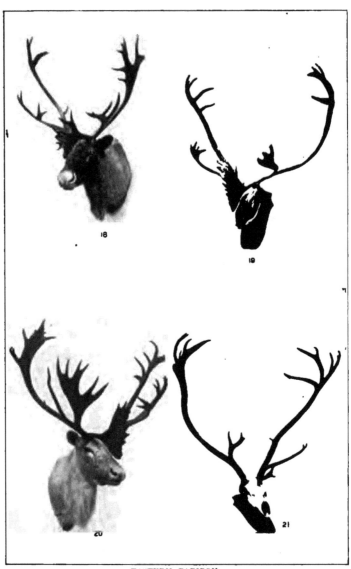

EASTERN CARIBOU

18. Black face caribou. (*R. montanus*.) Revelstoke. National collection. Length, 34; spread, 28½; circ., 6½; points, 13+19.

20. Newfoundland caribou. (*R. terranovæ*). Newfoundland (Wilson Potter). Length, 46½; spread, 38½; circ., 6½; points, 27+16.

19 Barren Ground caribou. (*R. arcticus*.) N. W. of Hudson Bay, 1909. National collection. Length, 51; spread, 40; circ., 4½; points, 12+15.

21. Greenland caribou. (*R. groenlandicus*.) Greenland. National collection. Length, 52; spread, 39½; circ., 5½; points, 9+11.

CARIBOU NEAR PAVLOF VOLCANO   *Photo. Gilpin Lorring*

Grant's caribou which ranges exclusively on the Alaska Peninsula west of Cook Inlet, is of the Barren Ground, or Arctic, type, as distinguished from the varieties which inhabit wooded country. The head is much smaller than that of the woodland caribou but carries longer, more slender and less palmated antlers.

then raise his nose in the air, stick out his tongue and try to pull something down into his mouth. This at first appeared to be some moss or a twig that seemed to have become entangled in his horns, but upon closer examination we saw that the animal was eating the velvet that he scraped from his antlers. After watching this performance for some minutes Collins shot him, and we actually found the velvet from the horns in his mouth.

"It was, of course, very disappointing to us not to see any brown bear that must have been in this vicinity in great numbers only a week or two before our arrival, for they had great trails beaten from the alder thickets to their favorite fishing pools, where they apparently would eat their fill and then return to the alders again.

"Without doubt the weather we had during our caribou hunt was quite exceptional for this locality, and a more enjoyable ten days would be hard to imagine.

"The data of this excursion show that fifty-seven head of caribou were seen, and out of that total we secured our allowance of three heads each.

"If men were contemplating a trip to this section it would add much to their comfort and convenience to equip themselves with some sort of a camp stove. If it were possible to carry fuel a kerosene stove would be the best, as we had to range a good deal to gather alders for the fire."

CHAPTER XII

WE had spent ten days at Pavlof Bay according to our schedule and it was now the eighteenth of September, a week or two later than Klein-schmidt had planned. Our next and last excursion after game was to take place in the Kenai Peninsula, that considerable tongue of land which separates the waters of Cook's Inlet from those of the Gulf of Alaska. At the town of Seward we were to leave the "Abler," which would go directly back to Seattle while we spent a month in the interior. For a thoroughly satisfactory hunt there forty days was none too much. But the vicissitude of our summer's voyage had used the time at our disposal.

Had the weather been favorable it would not have taken us more than four days to get from Pavlof Bay to Seward, but in fact we were eight days in arriving there.

In the first place we had to put in at Pirate Cove on Popof Island and take on board a large number of gaso-line drums which Kleinschmidt had left there in the spring. On account of head wind, we had to anchor for the night in Coal Bay, about a mile to leeward of a large reef on which the steamer "Dora" had been wrecked, and which tossed the white spray of its breakers high into the air. Some twenty-four hours, however, after leaving Pavlof Bay we arrived at the beautiful little harbor of Pirate Cove and proceeded at once to load the iron barrels. This tiny harbor was one of the oldest fishing stations on the Alaskan coast, and from it a fleet of sailboats and dories issued all the year round to catch cod for the packing factory operated there by the Union Fish Company. The fishermen received fifty dollars a thousand for the fish, regardless of size. While some were very large, the average was as low as four pounds.

Several of the fish company's officials came on board and spent the evening with us. To these was added the great Norwegian hulk of one Oscar Olsen, one of the independent residents of Alaska, of whom we had met so many. He told some remarkable stories of his hunting exploits, among them a tale of a sixty-three point caribou which his partner had shot on the other side of the Alaska Peninsula. But his best was that of a bear which he had followed near Chignik.

"I was prospecting in from Chignik," said Olsen, "and I had discovered a volcano or two and some hot springs which were not on the map, when I came upon the biggest bear track I ever saw. At first I thought the ground was wet when the bear went by, because it looked impossible for any of the big brown bears to have a foot so large. But I followed it for a mile or two and was satisfied that it was a bear's track." Olsen stretched his huge hand to its fullest span and laid the end of one little finger on the corner of the table. At the point where his thumb touched the edge of the table he placed the thumb of the other outstretched fingers, then crossed the first hand over and measured off a third span. This enormous measurement he completed accurately by laying the four fingers of his hand beside it, making a total length of more than thirty inches. "There," said he, "is the exact size of that bear track. I went and got my partner Anderson, and showed it to him."

" 'Oh, pshaw!' said Anderson, 'that ain't a fair track; that was where he sat down.'

" 'Well, is that a fair bear track?' I asked, taking him to a place where the ground was dry when the bear had walked on it.

" 'Yes, by God!' said Anderson, looking down at it closely, 'that's a track and you haven't even counted the claws either.'

"Well, I followed that bear for many miles and at last I came up pretty close to him, about two hundred yards away.   He was so big that I looked at my little rifle, a .30–30, and I said to myself, 'Olsen, this little gun is too small to shoot at that bear,' so I turned around and went home."

In walking about the hills near Pirate Cove we came upon two little pine trees looking very lonesome in the great waste of tundra.   They were the first we had seen since leaving the lower regions of the Yukon River, but our pleasant feelings that we were once again in the land of timber were dispersed when we learned that these had been planted ten years before by one of the residents. Westward of Kodiak Island, which still was several hundred miles before us, there is in fact no natural timber on the Alaskan coast.

But the vast extent of the almost unknown Alaska Peninsula, with its adjacent islands, is rich in minerals, game and fur-bearing animals.   The Apollo Mine, on Unga Island, adjacent to our present port of call, had produced about eleven million dollars in gold during its existence.

We cleared Pirate Cove with a good breeze following us, and in several hours had made considerable headway toward Shelikoff Straits, when suddenly Captain

Larsson rushed into the saloon exclaiming, "We've got a stowaway on board, and we'll have to go back to Pirate Cove to put him off."

We expostulated vigorously, but the captain explained, "We have nineteen men on board, which is one more than the law allows us, so I'll get into trouble if I carry this fellow." Out he went and put the schooner about to beat back against the wind to the fishery station. It would certainly take all day to reach it, as the sea was beginning to run higher than the "Abler" could cope with.

Presently, however, Larsson reappeared. He had thought the matter over and devised a plan which would satisfy his scruples.

He addressed himself to Dr. Elting: "If you will examine this fellow and pronounce him a sick man, as he claims to be, we can take him with us."

Elting jumped up at once, and went out to look at the stowaway.

"I guess that will be a sick man," remarked Lovering.

Elting came back in a few minutes and took his seat again. "The fellow is sick," he announced. "I told the captain that he could not get proper medical attention at Pirate Cove and we should have to take him with us."

The schooner once more swung off on her course toward Kodiak Island. The stowaway was put to work assisting the crew and by the end of the voyage was ready to admit that he had fully earned his passage. It was indeed lucky to have him, for a slight accident to one of the other men next day made us short-handed.

Paul, one of the sailors, caught the first finger of his right hand in the block of the main-sheet and ripped off a good piece of the end of it. "Oh, that's nothing," he said, stoutly, as Elting was dressing the painful wound; "I'll be thankful if I get to Seattle with only that much of a loss."

The old "Abler" was now pounding in the seaway raised by the wind hauling to the southeast, nearly ahead, and we were tacking off and on in an effort to hold the progress that we had made on the preceding day. Fog shut us in once more, and in such familiar atmosphere we came up with Kodiak Island, passing many rocks which projected above the surface, and were surrounded by numerous seals. Our first glimpse of Kodiak was the sandy beach on the south coast called Low Cape, and we had run within a half mile of it before the fog thinned sufficiently to reveal it. Shifting our course to the westward we ran up Shelikoff Straits in a favorable breeze which sucked around the south end of the great island.

Our fourth day out from Pirate Cove was beautiful. Afognak Island, closely fitting the northern end of Kodiak, rose steeply from the sea, clothed with the welcome greenery of many trees. Ahead of us a group of sinister rocks entitled "The Barren Islands" jutted hundreds of feet above the waves. We speculated idly, as we went by, upon the miseries of living on them, little dreaming that we were soon to face the possibility of landing there in spite of our utmost efforts to avoid them.

Most of the day we spent clad in oilskins, putting into barrels our walrus head skins and other trophies secured thus far, and after the greasy work was over we trailed the garments overboard at the end of a rope to clean them as much as possible.

We were eagerly anticipating our arrival in Seward. "Tomorrow night," said the mate, "I will have my hair cut in Seward." But the mate's usually reliable prophecies were for once brought to nothing. In fact the trouble began almost as soon as he had uttered this boast.

By six o'clock that night we were abeam of the Barren Islands and had them, as we thought, safely under our lee. We were making steady progress toward our destination. As the evening went on the sky became overcast, the air grew thick and hazy and an hour before midnight the wind hauled to the southeast and began to blow hard. All through the night wind and sea increased. The haze thickened, the wild spindrift, blown by the fury of the gale, rose from the fleecy crests of the billows and filled the whole air. It was impossible to see more than four hundred yards. Staunchly the "Abler" battled against the raging elements. All night she heaved and plunged, wallowing in the angry sea. The captain had long since put her about and instead of trying to brave his way toward Seward was running back toward Afognak Island, holding as closely to the wind as possible and forcing the motor to its highest speed. All night long we could sense the struggle, between the fitful snatches of sleep that the tossing vessel allowed us. It was clear to every one on board that we were in a bad position with the Barren Islands and the half-sunken rocks off Afognak under our lee.

We turned out to breakfast and found only Larsson, Ed Born and Kleinschmidt in the saloon. A few cold dishes were on the table. Nothing was prepared by the cook. He was panic-stricken and had quit completely.

"Well, captain," we asked cheerily, "where are we now?"

"We're about three miles to windward of Sea Lion Rocks, trying to keep her off them," answered the captain

in a despondent voice. A glance at the chart showed that
the Sea Lion Rocks lay just off the northeast coast of
Afognak Island.   Ed Born had lost his usually cheerful
disposition and was serious.

All day long the wind blew a three-quarter gale and
not once could we see farther than a quarter mile through
the flying haze, while the "Abler" beat back and forth
on long tacks, striving to hold her own and yet losing,
as we all knew she must lose, on every tack.   Slowly
but surely we must be driven to leeward and then, perhaps
without warning, crash upon the rocks.

"Don't call me if she strikes," said the mate with a
grim smile, as the captain relieved him and he prepared
to go below to sleep.   "I want to be nice and warm in
bed when the finish comes."

"If we come in sight of a rock or an island there won't
be time to turn around before we hit it," replied the
captain, "to say nothing of bothering to call you."

We spent much of the day lying in our bunks waiting
to see what would happen.

It caused considerable amusement, however, when
Kleinschmidt went to Dr. Young and said, "Papa, you
had better get your clothes on; we may strike a rock at
any minute," and the old gentleman got all dressed to be
ready.

No lunch was served, except a few cold dishes that we
discovered for ourselves.   During the day a large wave
came over the bow and happened to catch Martin,
the sailor who had tried to leave us at Nome.   It crushed
him against the windlass and broke two of his ribs.
This effectively prevented Martin from deserting the
ship at Seward and earned him the distinction of being
the only deck-hand who went with the "Abler" on the
entire trip from Seattle to the Arctic and back again.

As the storm continued all day without apparent intention of abating, a council of war was held in the cabin between Larsson, Kleinschmidt and Ed Born. Among them it was suggested to change the course and try to run before the wind between the Barren Islands and Shuyak Island. "If we can hit the large passage between them," said Larsson, "it will give us a great deal more sea room to drift in before we fetch up on the coast of the Alaska Peninsula, on the other side of Cook's Inlet, and we might even be able to get under the lee of the Kenai Peninsula and run into Kachemak Bay."

But then the question naturally arose, "Where were the Barren Islands at this moment?" Nobody knew. Nevertheless, Larsson was for trying it.

"I will not do it on my own authority," said the captain. "I will call the mate and see what he thinks." The mate emerged from his cabin next to the engine room and the plan was put before him.

He heard them all through. "If you want to commit suicide, go ahead and do it," said the mate. "I will not be a party to any such thing." So saying he went back to bed.

The vessel was kept straining to windward. All this time by the greatest good fortune Jenny, the motor, never once halted. It had been her custom to hesitate, to pause, to catch her breath, to stop entirely and wait for the tender hand of her engineer to coax her again into activity. But now in our time of utmost need she responded with a delicacy, a consideration of feeling which one would not have looked for in so hard a heart as hers, and kept bravely turning the propeller without once ceasing. Ever since leaving Pirate Cove she had, in fact, been doing this. Her clutch was wedged full of wood, for it had long ago completely worn out, and it was impracticable, therefore, to disengage it, and of course equally impossible to reverse the engine, even if we wanted to.

We had been in a state of tense anxiety for two days when at last hope broke through the gloom. A clean speck of sky showed in the southwest and it grew larger late in the afternoon of the second day of storm and promised that the wind would shift within a half day and blow from that quarter. It cleared also, considerably towards the southwest, and at least so far as we could see in that direction no rocks were visible.

Reflecting the cheerfulness which came with this good sign Ed Born gave us a can of raspberries from his private stock. We had not for a long while enjoyed such a tidbit because the sailors in the forecastle had systematically rifled the ship's stores and eaten all the best of the tinned goods before this time.

As soon as the wind changed, which was about midnight, the "Abler" was put on the starboard tack and ran like a hunted thing out to sea for twelve hours. When the morning broke clear and sunny no land was in sight. An observation at noon showed that we were some sixty miles off Afognak and that we had, during the storm, passed and repassed close to the fatal rocks. How we missed some of them never was explained, and neither the captain nor the mate made any attempt to trace on the chart the actual course we had taken during the two days of storm. It is probable, however, that the strong tide setting out of Cook's Inlet had carried us to windward at the hours when its help was most needful.

By noon, then, we were headed directly for Seward. The wind blew fair all day and all night, and at dawn the gaunt rocks of Cape Resurrection pointed the narrow entrance of Resurrection Bay. On the left we could see some of the numerous mouths of the great Kenai Glacier which covers the mountain tops of the Kenai Peninsula, on the western side of which we were to do our last hunting. Up the long stretch of beautiful Resurrection Bay we sailed until the little town of Seward was in sight and we made fast, without further accident, to the pier at the foot of the main street.

It was the twenty-sixth day of September when we stepped off the "Abler" for the last time. Our long voyage of two months and a half had taken us more than 4,400 miles through both good and evil fortune in various details of the journey, but in spite of everything that had at times seemed destined to prevent us from attaining our objects we had succeeded in accomplishing practically everything that we set out to do. It was with feelings akin to regret that we said good-bye to the good fellows on the schooner: Kleinschmidt, the Borns, the captain and the mate, who had each in some way contributed to make our cruise successful.

There is sometimes disagreement among men who are associated at hazard in such enterprises, and we on the "Abler" were by no means immune from it. There were conflicting interests on board and quarrels were as frequent and as gusty as the sudden storms of the Arctic in summer. But they blew over quickly and when we left we grasped the hand of each man with honest good feeling.

As a farewell token we sent on board a case of whisky and a case of port of which to make "smotherins" and as a consequence the "Abler" did not sail for two days. "It's blowing too hard outside," Captain Larsson would exclaim genially when we met him on the streets of Seward.

Eventually, however, the "Abler" got off and made a good trip of ten days from Seward to Seattle, while we were on the Kenai Peninsula engaged in our last hunt of the season.

PIRATE COVE, AN OLD ALASKAN FISHING STATION   Photo. A. M. Collins

From a hill 2,000 feet above the water, the tiny harbor of Pirate Cove, on Popof Island, presented a charming picture. At this place a large and reliable catch of cod was brought in dories the year round, to be dressed and put up for shipment. The small photograph shows a scene at the dock.

TRAVEL AND RESIDENCE IN ALASKA

Above: Relaying goods across a damaged bridge over the Resurrection River, near Seward, on the Alaska Northern Railway.

Below: Cottonwoods cabin and cache on Skilak Lake, Kenai Peninsula; a typical Alaskan trapper's winter home.

CHAPTER XIII

THE Kenai Peninsula is a large, roughly triangular piece of land jutting out from the sharply irregular coast into the Gulf of Alaska. It is separated on the west from the mainland by the waters of Cook's Inlet and on the east by the much indented shores of Prince William Sound. At its base the peninsula is nearly cut through by bays which run into it from both west and east. When Captain James Cook sailed up the coast of Alaska in 1778, and entered the waters of Cook's Inlet, he navigated them to the head where they forked, one part running east and the other north. The old adventurer was under orders to find the Northwest Passage around America and here thought he had discovered it. But when he had reached within twelve miles of Portage Bay, which makes in from Prince William Sound, he was forced to turn back, appropriately naming this body of water Turnagain Arm. Cook's Inlet is remarkable as having the greatest rise and fall of tide, forty feet, of any place in the world except the Bay of Fundy in Nova Scotia.

Into the head of Cook's Inlet flow several rivers, chief among them being the Susitna, which flows past the vast slopes of Mount McKinley, and the Matanuska, which in a general way parallels the Susitna on its eastern side. In the drainage systems of these two rivers lie some of the most important mineral deposits and possible agricultural lands in the country. But owing to the fact that Cook's Inlet is, for a great part of the year, choked with broken or solid ice and on account of the inconvenience to navigation presented by the great rise and fall of tides, permanent routes for tapping this rich district must start from the eastern side of the Kenai Peninsula.

Prince William Sound, therefore, is generally regarded as the scene of Alaska's future development. This beautiful body of water has an extremely irregular coast line. Its great fiords run far into the coast and a number of islands protect it from the full fury of the open ocean. In the number and grandeur of its glaciers Prince William Sound is unsurpassed by any other locality in Alaska. They lie on nearly all of the snow-covered mountains and flow imperceptibly down to the heads of the great fiords. The sea never freezes here in winter and there are numerous harbors well protected from the weather.

Several towns of importance were situated on the shores of Prince William Sound at the time of our visit. I say "were situated" advisedly, because by the time this book is published others may have sprung up, as is common in Alaska.

Most easterly of these is Cordova, situated upon a shallow bay of the same name. This place was established as a terminus for the Copper River and Northwestern Railway by the Guggenheim Exploration Company, which spent about $17,000,000 constructing the lines from Cordova up the valley of the Copper River as far as the town of Copper Center, with a branch line to the Bering coal field and the great Bonanza copper mine near Kennecott. It leads also toward a new gold strike, discovered in 1913 on the Shushanna River, one of the tributaries of the White. The "Guggs," as this syndicate is familiarly called, began life as the sons of a poor peddler in Philadelphia. They migrated to Colorado and became interested in the lead-smelting business, eventually extending their operations to various other metal traffics. By this time they had obtained great interests in Alaska and owned or controlled many of the most important mining and transportation properties. It was the fear that these and similar large groups of capitalists would secure control of most of the natural resources in Alaska that led the administration in Washington to withdraw coal lands from entry in 1906 and to create vast forest reserves in southeastern and southwestern Alaska. That this fear was not shared by all of the residents of Alaska is illustrated by the remark of one of the individual mine owners in Nome who said, "Washington is afraid that the 'Guggs' will buy us all out. Our only fear is that they will not."

After the embargo of 1906, development work in Alaska was at a standstill. The Copper River and Northwestern Railway proved to be an unfortunate investment as a common carrier, although it was said that the Guggenheims had taken out enough copper to pay for their total capital outlay. Nevertheless the initials of the railway's name, C. R. and N. W., were locally interpreted "Can't run and never will." Although this opinion may be unjust, it was admitted that the great snowfall and the quantities of ice lodged by the glaciers on the Copper River made the line very expensive to keep open.

Valdez, a community of rather more than one thousand people, is situated at the head of the bay of that

name on a low flat between the water and the great
Valdes Glacier which is thirty miles long. Near it, Fort
Liscum is an important military station. Between
Cordova and Valdes are several mines producing mostly
copper, Ellamar and Fidalgo Bay being the principal
ones. At the western edge of the bay the Latouche
copper mine is a valuable property and steamers call
frequently at all of these points.

But our attention for the ensuing month was to be
centered upon the Kenai Peninsula. Seward, its most
important town, was a struggling village of two hundred
and fifty souls, nearly a tenth of its one-time size.
Although we found an unusually substantial and interesting lot of men among its business people, the possibility
of amusement in this place was very limited. There was
not even a moving-picture show. A scrap of conversation heard on the dock one evening put the situation as
tersely as may be. Two men were walking up toward
the town, one a very large man, the other a small fellow.
The following dialogue ensued:

The very small man (in a complaining tone): "I'm
the only fellow that can furnish any excitement in this
place."

The very large man (contemptuously): "Well, you
don't furnish such a lot of excitement."

The small man (defiantly): "Well, I would if I could
only get drunk."

There was much for us to do. Our guides were on
the pier when the "Abler" docked: Ben Swesey for Dr.
Elting, "Colonel" Revell for Collins, Crit Tolman for
Lovering and "Wild Bill" Dewitt for me. Our first care
was to make lists of provisions for the month in the
interior, and to have them ordered and packed. We

must also purchase stoves, tents and sundry camp necessities.

Our first few meals consisted mostly of ham and eggs. We reveled in the first good bath since leaving Nome, enjoyed the almost forgotten luxury of sleeping in a real bed, read stacks of letters from home and interviewed Dick Lane, manager of the railway, in regard to sending us on our journey as soon as possible. There were also the trophies of our Arctic hunting and our caribou heads to be packed and shipped by the next steamer; and in connection with this duty we made the acquaintance of the new game warden, Dr. Baughman. Mrs. Kleinschmidt and her two attractive children had been awaiting their wandering Ulysses at Seward during the summer, with the intention of returning to Seattle on the "Abler," but these plans were changed and while Captain Kleinschmidt went back on the schooner his family returned on one of the regular steamers.

We were now delayed for several days by repairs necessary on the Alaska Central Railroad. This highway of transportation, on which about six million dollars had been spent by the promoters to construct seventy-two miles of track, was described in its present condition as "two streaks of rust." It had been bankrupt for some years, and now a citizens' committee was operating gasoline motor cars for twenty-nine miles of its length, paying no rental and charging sufficient tariff only to keep even with the running expenses. Tickets were issued in the form of receipts for "Donation to Gasoline Fund." Tozier, the engineer and superintendent, was now repairing the bridge across Resurrection River, about three miles out of Seward, where a jam of logs had come down the stream and weakened one of the sections.

Lane said that we ought to be able to cross it within a couple of days. Meanwhile we paid several visits to him in his apartments in the large railway office building which had been built for a future development of trade that never came, and where he was nursing a sick man, Jim Hayden, one of the principal mine operators in the Kenai. Finally everything was ready and on the twenty-ninth of September we loaded our duffle on a flat car at the dock, which was pulled by a motor passenger car. Early in the afternoon we started from Seward. On reaching the damaged bridge we had to unload all the stuff, place it on small flat cars called trailers, push them across the bridge which was considerably bent in the middle, and hitch them behind the largest passenger car of the line waiting on the farther side.

It was a considerable company of us that made the up-bound trip. Collins and Lovering, who were to start hunting moose, sheep and bear from a common camp, had one cook, "Scotty," and two packers, Elgin Vaughn and Ike Hergard, besides their guides. Dr. Elting had one packer, Ed. Crawford, and Gus Kusche for cook. Kusche had sickened of the sea voyage and welcomed Elting's invitation to go with him into the interior for a month of sport and recreation. I had a cook, Alex Bolam, and a packer, Fritz Posth, besides "Wild Bill," my guide.

For something more than an hour we followed the course of Resurrection River until at mile twelve we had reached the summit of the pass. Dense forests, mostly of spruce trees, flanked the railway on both sides in the lower part of its course, and beyond them the mountains towered up, capped by snow and ice, glistening brilliantly in the clear air. Beyond the watershed we descended gradually, stopping once or twice to cut away a "sweeper"—a tree which had fallen across the track—and ran carefully over the bridge of the Snow River, which flows into the head of Kenai Lake.

At mile eighteen we reached this long, narrow body of water and at mile twenty stopped to put off my three hunting companions and their outfits. This place was called Grandma White's, in honor of an old woman who kept a road-house, and from here my friends were to take launches and proceed down Kenai Lake as the first stage of their journey into the wilderness. The rest of us, however, went on to Roosevelt at mile twenty-three and a half. "Wild Bill" and Charley Emsweiler had recently built here a log cabin for a road-house and with them I spent the night, as it was already dark when we reached the station.

Most of our stuff we placed in the station storehouse, since we were to leave in a launch the next morning from the pier at the station, and we walked about a half-mile to Bill's cabin.

It was a large house, this log cabin, two stories high. A new stove with all modern fixtures stood in one corner and up-stairs each had a bed to himself. Some anxiety was caused by the discovery that the rowboats which had been pulled up at some distance from the water, were swamped, the lake having risen several feet since the men went to town, but they were fortunately found undamaged.

Early the next morning, therefore, we turned out, loaded a large dory belonging to Alex Bolam, my cook, and Fritz rowed it to the dock. Bill took a light round-bottom boat which had been confiscated from some Japanese seal-poachers and sold by the Government. Our remaining things were placed on board the "Bat," a launch owned by Fred Bunce. We were soon off across the lake, but not before we had seen the long tow of our friends, who had made an earlier start from mile twenty. Their three rowboats strung out behind a launch were already several miles before us. But the "Bat" swiftly covered the narrow lake, twenty-four miles long, and arrived at its lower end, Cooper Creek Landing, just as the other men pushed off from the dock to run down the river.

Cooper Creek Landing was a city consisting of three or four tents, and a few hundred yards below them a new cabin erected by one Schultz, whose hospitality we accepted for lunch. At the landing our launches left us and returned to the railway station while we prepared to run the eighteen miles of swift Kenai River, which drained the upper lake into the lower or Skilak Lake. Thanks to careful navigation through the numerous rapids and around the threatening rocks, in the swift current which sped at an average of about six miles an hour, we reached the mouth of the river three hours after we started fom the landing, without loss or damage, although some of the boats shipped several large waves. Every boat except our two stopped for an hour or so at Frank Young's mining camp, about a mile below the landing, with the result that we beat most of them down to the lower lake. Only Crit Tolman passed us, because he had had an Evinrude motor attached to the stern of his dory, and with this most convenient little device he drove the boat bow first through all the rapids in safety. We, having only oars, must perforce go down through the bad places stern first in order to be able to row against the current and keep off the rocks. But not so stout Ben Swesey, who declared that he believed a boat was

VIEW ON THE KENAI RIVER, ALASKA

Photo. Gilpin Lowring

The Kenai River drains Kenai Lake into Skilak Lake, and for the 18 miles of its course between these two bodies of water is a rapid stream winding through rough country. The banks are much wooded, though in many places the timber is of small size. Considerable gold has been taken out and its valley is looked upon as a promising field for dredging.

LOADING BOATS AT SKILAK LAKE

Looking across the lower lake from the cabin at Cottonwoods Creek, in a northwesterly direction. A heavy snowfall had, by the end of October, changed the landscape from the brown and green of autumn to the gray and white of winter. Trophies and outfit were stowed in the boats for the trip homeward up the Kenai River.

made to go bow first and bow first his boat should go—
rapids or no rapids. Being a skilful riverman, Ben
succeeded where the other guides preferred to use the
more conservative fashion.

On emerging from the river and crossing the shallow
bar we hauled up on the beach at the head of Skilak Lake,
baled out the water which had come into our boats and
cut poles and rigged up tarpaulins as sails. It was half-
past four in the afternoon when we were ready to push
off again, but the wind, which at first was favorable,
soon hauled ahead and we took down the sails and rowed
the remaining six miles of our journey.

The lower lake, as the local inhabitants almost invari-
ably called that which is set down on the map as Skilak,
is broader but shorter than the Kenai Lake, and is subject
to violent wind storms which make it, at times, impassable
for small boats. We were anxious to get started on our
hunting and therefore pushed off without unnecessary
delay and by steady rowing reached Cottonwoods Creek,
six miles distant on the other side, at six o'clock. The
other three boats, with Tolman's motor-driven dory in
the lead, pulling them, passed us before we had arrived
at our destination. They were going twice as far down
the lake to a cabin at the mouth of King County Creek.
I did not have a chance to speak to any of my companions
again for a month.

"Wild Bill" steered the little Japanese sealing boat
in which he and I crossed the lake, to the mouth of Cottonwoods Creek where Alex had a cabin. The light, finely
modeled craft rowed so much easier than the dory that
we arrived about a half hour ahead of the two other
men and had a good fire going in the stove when they
pulled into the beach. Before turning in for the night

we unloaded all our goods and carried nearly all of them up to the cabin, about a hundred yards, and placed them under cover until morning. We had made forty-eight miles this day and were seventy miles distant from Seward along the route we had come, but a much shorter distance across the mountains, for we had bent to the southward after leaving the railway.

Our cabin was a most magnificent affair, about 11 x 14 feet in size, high enough for a man to stand upright in it without hitting his head. A large bed, which accommodated Bill and me, was built into one corner beside the door; while Fritz and Alex, having no bed, wrapped themselves under the same blanket upon the hard floor. On the opposite side of the door a stove had been set up and at the back of the cabin were a table, stools and storage place for the provisions on the numerous shelves. The windows had real glass in them; one in the rear wall over the table and one in the smooth board door. The door was inscribed with the names of previous wayfarers who had accepted the silent hospitality of the place. Opposite the front of the cabin and about fifteen yards distant, a high cache, or miniature cabin raised on tall posts, was designed to protect supplies from the porcupines and dogs.

This then was our first night in camp in the woods. Thick around us grew the tall spruces and cottonwood trees, through which the wind made delicious moan upon the night.

Bill and the other guides had among themselves arranged to hunt different parts of the country so that we should not conflict with each other, as the region to which our efforts were to be confined was rather a small tract of land and there were already several other parties in the field.

The large game of the Kenai Peninsula comprises moose, caribou, brown bear, black bear, sheep and goat. The goat has, however, been exterminated from all except the most northerly portion, while the caribou is nearly extinct and strictly protected by law.

The great pride of the Kenai Peninsula as a game country rests upon the moose. This magnificent animal, the largest member of the deer family living or extinct, attains in this country its greatest size, and here bears the largest antlers. The Kenai moose has been described as a separate variety and is called the giant moose. The two largest specimens of this splendid deer ever killed have been taken in the Kenai Peninsula, the antlers measuring in width 78½ and 77½ inches respectively. One large bull, which we measured, stood six feet seven inches high at the shoulders and other travelers record taller figures.

The Kenai brown bear has been described as a separate variety, differing in some particulars from those of Kodiak Island and other parts of the Alaska Peninsula, as well as from the representatives of the family found on Montague Island in Prince William Sound and the islands of the Alexander Archipelago near Sitka. Certainly it is one of the largest of all bears, a gigantic cousin of the grizzly, which it probably exceeds in ferocity. Owing, however, to the systematic hunting of this great creature each spring by the guides, it is becoming scarcer here than in other localities.

The first day's march was the longest and hardest of our trip in the Kenai Peninsula and was not made any easier by the previous inactivity for many days. We bundled together food enough to start a camp in the sheep country, with a couple of tents, cooking pots and sleeping blankets. After we established ourselves within range of the game, Fritz was to come back to the lake and bring up additional goods as they were needed. We left in the cabin, therefore, as a base of supply, most of our food and all the duffle which was not absolutely necessary for the first few days.

Sheep were to be our first object, although in reaching their habitat we should pass through country frequented by moose; for we desired to have our work among the mountains finished before snow fell and made the going difficult.

Accordingly all four of us took loads on our backs and began to scale the mountains which rose immediately behind the cabin. At first the path led through the dense wood at an easy grade. It grew so warm here that soon we stopped to take off most of the clothing which covered our backs, leaving only a thin flannel shirt. The cottonwood, birch, spruce and hemlock gradually thinned out to spruce and hemlock, until we reached the timber line. Here juniper, alder and moss replaced the larger trees. Much of the path was now extremely steep and slippery. When we reached the open upper slope of the mountain the cold wind whirled a heavy snow storm down upon us and we stopped in the shelter of some alders to strip and put on the clothing we had removed below. A short distance higher we arrived at the summit of Bear Pass, some twenty-five hundred feet above the sea level, having marched about four miles in as many hours to attain it. Below us spread a splendid panorama of Skilak Lake, but the full beauty of the more distant view was shut out from us by the falling snow.

Ten miles of barren upland, crossing two ridges and passing a couple of lakes, succeeded the stiff climb. Our shoes were soaked through by the swampy land under foot and the cold wind froze every piece of clothing on us. When we stopped for a rest, as we did frequently, we could remain seated only a few minutes because the sweat chilled us through.

Eventually we reached the southern edge of the plateau where a low dike connected two taller mountains. From this little ridge a splendid view lay below us. The Killey River, two thousand feet lower, ran from left to right across our vision as it issued from a narrow gap in the mountains on the left and meandered through lower country to enter Cook's Inlet at the town of Kenai. Far to the westward across the water of Cook's Inlet towered a vast serrated range of snow-clad mountains, the northern end of the Aleutian range, of which the highest peaks, Iliamna and Redoubt, were somnolent volcanoes.

All this was not revealed to us fully upon the first day, but we could see sufficient to give us an accurate conception of the character of the Kenai Peninsula in its central portion. The land sloped generally from east to west. The watershed lay close to the eastern coast, where the mountains were covered with the great Kenai Glacier, forty-five miles long. On the western slopes of this Kenai Range we were to find the white sheep of our search. On the lower foothills and timbered flats still farther westward lived the great moose and all through this country from the higher mountains to the lower land we were likely to happen upon brown and black bear.

The other three hunters of our party had penetrated farther south and east. Their design was to go around us, so to speak, and from this lookout we could fairly

14

trace the route that they were traveling. We could see some of the bed of King County Creek, clearly make out the channel of the Funny River, which ran almost parallel to the Killey and some miles south of it, and beyond this could see the edge of a higher table land separating the Funny River basin from the drainage system of Lake Tustumena, which the local inhabitants called Kusiloff Lake.

As we stepped upon the dike, shivering with the cold, trying to beat our numbed fingers and toes into sensibility, we were in position to look over almost the whole of the small territory thickly populated by the great moose. For these noble creatures had, in recent years, been crowded into a definite region. At times they migrated to one side or another, but generally they were now hemmed in the country lying between Skilak and Tustumena Lakes, between the Kenai Mountains and the low western coastal plain. North of Skilak Lake specimens were often obtained, but the general opinion was that such had migrated from the main territory.

Driven out of the southwestern end of the Peninsula by hunters issuing from Homer and Seldovia to supply the canneries there; forced to retreat from Kenai and Hope on the west and north, the moose had withdrawn near to the mountains, and we sometimes found them among the foothills at elevations exceeding three thousand feet, in isolated instances. Most of the animals we came upon, however, were ranging at one thousand to two thousand feet above the sea level. Many hundreds were killed yearly by the Indians, the guides and the professional meat hunters, and the continual persecution had herded the remainder together into a comparatively small piece of country; possibly only 1,500 square miles in area. This process of congestion led game wardens and guides, who noted the increased number of moose in the locality, to conclude that the stock was increasing in number. But unfortunately there was hardly any other reason to think that this was the case, and unless protective measures were to be taken we regarded it as reasonably certain that the noble moose would be exterminated from this part of Alaska. Fortunately two convictions for poaching were obtained during the summer that we were in the country, but the general sentiment of the community was not favorable to the preservation of the game, and serious offences generally went unpunished. Taking advantage of the malicious clause in the Alaskan game law, that natives, explorers, prospectors could kill at any time when in need of food, any resident of Alaska felt entitled to the privilege of shooting whether in need of meat or not. This was so generally understood as hardly to raise a laugh when joked upon.

While also the sheep had been driven back to more remote mountains than those on which they used to live, there was not so much danger of them being soon exterminated. For if much hunted, the sheep soon become wary and extremely skilful at escaping. Our first designs were directed against these beautiful creatures.

We had not sat so long upon the dike as the foregoing comments upon the moose might lead the reader to believe, for the cold wind still blew and after a few moments' rest we moved on. "We'll go down here," said Bill, stepping to the edge of the dike, and in truth we did go down a steep, slippery trail for about a thousand yards, and then were obliged actually to slide down the side of a particularly abrupt hill. Four moose watched us do so. This led us into a gully between the high mountains on the left and rounded knolls on the right, took us through an abandoned beaver dam which was very soft and swampy in places where we broke through the thin ice.   Our track then led over the brow of the rounded knolls to the right, from which we spied more moose directly on our way, and down into the green timber by the Killey River. The whole trail was blockaded by windfalls of burned spruce trees, so that every three or four paces, on the average, we were obliged to step from one to three feet high to get over the obstructions.   Toward the end of our eighteen-mile tramp this became extremely wearisome and we were all glad to arrive late in the afternoon at a little cabin on the banks of Benjamin Creek just above its confluence with the Killey River.

Quickly a roaring fire was built of the many dead logs lying about, and we warmed and dried ourselves as best we could.   Forked stakes were driven into the ground at each side of the fire, a green log laid across them, hooks manufactured from the crotches of trees, pots and pans brought out, and in a short time we were enjoying a simple but welcome meal.

Porcupines had gnawed great holes in the corners of this cabin, but we stuffed them up somehow, tacked a piece of cloth over the glassless window, spread the floor with freshly cut spruce boughs and all lay down to a dreamless sleep side by side on the floor of the cabin. There was barely room for the four of us, after we had cleared out all the débris which littered it when we arrived.   But it was many times easier to occupy the rough and imperfect little house than to set up a tent.

We were now deep down in the gorge of the Killey River, surrounded on all sides, except the west, whither the stream flowed, by mountains nearly a mile high.

SHEEP PASTURE IN THE KENAI PENINSULA

The mountain sheep nibble the green grass which flourishes on hillsides, generally below a patch of melting snow. "Wild Bill" posed here to illustrate the steepness of this slope near the head of Killey River.

A ROCK SLIDE IN SHEEP COUNTRY

Many hundreds of yards the hunter must travel on such slopes in pursuit of the Kenai sheep. This walking is tedious but not at all difficult.

Their summits were covered with unbroken snow and their sides near the tops showed many large patches through which the bare rocks peeped. Below the snow line we saw nine sheep on the opposite hillside while we were sitting at breakfast the next morning. We did not molest them, for we were to push on about six miles farther up the river to Steve Melcher's cabin. Alex and Fritz went back to the lake to bring up more supplies and a stove, while Bill spent the next day prospecting the trails that led up the river and I wandered off with camera and rifle to look at the neighboring country.

A stiff half-hour's climb took me up to the top of the bench, down which we had come the day before to the cabin, and led to the very edge of a vertical cliff overhanging the deep gorge of Benjamin Creek. More than five hundred feet deep, the precipices on both sides of the gorge dropped sheer to the turbulent bed of the mountain torrent. For more than an hour I lay on the edge of the rock listening to the ceaseless roar of the cataract below and searching the country for animals with my glasses. But there was no sign of game. Across the ravine the mountains ran down almost to meet the crags on which I lay. Looking up the Killey River one could see the snow-crested summits on whose flanks we were to look for sheep, but the bottom of the gorge through which the Killey River issued was blocked from view by wooded low hills and one could not trace the river bed exactly.

Bill slouched into camp as silently as he had gone out, carrying only the axe with which he had been swamping out a trail. It was a favorite pastime of his to wander off with an axe and cut out the alders and other obstacles in a path which we intended to follow a day or so later. When time permitted this, on account of its being inex-

pedient for us to push on without our supplies as in this
instance, his preliminary work made it much easier for
us to go loaded with our packs.   Bill had a good eye
for a trail.   Often he would halt on some little rise to
look over the country ahead of us, and wrinkling up his
nose as he squinted into the distance would stand motionless for five minutes.   He hardly ever spoke when we were
on the march or looking for game.   Then, if we were
confronted by an apparently insurmountable precipice,
he would presently say, without turning around, "I
suppose a fellow could put his feet on those little ledges
where the grass grows, about three inches wide, and maybe
hold on to the willows and pull himself up there."   By
this Bill would intend to say to me, "Do you think you
can climb up there?"

But preserving the impersonal form of the question, I
would generally reply, "Yes, I suppose a fellow could
do that," and up we would go.

Upon returning from this tour of exploration Bill
announced that we would cross Benjamin Creek at the
cabin and follow an old trail on the north side of the
Killey River which he had cut out for several miles.
Accordingly we packed a little food and enough of an
outfit to last for a week in the sheep country and started
off next morning, leaving a note for the other boys to
come on the following day.

We had felled three trees and placed them across
the creek at the cabin.   Over these we went dry shod
and followed Bill's blazes along the bank of the river.
After we had passed the point which Bill had marked
the day before, it became necessary frequently to stop
and look for the most practicable route, as the trail led
up and down over hillocks thickly strewn with fallen

timber. Bill had never been farther up the river than
the Benjamin Creek cabin, but had been in the country
on both sides of it, so he was acquainted with the general
lay of the land. We knew that we had to cross the river
at the cabin, but we did not know within a mile or two
exactly where it was situated. Consequently in diverging to the left and climbing a steep hill, because it was
not possible for us to follow the river bed through a deep
gorge about five miles above Benjamin Creek; we came a
little too far up stream, passing two small lakes which
lay on the bench several hundred feet above the river bed.
Eventually, however, we made our way down to the
roaring stream and located the cabin, which was well
concealed in the timber near the opposite bank. The
river ran with considerable force over a very stony bed.
It was out of the question for us to ford it, and numerous
tree stumps on both banks showed that former travelers
had cut trees and laid them across the narrow parts as
foot logs. Every spring, however, freshets had washed
away the slender bridges, and we must construct a new
one. It was easy to put a tree across the little channel
which separated the northern bank from a patch of rocks
in the middle of the stream, but we had more difficulty
bridging the main current on the other side. Finally we
laid a long, straight spruce tree trunk across a boulder at
the narrowest point and by bearing down on the butt
managed to push the top across to the opposite bank and
wedge the butt firmly between two large rocks. Bill
then crossed on this narrow roadway, cut another tree
on the bank and we laid it beside the first log. So we
reached the cabin, having taken nearly eight hours to do
a march that we afterward made in two and one half
hours.

An accident to my gun had, however, occurred in our difficult scramble over the fallen timber on the way up. I was carrying it in a case in both hands as I plodded along, when a snag tripped me. Down I came and broke the rifle at the grip. It was a cross-grained piece of wood. This accident threatened to delay our hunting for several days until we could get the other gun up from the lake. But Bill and I succeeded in repairing it.

Search revealed two small wire nails in the window frame of "Hotel Steve." These were carefully straightened to drive into the stock. To prevent them from bending or splitting the hard walnut wood we cut a half dozen little chips of soft spruce and drove the nails through a stack of these in such a way that just the points projected from the bottom of the pile. A light tap of the axe easily started the nail into the gun stock and as we drove it down we split off the top chip with a knife and drove the head down to the next piece. In this way we kept the nails from bending and finally had them accurately in place. A lot of pitch from the spruce trees was then gathered and melted in a pan with a little bacon fat. This we spread over the splice and while the pitch was still soft wrapped the part tightly with fish twine. The result was entirely satisfactory, and for the following month the rifle worked as well as ever and did not break or loosen again.

Before this accident occurred I had lopped the head off a plump grouse with a bullet as it sat in a spruce tree and thus made sure of our first supper. Epicure could not cry for a more savory morsel.

CHAPTER XIV

CLIMBING FOR WHITE SHEEP

IT rained considerably during the first night we slept in Steve's cabin and the roof leaked, but this was only a trifling inconvenience.

By the time we had finished repairing the gun Alex and Fritz arrived with the stove and more provisions, including four ptarmigan which they had shot with the .22 rifle.

Bill and I spent the afternoon looking for sheep. On this first excursion we did not cross the river but climbed an old trail directly out from the cabin to the first row of benches, which were here about a thousand feet above the river bed. When we had emerged from the spruce and cottonwood forest—for the cabin was situated just within the upper limit of the timber line—the going became difficult through the alders in the ravines. But we followed an old trail up one of the beds of the streams which here flowed down steeply and gained the top of a rocky knoll, commanding a considerable view. We saw signs of black bear and numerous white-tailed and rock ptarmigan before reaching the lookout. Our little hill was a spur from the side of the higher mountain and enabled us to see five or six miles up the valley of the Killey River as far as the Bear Glacier from which the river issued. About two miles farther up than we were standing a fine cataract plunged through a very narrow, rocky gorge. The snow line was drawn at an altitude

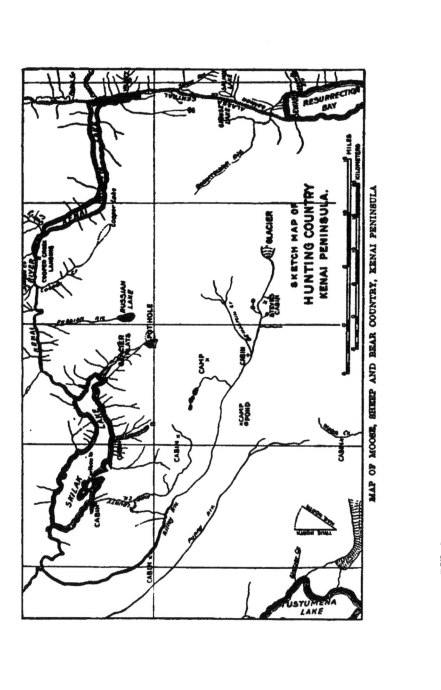

MAP OF MOOSE, SHEEP AND BEAR COUNTRY, KENAI PENINSULA

between 4,000 and 4,500 feet around the valley on both sides. Below us the ground showed rusty brown; green where little patches of pasturage were tucked away in the swales. On the hillside back of us a little troop of sheep, females and young, were nibbling at the green grass four or five hundred yards distant, and a prolonged scrutiny of the landscape through our glasses revealed altogether sixteen of the beautiful white animals on our side of the river. On the opposite slopes, across the river, however, from one to two miles distant, forty-eight more appeared as we watched the tiny patches of white until they moved or otherwise convinced us of their identity. This was not so bad—sixty-four sheep seen in the first afternoon—so we went back to the cabin in high spirits. At the creek, on the banks of which the house was built, Steve's old sluice boxes were lying around, for he had numerous mining claims here. We sent Fritz to Benjamin Creek again to get more cartridges for the gun and a few other trifles and Bill and I started for our first serious day's hunting on the opposite side of the river from the cabin.

"I think there's an old trail made there last year by Wilson Potter," said Bill, "used by him when he was hunting the other side of the valley. He killed three sheep on the hill opposite to the cabin."

Accordingly we started off early in the morning of our second day at Steve's cabin, crossed the river on our foot logs, and soon found the cuttings and blazes on the trees which marked the trail of a year ago. It led at right angles to the river straight up a little hill over the brow of which nestled the two lakes we had passed in coming up to this point, crossed a little swamp to another small rise, and then went straight up the steepest part of the hill to the top of the first row of benches.

"I guess," said Bill, as we struggled through the alders and devil's club, "that Potter and the Colonel thought they would get up to the top of this first bench in spite of every obstacle just to have a look around, for they went for it as straight as an arrow."

Finally we scrambled to the top of the steepest place and saw that we had but begun the real ascent.

Through cottonwood groves, willow patches and alders we made our way up another steep slope to the crest of the second row of benches, and from here we saw that what had appeared to us in the bottom of the valley to be the tops of the mountains was really but the sky-line of the edge of their lower foothills. Still higher above us soared the snow-covered peaks and far to the eastward at the head of the valley the loftier mountainous backbone of the peninsula clad with its coating of perpetual ice.

A few sheep were grazing on the steep slopes above us, but there were no rams with large horns, so we proceeded eastward toward the head of the valley, keeping a sharp lookout in front and below us. Down and up, down and up we picked what seemed to be the most practicable route over the inequalities of the hillsides. We were just below the snow line, although a light fall of the night before had put a covering of glittering crystals on the grass underfoot. For some distance we made our way from ridge to ridge, peering carefully over each sky-line to surprise any game, but there was no sign of life.

Then of a sudden we came upon the sheep.

We were walking down a slope toward the bottom between it and a jagged sky-line, when Bill saw one of the animals disappear over the next ridge. Carefully we climbed up the rocky bank to the top, and Bill went ten-

Photo. A. M. Collins

FOUR SHEEP AMONG THE ROCKS AND SNOW

Near the head of Watch Creek Collins was able to approach a little band of sheep within close range of his camera and against a background which showed that their apparently white fur was slightly yellow compared with the snow.

TWO SHEEP AT THE KILLEY RIVER

"We surprised the two young rams which we had seen crossing the river. We took a picture just after they had plunged across the stream."

derly to the edge for a look below. We were on a gentle downward slope toward the east. As Bill crawled along to get a better view of the lower ground between us and the river bottom he took off his black felt hat and let his long brown braids of hair fall over his shoulders. Slowly he crept on hands and knees, stopping every few yards to search the new ground revealed as he descended. Then suddenly he crouched low, turned and beckoned to me to follow him.

From his side I looked down. About three hundred yards below us, across a gulley, was a small troop of sheep feeding on one of the little green upland pastures of fresh grass. They were unaware of our proximity and we examined them carefully through our glasses without giving alarm. There were eight ewes and eight rams. Of the latter two were fully grown, with good horns, and were perhaps eight or nine years old. The others were younger, from two to five years of age, their horns running from short curving spikes to curves which did not make a full turn when we looked at them from the side. At least the two largest were well worth shooting, but we could see no way of approaching them any closer. The wind was blowing from them to us and we could not go to the left and descend upon them from that side for fear a sudden change in the air as it struck the face of the rocks might give them our scent, nor could we come to them from below the wind, for on our right the cliff broke away steeply and there was no cover to conceal us.

I suggested, "If we sit here a half hour or so, Bill, the sheep might feed up the hill toward us and give us a chance."

"Yes," said Bill, in his slow, noncommittal way, "they usually feed up or down hill, or else they go round to one side or the other."

Nevertheless we decided to lie for a time where we were, in the hope that the sheep might change their position and give us an opportunity. In fact if they moved almost anywhere else it might enable us to stalk them successfully.

From our position we were not able to see the side of the hill immediately below where we were lying, as a little fault in the ground jutted up and shut off the lower part of the hillside.

While we lay there looking across to the next ridge toward which we had been headed, suddenly four rams walked into view up the slope from a place of concealment above the meadow where the first troop of sixteen had been observed. Two of these were fully as large as those in the herd below, and as they marched with slow and stately stride up the little ridge, holding their heads very erect and stiffly drawn back, I rubbed my eyes to make sure that these newcomers were not four from the lower lot of sixteen. But a glance showed that they were a different group entirely. We decided at once to try to get them and so soon as they had walked over the ridge and disappeared on the other side we started to cross the gulley between us.

Hardly had we run half the distance, however, when we discovered three more at the place where these four first showed: one ram and two ewes. The former was lying down chewing his cud. By this time we had crossed the bottom of the gulley and were a short way up the opposite hillside. We stopped, half turned and looked back.

Then for the first time we saw, lying lower down on the very slope that we had last been sitting upon, two good rams asleep. One was facing us, the other headed away. We crouched immediately and examined them with our glasses. One had larger horns than any we had yet seen. The other's were nearly as good. Having once assured ourselves that the animals were asleep and had not seen us, we crawled back as quickly as we could to the slope we had left and now thus concealed by the swelling of the ground, I took rifle in hand and crawled toward the little ridge in the surface of the hill which shut them out from our vision. This brought me within a hundred yards of the animals. As I lay there beside a small boulder, one of the sheep woke and jumped to his feet. Possibly a little swirl of the wind had given him a whiff of me. As he stood on the alert, turning slowly this way and that, I had good opportunity of examining his head with the small glasses which hung always about my neck, and saw that the horns made slightly more than a complete circle and that they were symmetrical and unbroken. The other sheep also rose and stood uncertain what to do.

Bill had crawled nearly to where I was and advised not shooting at the second of the sheep as we might get better ones; but the first, at any rate, was destined to be bagged. At the crack of the rifle he humped himself together and stood, swayed and fell over backwards, rolling head over tail about thirty yards down the hill before lying dead.

The other was astonished at his mate's performance. Instead of taking flight at once he stood and looked curiously at the dying animal until it stopped and lay motionless. Then, somewhat perplexed, but apparently not frightened, he began to walk slowly toward me. I considered him carefully. The horns were not so heavy as those of the first sheep, but they were nearly as long.

"Bill," I whispered to the guide, "I think I'll take this fellow too and then we will spend the rest of our time hunting for one that is better than either of these." Suiting the action to the words I fired. The sheep was now standing stern to. The bullet struck him in the rump and his quarters dropped. We got up at once and started to cross the gulley toward the four rams which had disappeared over the ridge, but after we had gone a few steps, we looked back and saw that the second was still able to drag himself a little, so I finished him. All this took place while we were in plain sight of the herd of sixteen grazing on the meadow below us.

When we crossed over to where the four had been last seen we could not find them. Later we discovered that they had gone up into the snow and were making their way over the divide into the country at the head of Benjamin Creek. But a few yards farther and we were able to look over the other side of the ridge down to the lower ground somewhat east of the meadow where the first-seen herd of sixteen had been feeding, and there they were, all together, grazing on a new pasturage as unafraid as when we had first observed them, in spite of the fact that three rifle shots had been fired within a quarter mile of their position, and that two sheep had died in full view of them. But a careful inspection showed us that none of these had better horns than those we had killed and we decided to postpone to another day our attempt to find a larger animal to complete the three which I was allowed to secure under the regular hunting license. Still other bands were grazing farther eastward and we did not pursue any of them.

Back to our victims we went, and as the first shot had been fired at noon we had lunch of cold broiled ptarmigan, then skinned and butchered the animals. The horns of the first sheep measured as follows: length on curve 38½ inches, girth 13½ inches, spread of tips 20½ inches. Those of the second were: length 35½ inches, girth 12¾ inches, spread 20¾ inches. We estimated the weight of the larger animal at more than 250 pounds.

The white sheep (*Ovis dalli*) of the Kenai Peninsula has narrow-spreading, close-curling horns of considerable length, while its close relative of the White River country bears wide-spreading horns which are even longer. The White River variety is unquestionably the handsomer and is hardly surpassed by any wild sheep.

Bill cut about fifty pounds of meat and fat off the larger ram and with the two heads and this load we started homeward at two o'clock. Orders had been left for Fritz to follow our trail, after he returned from Benjamin Creek cabin with the supplies which we had sent him for, and we were not more than ten minutes on the road when he came in sight.

We counted fifty-six sheep this day, twenty on the side of the river where the cabin was and thirty-six on that where we had done our hunting.

As we now had plenty of the best meat we stayed in camp all the ensuing day, skinning out the heads, washing the scalps in cold water to get the blood off and enjoying the good living which our luck had brought us.

The next day that we did go out was blank in game, as we did not fire a shot, but one of the longest and most enjoyable tramps that we took during the month of our hunting in the Kenai Peninsula. Altogether we saw about one hundred sheep. Following our track of two days before we went beyond the point where we had shot the first two and traveled the slopes of the moun-

15

tains close under the snow line for several miles up the river. The wind was drawing slightly up the valley, and stirred the game ahead of us as we went. Numerous ewes and small rams jumped up and disappeared, but we saw none better than those we had already shot. At lunch time we had gone perhaps nine or ten miles from the cabin and lunched at a point where the valley broadened and turned to give an uninterrupted view of the great glacier where the Killey River headed. In a crevice of the rocky cliff we ate, protected from the keen wind.

The view from here was superb. Down in the broad valley the river wound its tortuous way through the flat bottom and just below us entered the gorge of the waterfall which we had seen from the opposite side on our first afternoon's walk from Steve's cabin. At this point we saw two young rams cross through the water to our side. High above them under the snow line lay three more which looked at the long distance, nearly two miles, as if they might have good horns. Farther to the right, somewhat down the river, a lone ram was feeding in one of the steep pastures under a big patch of snow. He too was worth investigating. Many others were in sight; a large troop of ewes came to the sandy flat above the waterfall and nibbled the grass on the farther river-bank. Higher up on the hillside, and too distant for us to attempt to reach them during the remainder of the day, other flocks lay planted against the mountain, generally below some patch of snow which fed a little rivulet of water.

As we lay in the cleft of the rock, smoking our pipes and looking over the panorama from the brownish red and green verdure below us to the dazzling white snowy ice of the eastern mountain tops, we tried to imagine what this country looked like when it was completely encased in its former glacial ice. That the whole place had been covered by glaciers was evident, not only in the scarred surface of the rocks but also in the contrasting deposits of stone lying about us. Each little hill of the benches on which we had been traveling was capped by a single, large, rounded boulder, exactly balanced on the pinnacle of the summit. These were all of granite, while the composition of the hills beneath them was entirely different. Bill remarked that he had not found any granite outcrops within twenty miles of this place. The ravines between the hills were choked with similar granite boulders which had evidently been brought from a great distance by the prehistoric glaciers. When the long-enduring coating of ice had finally melted and the all-covering glaciers had disappeared, the granite moraines which they had borne upon their surfaces were deposited upon the ground beneath. At least one, of course, rested upon the very summit of each hilltop. The others rolled down the sides and became gradually covered with soil. Of those which still remained, balanced upon the points, a comparatively light touch might have sent anyone rolling down to a more stable resting place. But no such impulse had been given them, and they still remained, precarious tokens of a long-forgotten epoch.

We decided, if possible, to try to cross the river at the waterfall or just above it and investigate the lone ram on the other side, on the way looking after the three which were lying up near the snow line. In doing this we surprised the two young rams which we had seen crossing the river and came over the edge of a cliff upon them at twenty-five or thirty yards distance. Hastily getting out the camera, we took a picture just after they had plunged across the stream and were about seventy yards away on the other bank.

But it was not so easy to cross the rushing river as it had seemed from the heights above.   Indeed, after almost an hour searching the banks we finally found that we could do so only just below the waterfall.   Here the main channel plunged into a very narrow passage, a mere slit between the rocks about three feet wide. Across this we jumped over the boiling torrent, and had a hard climb up the steep benches on the other side to reach the snow line.   This took another hour, and when we got there the three rams which we had been aiming to find had disappeared.   We could not see them in any direction.

Around the benches we went, therefore, keeping a lookout for the lone ram we had seen grazing there earlier in the morning.   But when we came upon him he did not look worth a very great effort to secure.   His horns had evidently been worn off and although they appeared rather heavy, the day was so well advanced that we watched him scramble to his feet and climb up the steep mountain without much regret.   Afterward we were inclined to reproach ourselves that we did not go for him. But at that time we had great hopes of securing an exceptionally fine specimen by more extended hunting.

A careful survey of the country between this point of the benches where we were standing and the course that we must take to reach our cabin showed a discouraging prospect.   The low land was full of thick alder patches and swamps with numerous willow fields.   It was impracticable to follow the crest of the benches, as they made a wide sweep around to our left and some of the rock

VIEW TOWARD THE HEAD OF KILLEY RIVER

Looking eastward from the benches opposite to Steve's cabin we could see the mountainous backbone of the Kenai Peninsula, just beyond which lay the Gulf of Alaska. From a glacier in these mountains the Killey River sprang.

TWO BEAR CUBS IN ONE PACK BAG

"The little fellows had very good fur. Bill put both the carcasses entire into his pack bag and for the rest of our trip we enjoyed roast bear meat more than any other delicacy that we had. Very rich and fat it was, similar to but more tender than young pork."

slides and precipices looked almost impassable. At any rate it would have been a long way around to reach home. We therefore slipped down over the brink that we were standing on, several hundred feet to the valley below. Loose stones in quantities gave way beneath our feet and we slid rather than climbed, holding to the alders and willows as we went down, until we emerged in the flat below. Here we found ourselves from time to time in almost impassable patches of alders, but with patience we managed to work through all of them, following the general course of the river. At the edge of a deserted beaver dam lay a very large pair of old moose antlers which probably measured about sixty-seven inches in their dried and broken condition. Then we struck one of Steve's former trails, much grown up, as it had evidently not been used for many years, and arrived weary in camp at dark.

Our fifth day at this cabin yielded us two black bear cubs. Evidently our repeated trips around the valley had sent the sheep up into the snow or over the hills which enclosed the river basin, for we saw very few. Numerous ravens were hovering in the air above the spot where we had killed the two sheep, and as we came over the rising ground and got a view of them, three eagles were sitting there so gorged with meat that at our approach they could hardly take to their wings. Scarcely anything was left but the bones of the animals.

While we stood there two black spots on the hillside above us moved rapidly across from left to right going up the river. They looked like a grown she-bear and a nearly grown cub and were traveling at a great pace across the rocky slide. When they had, however, gone out of view around a turn on the hillside, and we had felt that they had disappeared forever, suddenly they came into sight again, making toward us. We dashed uphill to meet them at a point which we saw their course would bring them to. I dropped flat on the ground to get my breath again. So rapidly did they come that we had hardly gained the cover we were aiming for when they disappeared into the depression just beside us. The next thing we knew they were passing below us a few yards away. Jumping hastily to the edge, I shot them both and then discovered that they were young cubs, a year and a half old. The little fellows had very good fur. Bill put both the carcasses entire into his pack bag and for the rest of our trip we enjoyed roast bear meat more than any other delicacy that we had. Very rich and fat it was, similar to but more tender than young pork. Indeed, it was so good that I almost regretted refusing to shoot a third cub which we came upon later in the morning of the same day—evidently a little fellow belonging to the same litter—which had strayed away from its mother. We saw it from a high perpendicular cliff, playing in the alders just below us, and threw some stones down to scare it off. The little bear took to its heels and we watched it run for more than a mile and a half, stopping every now and then to look back as if afraid that we were still upon its tracks, and pausing for breath at some unusually stiff climb which it had to make. When we reached camp in the evening the boys said that they had seen this bear still running a mile or so beyond the point where we had lost sight of it.

Yet looking for a third very good sheep to complete our bag, we started out on the sixth and what was destined to be the last day of our hunt in the sheep country.   Hardly had we got across the river and begun ascending the benches on the opposite side from the cabin when two tiny black points on the sky-line of the ragged mountain edge behind and above the camp caught our eyes.   They were two men, one of them carrying a gun, in the snow just above us.   We saw them proceed along the ridge in a direction up the river, occasionally lying down in the snow, looking about with their glasses and acting as though they had seen game.   It needed but a short examination to convince us that it was Elting and his guide Ben, evidently on their first day's hunt after sheep, after a long detour to reach this place.   As we came back into camp that evening we could see a column of smoke rising from the forest near a little lake on a bench above the Killey River about two miles below Steve's cabin, which confirmed our view. And indeed it later proved, when we met Elting, that he was just beginning to hunt sheep on this day.

We had now decided that in order to find remaining specimens we must go up into the snow and hunt there. Straight up we went, a stiff climb of about two thousand feet.   The light dry covering of snow filled all the hollows of the hill slope, leaving only the points of the jagged stones projecting above its surface.   Numerous fox tracks crossed and recrossed the hills as we proceeded westerly along the snow-covered slopes.   A herd of seven rams and some ewes appeared on one of the benches below us, but separated from us by a considerable ravine.

The men across the river had in the meantime been moving up-stream along the benches in the snow and we had lost sight of them.   Just before noon, however, as we were about to start approaching the sheep that we had discovered, they began to fire.   At the first shot the

sheep below us looked up and across the river to the
point, some three or four miles away, from which the
reports came.   As shot after shot rang out they shifted
uneasily and began to move up hill, stopping frequently
to look toward the place of the shooting.

To cut off our game we had to run about three-
quarters of a mile to the bottom of the gulley, down a
steep slope covered with snow above our knees, then climb
the opposite bank.   We did so, taking almost an hour
to accomplish it, and as we drew ourselves carefully to
the fringe of bare rocks which showed through the snow,
saw to our annoyance that the whole troop of sheep had
crossed the canyon far below us and were ascending the
slope which we had left.   Helplessly we lay in the snow
watching the seven rams, who had left the females,
proceed slowly in single file up to the ridge from which
we had first spied them, for we were in plain view and
could not move without letting them see us.

Another band of fourteen had already gained the sky-
line of the divide far above us and four small rams were
farther west, gradually working in the same direction.
There was nothing to do but avoid giving the alarm to
those which we had unsuccessfully tried to stalk, and we
spent the time in eating lunch.   Then we went westward
to a point which overlooked the course of Benjamin
Creek in its lower channel, and from here we could see
the top of the cliff forming the deep canyon just above
the cabin in which we had made a camp.

Heavy clouds, however, soon began to shut off the
view toward Cook's Inlet and betokened a storm.   We
retraced our steps just as a blinding snow squall struck
us, accompanied by thick fog which shut out all objects
at a hundred yards distance.   Back we followed our

KENAI WHITE SHEEP HEADS

The first rams killed; photographed at Steve's cabin on the Killey River. That on the right is a good average head, for size and symmetry, the measurements being: length, 38½; spread, 20½; circumference, 13¼. The men, Fritz on the left, and "Wild Bill" at the right, accompanied the author.

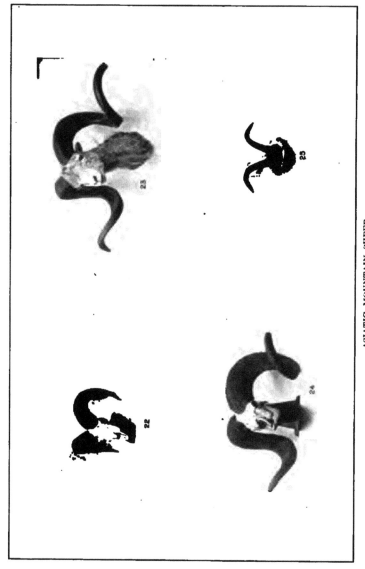

ASIATIC MOUNTAIN SHEEP

22. Kamchatka sheep. (*Ovis nivicola*.) Kamchatka. National collection. Length, 27¼; spread, 17¼; circ., 14. 23. Marco Polo sheep. (*Ovis poli*.) Southern Tibet. National collection. Length, 60¼; spread, 50; circ., 15¾. 24. Siberian Argali. (*Ovis ammon*.) Altai Mountains, National collection. Length, 59¼; spread, 40; circ., 19¼. 25. Chukchi Peninsula sheep (not described). Horns of 2-year ram obtained at Penkegnei Bay, Siberia, 1913.

AMERICAN MOUNTAIN SHEEP

26. Lower California sheep. (*O. crimsobrica.*)
L. Cal. (Wilson Potter). Length, 40 1-16;
spread, 25½; circ., 16½.
29. Kenai sheep. (*O. dalli.*) Kenai (E. M.
Scull). Length, 38½; spread, 20½; circ., 13½.

27. Rocky Mountain bighorn. (*O. can-adensis.*) Alberta (Wilson Potter). Length,
43½; spread, 18½; circ., 17½.
30. Yukon sheep. (*O. dalli.*) White River
(Wilson Potter). Length, 44½; spread, 34½;
circ., 14½.

28. Black sheep. (*O. stonei.*) Casiar
(Wilson Potter). Length 43½; spread, 30½;
circ., 14½
31. Saddle back sheep. (*O. fannini.*) Atlin
(Allen I. Smith). Length, 35½; spread, 24½;
circ., 13½.

FORCING A WAY THROUGH THE ALDERS

At times the difficulty of getting through the thick alders in the Kenai Peninsula was extremely exasperating. On steep ground, however, they were welcome as aids in climbing.

tracks through the canyon and up the long hillside that we had descended. As we came to the top our traces were pretty well covered by the drifting snow. I was peering this way and that.

"Don't move," said Bill. "I'm not looking for our tracks; I'm looking for these sheep. There they are!"

We were, in fact, within one hundred and fifty yards of the herd of seven rams which had lain down in the shelter of the little knoll from which we had first seen them. It was almost impossible to see them through the fog. As I crawled carefully nearer, some of them rose. They looked as large as camels, but very ghostly, and we could just discern their outlines.

The best ram was still lying. Others about him were scrambling to their feet. Finally he too stood up and I fired; he turned and faced us. Another shot and he ran. At the third he stood, evidently badly hurt. A fourth shot knocked him over backwards, dead. Then the others broke and ran, some jumping fifteen feet, according to the tracks that we afterward measured. I paced one hundred and twenty-five yards to where the ram had been first hit. It was a miserable exhibition of shooting, as the first bullet had broken his lower jaw and nicked the horn on one side; nor was the trophy as large as either of the first two which we had obtained. But the interesting conditions in which the animal was brought down made the specimen appear even more valuable. The horn measurements were: length $33\frac{1}{4}$ inches, girth $12\frac{1}{4}$ inches, spread $17\frac{3}{8}$ inches.

For the last time, then, the next morning we washed our faces in the gold pan, which had been our basin since we arrived here, and packed down to the cabin at Benjamin Creek, making the six miles in two hours and

twenty-seven minutes, loaded, at a fast walk all the way.
The last sheep skin was put in the creek to drain clean
of blood and by morning was frozen stiff.   We were
through with the sheep and were now to try stalking
moose.   The beauty and interest of the country we had
just been in appealed to me strongly, and it was with
great regret that I turned my back upon it.

CHAPTER XV

JUST off the trail leading from the lake to the cabin at the fork of Benjamin Creek and the Killey River and about a half mile lower than the dike from which we had obtained our first broad view of the river bottom, a little patch of cottonwood trees grew around the sides of a small basin amid the hills. Here we pitched two tents and kindled a blazing fire.

It was the first night that we spent under canvas. The weather had turned bitterly cold; a thin film of ice formed in a few minutes on the water in our buckets. Lying in the little, thin miner's tent with my head and feet touching its cold walls, I could almost feel the warmth of life oozing out through the thin blankets which formed my sleeping bag. In the 8 x 10 duck tent the other three men slept like logs in their warmer coverings.

We had counted eleven moose on the way as we moved from Benjamin Creek to the cottonwoods camp, and just as we were coming into the place where we were to pitch, a large bull was plainly visible hardly a quarter of a mile beyond the camp. So close was he, in fact, that we had to stalk behind the willows to get into our shelter. Bill and I, of course, immediately after arranging matters for the night, set out to have a closer look at this specimen, and we got within one hundred and fifty yards of him. There was no doubt that it was a very good bull, but the hope of finding a larger one before our time expired withheld the hand from the trigger. As we returned to camp after this stalk we were careless of showing ourselves to the moose and consequently he caught sight of us and followed us much nearer. Then, getting below wind of the fire, he made a circle through the foothills and emerged on the lower ground in the direction of Benjamin Creek cabin. We saw him there the next morning on arising, and went down over the benches to have another look at the animal. This time we did not exactly locate him among the fallen timber before he had heard us and dashed off at a great rate down over the hillocks nearer to the river bottom.

On the third morning the same moose was still to be seen approximately at the place where we had last observed him. We were pretty well satisfied by this time that the horns would make no mean trophy and Bill said to me, "If you're going to shoot two moose I think you had better take this one." Accordingly we set after him.

From the little knoll immediately at our camp we could spy for many miles over the lower country between us and the Killey River and also more dimly over to the country along the Funny River. Much of the immediate foreground was burned-over country, where the naked trunks of the spruce trees had fallen and lay crossed and tangled like piles of jackstraws. Little tongues of green timber ran down into the broken country from the hills north of us, very many patches of dense alders beset the sides and bottoms of the numerous ravines, but here and there were old moose trails which led by apparently practicable routes toward the spot where our game lay unsuspicious of danger. The

Photo. Gilpin Lovering

KENAI MOOSE IN HIS FEEDING GROUNDS

The moose browses the tender tips of willows and other bushes. This view shows not only a good picture of a free and uninjured animal but also a characteristic panorama of the country in which he ranges in the Kenai Peninsula.

CAMP IN A COTTONWOOD GROVE

A rope slung over a tree limb was sufficient to raise the little miner's tent. For the wall tent we usually put a ridge pole across two pairs of leaning poles and guyed them to trees. The stove pipe opened and nested compactly for traveling and proved a great comfort in camp.

moose was now resting, now browsing, in a little meadow full of fallen timber between two low rounded ridges. From the great height on which we stood we could look down into this glade and see him distinctly. But we were well aware that when we had once left the summit and had plunged into the tangled bottoms we should be lost unless we had easily recognizable landmarks to steer by. There were, fortunately for this purpose, seven large boulders on the side of the little ridge between us and the moose and we aimed to arrive at this point.

The first part of the journey was difficult, owing to the numerous alders which surrounded the little hill on which the camp was placed, but we worked successfully through these and kept on the highest ground possible, while heading in the general direction of our prey, in order that we might, from time to time, try to look again for him and make sure that we were traveling right and that he had not shifted his location. Several small hills gave us a chance of spying down into the little meadow where the moose had been, but we were now lower than at the camp and, whereas from the greater elevation there we could look through the thinner parts of the tree stems, from here we saw a maze of thicker trunks. Consequently it was very hard to make out the animal, and at some of our stopping places we did not succeed; but as we drew nearer we located him ranging to and fro and at last lying in the bottom of the little hollow. Carefully we went down across a swampy meadow and reached the ridge of the seven rocks.

Coats were here laid aside for a crawl. Our first attempt brought us about fifty yards too far to the right of the moose, so we retraced our steps and went farther along before we climbed up on the ridge again. Now we were at the best place. On hands and knees we mounted the little hill, lifted twigs out of the path before putting hand or knee upon them, because the wind was light and baffling. At last we gained a good viewpoint. Several small evergreen trees and a few bare limbs were in the way, but it was possible to shoot between them and hit the animal without having the bullet turn aside before it struck its mark.

We were hardly more than one hundred yards away from the moose, and looked at him carefully with our glasses. He was lying with his back to us and it was not possible to see the brow points on both sides, but the blades of the horns looked large and they seemed to have a wide spread. The rifle was trained upon his shoulder, when suddenly the moose stood up. Bill said, "That is not the same one," but it was too late. We had made the stalk with the purpose of killing this animal, because we had felt sure it was the one we had marked down, and firing the fatal bullet was the only logical conclusion to our long and stealthy approach. The shot rang out and the moose stood still. "He's dead," cried Bill as the beast did not move. But to make sure of him I put another bullet at the same place and the great animal went down to his knees and then fell over.

With what emotion the hunter runs to his slain victim to examine the prize; with what exultation and regret that the chase is ended; with what hope that the trophy may surpass his expectations and fear lest it prove to have been deceptive! With all of these feelings I ran down the slope, jumping the fallen trees, to the side of the huge beast.

But alas for Nimrod's dream! This was by no means the moose we had followed with our glasses for three days. Three points were broken off, and the blades were folded so that the spread was comparatively narrow. To say the best about it, the growth was fairly heavy. I will not describe how bitter was my disappointment; but I swallowed it as best I could and spent the rage in skinning out the head.

We measured the game first. He stood 6 feet, 7 inches at the shoulders; the antlers were 53 inches in spread, the blades 33 inches long, and 15 inches wide.

As if to put the final touch of irony upon this mistake, our scent as we started back to camp roused another large moose not more than a quarter mile distant from the scene of our kill and he raced up the hills ahead of us. This one looked and probably was the game we really had intended to shoot.

The freezing weather had continued with about thirty degrees of frost, so we put the stove into the large tent on stakes capped with milk cans. About five in the morning I awoke, finding my toes were about to freeze, and went into the other tent, stoked the fire and warmed myself to life. Then back I went to the little tent and by breakfast time was cold again.

Bill and I took a prospecting tour around the hills above the camp to a point which overlooked Benjamin Creek, about a mile above its junction with the Killey River. From here we could see Tom Towle's cabin and the several forks of Benjamin Creek far up in the mountains, but no game except one porcupine. Alex and Fritz had meanwhile brought up the moose head and scalp and made everything ready to move camp the next day. It was still cold; so cold that a little squirrel, perched on one of the cottonwood trees, was too numb to run away and let Alex approach within eight feet and take his picture.

Bill, Alex and Fritz took loads the next morning and packed them about six miles over the table land to a cabin at the head of King County Creek, while I spent all of the time that they were gone in skinning out the thick lips and ears of the moose scalp. They returned to our tent about the middle of the afternoon and we had some lunch. Then all of us took the rest of the duffle and toiled up the hills to the dike from which we had obtained our first glimpse of the Killey River. Leaning against a great rock here were the horns of my moose, which Fritz had carried up to this point the day before, instead of bringing them into camp.

Our trail led across the level plateau, diverging slightly to the leftward from the trail which we had followed in coming from the lake to the dike. Several old fragments of horns of the Kenai caribou lay along the path, but we saw no other sign of this nearly extinct animal during our stay in the peninsula.

There was three inches of ice on the two small lakes which we traversed and we could see by layers of bubbles which rose at the same place that it had frozen an inch on each of the past three nights. The ice was perfectly clear. Small fish were swimming about in the waters beneath it. We could see the bottom now coming into view, now sinking to unknown depths, and the effect was exactly as if we were walking on a vast sheet of plate glass. A brilliant moon overhead, while we were going the latter part of this march, reflected a clear light on the frosty ground.

We descended but a little way from the table land to reach the cabin at the timber line near the head of King County Creek. This stream rose at the foot of the hills adjoining the plateau on the north, flowed south and

bent around to the west and north and entered Skilak
Lake about six miles below the cottonwoods cabin at
which we had left our main store of supplies. It was
from the mouth of King County Creek that Elting,
Collins and Lovering had entered the hunting country.
At our present camp we were some five or six miles
distant from the trail which they followed in coming in.

Our attempts to locate moose in the neighborhood of
this camp were immediately successful. Bill and I
climbed from the cabin up to the moss-covered hills near
which we had come down from the sheep country, and
began to see the game. One after another the majestic
animals emerged from the scanty shelter of the green
timber which fringed the slope of the hills and stepped
into view unaware of our presence.

Of the first dozen bulls and cows that we saw none
was worth consideration, so we moved along the bench
overlooking the green timber in which they were hiding,
and went in the general direction of the last camp we had
just left, but lower down on the table land. Moose
appeared on all sides, not only near the timber but up
on the bare moss of the table land. At last we climbed
a gaunt hill which commanded a good view. Below us
the slopes toward the Killey River and the cabin were
covered with fallen timber, interspersed with patches of
growing trees.

Presently several good bulls appeared in the nearer
edge of this fallen timber and we stalked them across the
canyon and through some live woods, finally arriving
within two hundred yards. One smaller bull lay facing
us and we could not make a closer approach but peered
with our glasses through the boughs of a little spruce.
It was not always easy to make out the whereabouts of

16

the other moose on account of the numerous snags which stood between us, but the animals were moving and presently we identified at least four good heads. Two seemed to be exceptionally large. One of these had a very light-colored skin and the horns were light yellow. The other moose had broader antlers and a dark skin. These two largest made as if to engage in a fight with each other, but presently abandoned this intention and after clashing their horns together a few times, fell instead to browsing upon the willow tips. It seemed inadvisable to fire on either of these animals, for we had not well looked over the country and we had already seen about fifty moose. Accordingly we crawled carefully back over the many windfalls, through the green timber and up the canyon at the foot of the bare lookout from which we had seen the large moose and got home after the moon rose. well satisfied with our first day's reconnaissance.

Alex and Fritz had meantime been to the lake, taking the moose scalp with them, and brought back enough provisions to last us another week. Once more we enjoyed the luxury of fresh raised bread. Hot cakes we had, of course, every morning from the sour-dough which was prepared each day. Fritz now got the moose horns from the dike and carried them to the lake while Alex shot a half dozen grouse for supper. Bill and I took the same walk as on the day before and saw about fifty moose, including five or six large ones. The wind was not very favorable for stalking them and we came home betimes.

On the next day we investigated the same country from a different side. Instead of going over the hills to the north of the burned slope, we struck west from the cabin and surprised many a moose in the green woods. A light snow fall and a damp wind had sent them to the shelter of the big trees and we could hear the bulls brushing their horns against the bushes on all sides of us. A cow stood not twenty yards away and watched us curiously until she got our wind and dashed off. About four miles lower we crossed King County Creek, made a lunching place in the canyon by brushing away the snow, and came home early. The precipitation continued steadily all afternoon and night and about five inches of snow had fallen when daylight came again.

It was now clear, but the going was slippery in our shoe pacs, especially when we had to place a foot on the snow-covered trunk of a fallen tree. Nevertheless we plodded along, starting off the same as the day before, but traveling through the burned timber instead of following the green woods which led down the creek. Our intention was to strike across the burned-over slopes to reach the point where we had seen the four large bulls four days previously. In doing this we came close to many and saw altogether about the same number as we had noted on the first days of our searching. One young bull had one horn broken off short. A herd of about thirty let us approach within a hundred yards without taking fright and then scattered uphill away from us. As we stood on the brow of a little rise close to the spot that we were aiming for, we saw a moose lying down. He had the same light-colored skin and yellow antlers that had marked the large bull of our first day's excursion. We approached closer and found that another was lying near him. It was exceedingly difficult, once we had left the ridge from which we had first seen them, to locate the animals again. Despite standing upon fallen

trees we were for a long time unsuccessful. Then suddenly one stood up and the other followed him; both
took fright and ran off.

As we returned homeward a pair of moose standing
partly concealed by a large tree attracted our attention
and we approached them very closely. From the horn
which projected on one side of the tree it was evident
that the antlers had a wide spread. Estimating the total
span of the two ears when stretched out straight from the
head to be thirty inches from side to side, it looked as if
the horns would run as much as seventy inches. The
other animal was nothing like the average. As we approached closer without giving fright to them, Bill was
certain that something was amiss. "He can't be any
good if he lets us come so near," said the guide. "By the
way, what's that across his forehead? It looks like the
bough of a tree." We got within twenty yards of the
two animals, screening ourselves behind some standing
spruces. Then we discovered that one antler of the
wide-spreading head had been broken off short. The
limb of a tree had become entangled in the horns of the
other side and wedged across the moose's forehead so
that he could not get it loose. We stepped into plain
view and both moose, much surprised, looked at us for a
moment, then turned and fled.

Tracks of bears, foxes, weasels and porcupines were
numerous in this part of the country and we found one
of the last in a tree. Bill always poked the porcupines
with his walking stick, at which they flicked the tail up
angrily trying to fill him with quills. The porcupine
excited the hatred of all of the guides because of his habit
of eating up cabins, and sticking dogs' mouths full of
spines.

THE GIANT MOOSE AT HOME   *Photos. Wilson Potter*

These remarkable photographs were taken in the Kenai Peninsula at a few yards' distance. Mr. Potter "called" the moose to the camera and occasionally brought them several miles. These two animals carried large antlers but were sent away after their portraits had been secured.

Photos. Wilson Potter

YOUNG BULL MOOSE OF THE KENAI

"Calling" moose has not been practised largely in Alaska and Mr. Potter used this method successfully in photographing them. Sometimes he had difficulty in undeceiving the animals after he had lured them to him. The moose in the upper picture stood only 12 feet away.

It was now just a week since I had brought down the first moose. The snowfall made it likely that we might have difficulty in getting up the Kenai River, and we had but little time in which to explore any other country than this. While we had seen a good many moose in the burned-off district we had been traveling through, doubtless we had counted the same animals many times on different days. As for an exceptionally wide and heavy head, we had marked none better than the first lot of four since moving to King County Creek. It was clear and a cold, nipping wind sent the moose to the shelter of the green woods. Fewer were visible than on our previous days' tramp, but we came upon about forty. One of these had a remarkable growth of brow prongs, but the rest of the antlers were not very well developed.

At last, however, we saw the light-colored moose which we had unsuccessfully stalked the day before. He was in a herd of several bulls and cows. We looked at him carefully through our glasses. We could not delude ourselves with the fancy that the horns were very wide-spreading. Contrariwise they were narrow, for the shovels rose somewhat straight from the beam and were folded almost parallel instead of being laid out flat as the wide-spreading horns are, and furthermore the points rather curled in toward the front than lay out toward the sides. The shovels were apparently broad and heavy and the brow prongs, instead of being long spikes separated from the blades, were outgrowths of the lower ends of the shovels themselves, so that the whole appearance of the horns was massive. The moose was moving about slowly among the trees and only small patches of him showed at any time. I sat down behind a snag on which I rested the rifle, and after carefully choosing an opening with my glasses so that the bullet would not hit any twigs, waited a favorable instance when the moose's fore-shoulder showed, and fired. He fell instantly out of sight. The distance was between two hundred and two hundred and fifty yards and was the longest shot I had taken during the whole summer. When we got up to him the moose was still alive, but paralyzed with the bullet through the lower part of the neck; another shot finished him. The spread of horns was under 51 inches, the blades 38 inches long and 16½ inches wide.

We melted snow in a milk can, made tea and lunched there, then skinned out the head and hung it in a bare tree and went back to the cabin. Men's tracks had crossed ours and on reaching home we found that Lovering and his guide Tolman had visited the cabin and had taken tea there. They were tracking a bear and were within a quarter mile of us when they heard the shooting and supposed that we had come upon the bear. They told our men that they had been living for some time on meat and salt, the rest of their delicacies having been consumed, and they especially enjoyed some fruit which Alex served them.

More snow fell and the haze made spying difficult. Only three moose were visible the next day as we went to the carcass to bring in the trophy. Fritz took the horns to the lake while Alex brought the scalp to the cabin and for the rest of the day we worked at this. The moose's tongue when boiled was excellent supper, but a strip of loin which we essayed to eat was entirely too tough, as the rutting season had practically passed and left the bulls very thin.

Nor were we lucky in finding any bear on the moose carcass when we went to it a day later. No fresh bear sign had been made since the last snowfall, and the moose were still in hiding. The rain and snow continued, but the air grew dryer later in the day as we made ready to pack our stuff down to the cabin at the lake. My old trousers which had served well for three weeks were now worn out and I had been wet below the hips all day long.

All our remaining food except a little sheep and bear meat we left in the cabin with a notice written on a smooth stick, "Help yourself," and blocked up the doorway with the logs which had been cut to fit it. In a hard snow storm we started across the mountains to the lake and with frequent halts for rest tramped our way through snow, which was three or four feet deep in drifts, to the summit of Bear Pass. The wind whistled through the draw in the mountains with greater force here and almost blew us down the steep hill on the lake side of the pass. Nevertheless Bill managed to shoot a ptarmigan with the .22 rifle before we went over the ridge, and when we reached the timber below added a grouse to the supper. Alex forged ahead and reached camp a half hour before the other men. Fritz, wearing shoe pacs, took many a tumble on the slippery hillside, but we did the eight miles in time to get a good midday lunch at the lake and to weigh the packs which the men had carried. Fritz had ninety-five, Alex ninety, Bill seventy and I sixty pounds.

We resalted all the skins and I then read through a catalog of sporting goods, the only reading I had done in the month.

We had been gone just twenty-five days and we now took stock of all our provisions to see exactly what we had consumed.

Provisions

The following is accordingly a list of the supplies actually used by four men in twenty-five days:

Fresh meat, about 135 pounds from game animals and birds; sugar, 35 pounds; beans, 10 pounds; farina, 5 pounds; corn meal, 3 pounds; rice, 8 pounds; dried fruit, 15 pounds; oatmeal, 10 pounds; salt, for table and cooking, 5 pounds; potatoes, 50 pounds; onions, 30 pounds; canned fruit, 12 cans (2 pounds each); syrup, 5 quarts; lard, 10 pounds, in addition to 14 pounds of tallow obtained from game animals; coffee, 7 pounds; bacon, 10 pounds; candles, 40; grapenuts, 6 packages; cake chocolate, 9 pounds; Lenox soap, for washing, 2 bars; tar soap, for toilet, 1 bar; canned tongue, 3 cans; canned beef, 3 cans; canned chicken, 4 cans; evaporated milk, 45 cans; butter, 12 pounds; tea, 1 pound; sardines, 12 cans; dried salmon, 5 pounds; yeast, 1 package (we used a "starter" for making bread); baking powder, $2\frac{1}{2}$ pounds; powdered cocoa, 3 pounds; soda, 1 pound; raisins, 3 pounds; eggs, 11 dozen; pickles, 2 pints; vinegar, 1 pint; pepper, 3 ounces; tobacco, 5 plugs, mostly used by Bill; matches, 25 cents worth; salt for skins, 100 pounds; flour, 75 pounds.

The following is a list of the articles actually used on the trip with the exception of the personal bedding and clothing of my three men:

Personal Outfit

Two flannel shirts, 2 suits underwear, 1 Duxbak hunting jacket, 1 Burberry raincoat, 2 pairs heavy socks, 2 pairs light socks, 1 pair shoe pacs (leather uppers on rubber shoes), 1 pair calked boots, 1 cap with ear flaps,

ANTLERS OF A KENAI MOOSE

This specimen, the author's second moose, bore weighty horns, though narrow in spread.
At the third week of October the rut had passed and left the flesh of the bulls very tough and
lean.

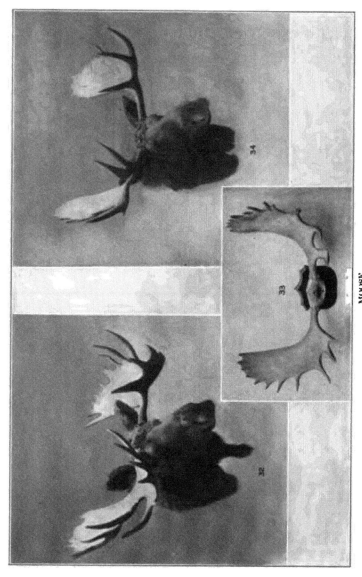

MOOSE

32. Yukon moose. (*Alces americanus.*) White River, Yukon T., 1910 (Wilson Potter). Spread, 59½; circ., 8½; points, 15+13.

33. European moose. (*Alces machlis.*) Northern Europe and Asia. National collection. Length, 31½; spread, 45; circ., 6½; points, 11+12.

34. Eastern moose. (*Alces americanus.*) New Brunswick, Can., 1901 (Wilson Potter). Spread, 52; circ., 7½; points, 7+10.

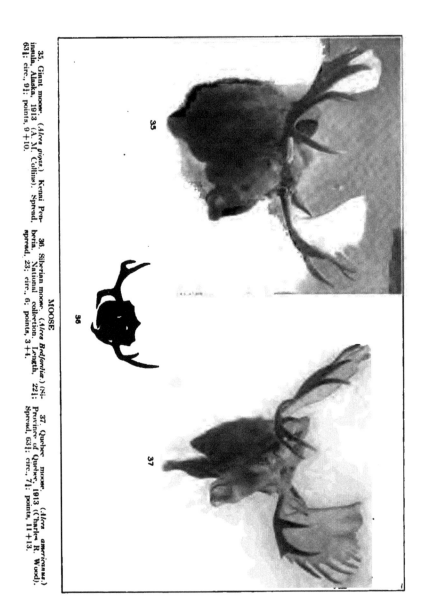

MOOSE

35. Giant moose. (*Alces gigas*.) Kenai Peninsula, Alaska, 1913 (A. M. Collins). Spread, 63½; circ., 9½; points, 9+10.

36. Siberian moose. (*Alces Bedfordiæ*.) (Siberia. National collection. Length, 22½; spread, 23; circ., 6; points, 3+4.

37. Quebec moose. (*Alces americanus*.) Province of Quebec, 1913 (Charles R. Wood). Spread, 63½; circ., 7½; points, 11+13.

Photo. A. M. Collins

HOW ONE MAN CARRIED A MOOSE HEAD

Collins' guide, "Colonel" Revell, took on his back a moose head with the skin still attached, weighing 120 pounds, and carried it 12 miles into camp.

1 soft hat, 2 pairs woolen gloves, 2 pairs cotton gloves to slip over woolen, 1 belt, 1 pair trousers, 1 pair breeches, 4 handkerchiefs, 1 sleeping bag, 1 clothes bag, 1 soap, toothbrush and powder, razor, brush and shaving soap, mirror, brush and comb, 1 towel, 1 pipe, 1½ pounds tobacco, 1 pouch, cigarette papers, needles, thread and buttons, knife and whetstone, tape measure, green spectacles, mosquito head net, binoculars, kodak, 5 films, 1 Mauser rifle and 15 cartridges, gun oil and rod, .22 rifle and 250 cartridges, notebook and pencil, 1 can fly dope, scales, 3 hanks fishline, 6 small oiled bags for duffle.

Camp Kit for Four Men

One wall tent, 8 x 10 ft., of 8 oz. duck, 1 miner's tent, 7 x 7 ft., paraffined silk; 1 pack cloth, 1 folding lantern, 1 stove, 1 canvas bucket, 2 frying pans, 3 pots, 4 each plates, cups, knives, forks, large and small spoons, 1 can opener, 2 axes, 115 ft. ⅝ in. rope for towing boats, 100 ft. $\frac{3}{16}$ in. rope for packing and tents, 2 Duluth pack bags, 2 pack boards.

An hour spent rambling through the woods by the cabin resulted in two grouse and revealed the numerous rabbit tracks. More interesting than these, however, was an ermine, or weasel in its winter coat, pottering about on the snow. As I stood quite still the tiny animal ran toward me and stood up on its short hind legs to look. Its slender white body was about ten inches long and its black tail made a distinct mark against the snow. Nor did it move until I stirred and then it dashed away to safety.

Realizing that we had two boats, a heavy dory and a

light, round-bottom skiff to pull against the current up
river on our homeward journey, we allowed nearly a
week for it. It took us, in fact, five full days from the
time we left Cottonwoods Creek cabin until we reached
Cooper Creek Landing at the lower end of Kenai Lake,
or four days and a half to ascend eighteen miles of river
which we had run down in less than three hours.

On the first day we crossed the lower lake and made
three miles up river, to Vaughn's cabin. Magpies, camp
robbers, rabbits, eagles and mergansers were the only
living things we saw, and we added to the cooking pot
one of the rabbits, which were rapidly turning white for
the winter.

Most of the first three days Bill, Alex and Frits towed
the boats one at a time, hauling one up several hundred
yards around or through the rapids, making it fast and
going back for the other. As we had plenty of time and
Bill was wearing my long rubber boots, I went dry shod
on the banks or through the woods, looking for little
game with the small rifle. Mallard ducks rose fairly
numerous as we toiled upstream. The second evening
showed we had done four miles more and we pitched
tents on an old camping ground beside the river. The
stars were very bright and it was a cold night.

The third day was tedious. We covered hardly a mile
and a half in the forenoon and were towing both boats
together, when in the middle of the afternoon the current
caught them as we were crossing a shallow rift. It swept
the seal boat with its heavy load broadside to the stream
and rolled it over on its side upon the rocky bottom so
violently that a stone went through one of the planks.
As quickly as possible it was dragged ashore, all the
stuff taken out before much of it had got wet, small trees

cut to make skids, and the injured boat hauled up on the beach for examination and repair. We pitched a tent in the snow, hung our damp blankets and clothing over ropes around the big fire, and by bed-time were comfortable again. With the use of a piece of board, some canvas, pitch, grease and nails, Bill patched up the hole in the boat and we were ready to start early next morning.

After that I took a hand at the line wherever I could do so from dry ground, in order to keep warm. The wind blew hard against us all the fourth day and with one end of the long rope cutting into one's shoulder and the weight of the two boats laden with over a thousand pounds of stuff worrying in the swift current at the other end, it was not easy to make progress up stream.

Since we had come down the river, moreover, the water had fallen several feet and left too shallow many of the side branches where the current would have been easier. Further, we were obliged in places to go ahead of the boats with an axe and cut away falling or fallen trees which overhung the river bank—in other words, to swamp out a clear trail for the towing of the boat.

A long, thin spruce tree had been cut and trimmed of branches and the heavy end of it tied with a rope to the bow of the leading boat, in such a way that Bill could walk on the bank or in the shallow water and hold the head of the boat out or in from the bank as conditions required, while the other two men pulled on the long rope, a hundred and fifteen feet farther up stream. Without this gee-pole it would hardly have been practicable to get the boat around the snags and rocks which lined the banks at many spots.

On approaching a riffle, where the water dropped

more suddenly and was swifter, one of the boats was
tied to the bank just below the rapids, the line was
passed up as far ahead as possible and all hands pulled
on it, Bill steering the boat with the gee-pole or with
his hands on the bow until it was safely brought up;
then we went back for the other. In this work the boys
had to wade frequently across places that were deeper
than the height of their boots, and by nightfall all of us
were usually wet from the waist down, if indeed not also
thoroughly soaked above this from the melting snow on
the bushes.

In spite of this and of the wetness of the wood everywhere we could always fell a dead spruce tree, cut a log
of it and get the heart wood out with an axe. Small
pieces of kindling split from this were then whittled with
a knife until a large bunch of shavings hung fast together
on each. A pile of these shavings judiciously nursed
with a match always produced a roaring fire in a few
minutes, and after a hot bed of coals was formed we
could throw on the wet logs with confidence that they
would soon burst into blaze. Sometimes the frying pans
were set directly on the coals or two green logs were cut
and placed parallel above the fire so that the pans would
rest on them. Pots were slung from a cross beam laid
over the fire on stakes, and we never failed to have a
good meal at the end of each day's work. Sometimes we
found abandoned cabins and made use of them instead
of pitching a tent, which saved the considerable work of
cutting stakes and pegging out the tent. In cabins we
set up our stove.

In the hurry of getting a fire started Fritz caused
much amusement in the cabin at Schooner Bend, a house
where he had wintered and which he called one of his

TOWING BOATS UP THE KENAI RIVER

The guide steered the forward boat by a gee-pole fastened to its bow, while the other men toiled ahead with a long line. We were obliged many times a day to cross from one bank to the other in order to find a clear course for towing and frequently had to make the way practicable by cutting down trees with an axe.

MIDDAY LUNCH ON THE KENAI RIVER

After a strenuous forenoon towing the boats against the swift current, we landed at a convenient shingle, collected driftwood and lunched beside a blazing fire with the temperature well below freezing. Bill, Alex and Frits are unpacking the food and dishes.

homes. Our stove was set up and Fritz started a fire, leaving the oven full of the things which we usually packed in it. In a few moments there was a mild explosion and a dense cloud of smoke filled the cabin. Quickly ripping the oven out of the stove Alex sorted out of the débris a burned dish rag, some knives and spoons which were fortunately not damaged, and two cans of evaporated milk which had exploded. The tins had burst open at the top only and the milk, plenty warm enough for the coldest weather, was uninjured.

Now we were only five miles from Cooper Creek Landing and the river was not so bad. Two hard rapids still lay before us, but the path on the bank was clear and most of the water offered comparatively few obstructions. Tom Towle was on his way to the landing and we got him to tell Bunce, the skipper of the "Bat," to wait for us until we arrived, so we could make a close connection and not have to lose several days for him, as we thought we might have to.

Five boats passed us on their way down the river on this last day of our slow return, most of them with men who were going out to trap during the winter. One, however, was William Hesse, who had sworn to get some moving pictures of live moose if he had to stay in all winter. Other boats contained two English sportsmen, Cadbury and Vereker. More Englishmen than Americans hunted in the Kenai this season.

In the month that we had been away in the interior a large log cabin had been built at the landing as a roadhouse for strangers. We were enjoying a big meal here when Lovering turned up, completely soaked through after a ten-mile march up the river. He had left his boat and men below to come up and be sure that a launch would be ready to meet them. The "Bat" was on hand, but the lake was rough and her skipper wished to postpone our starting. However, by noon we were off in the hard rain with the wind against us. Our two boats towed behind pretty well after the cargoes had been shifted to let them ride the waves, and we made good weather of it up the lake to the road-house at mile 23½ on the railroad.

Instead of having to wait at the station here as we expected until we could get a special car up from Seward, we learned that one had gone up the road and was expected to return in about a half hour. As quickly as possible, therefore, I divided among Bill, Alex and Fritz the grub which we had left over and some of the larger things that I did not want to take down the railway, and we all boarded the car when it came.

Darkness had fallen before we got over the divide and the rivers were swollen with rain. A telephone message had been received at Roosevelt from Seward saying that there was a washout at Resurrection Bridge, which had been repaired since we first came up. Accordingly, when we reached that point the crew got off the car and with lanterns went ahead to come back and report that all was right. Slowly we went across the bridge and proceeded cautiously toward the town with a large headlight blazing out into the darkness.

The telephone message, as it afterward turned out, had intended to convey the information that a washout had occurred on the line between Seward and the bridge over Resurrection River. We were going slowly along when suddenly the car lurched as if it had run over something, rolled from side to side and lamps fell out of the roof on the heads of the passengers. It felt as if we had left the tracks and since there was a twelve-foot embankment on the right-hand side and a twenty-foot drop on the left down into the waters of Resurrection Bay, we waited for a few instants with an uncomfortable expectancy. But the car was brought to a stop, still on the tracks. Examination showed that the earth had been washed out from under the rails by an unusually high tide. It was almost miraculous that we had come over in the heavily laden car without being derailed. Further traffic was held up on the line for several days until this damage could be repaired.

Elting was obliged to hire dog-teams and sledges at the upper lake and come over the pass on the snow, but when Collins got to the same point a day later, the railway was again in operation.

We had all our trophies put in boxes and barrels for the long freight out of Alaska, gave to the Game Warden affidavits that we had not violated the laws and boarded one of the regular steamships plying along the coast to Seattle.

CHAPTER XVI

ADVENTURES IN THE KENAI PENINSULA

ELTING had an interesting month in the interior, his experience being briefly as follows:

Collins, Lovering and Elting went down Lake Skilak to within about three miles of its lower end, where they camped and made a cache for their provisions and extra duffle at the terminus of the King County trail. They then packed in along the King County trail about fifteen miles to the Killey River, which was crossed in a canvas canoe belonging to Col. Revell. They then proceeded about four miles beyond Killey River where Elting established his main camp while Collins and Lovering went on three or four miles farther.

After placing their main camp, Elting and Ben, with the assistance of Ed Crawford, the packer, and Gus Kusche, the cook, made a side camp just at timber line, from which Elting was to hunt sheep. Three days were spent in hunting the sheep mountains, but no good rams were seen and only a few ewes. On one of these days a medium-sized black bear was seen feeding on blueberries across a canyon and after a short stalk was killed. The hide was in fine condition and the meat very toothsome.

Deciding that satisfactory rams could not be found from this camp, Elting and Ben returned to their main camp, when, with the assistance of Ed Crawford, they proceeded ten or twelve miles up the Killey River, through swamps and over ridges, most of the way without any trail. It required eight hours and a half of practically continuous traveling to cover this distance, and a camp was finally made at Guest's Lake on the same side of the Killey River as Steve's cabin. From this camp they scoured the left-hand side of the Killey River, but sheep were not numerous. On the first day a band of about twenty-five ewes and rams was seen a long way off, and after several hours of hard stalking in the snow, they were able to look them over. There were only two good heads in the band. The sheep became frightened and started away and Elting opened fire at about 300 yards. After several shots one of the two best rams was brought down at from 350 to 400 yards. This proved to be a very good specimen, nine years old, with the end of one horn slightly broken off. The horns measured 13 inches in circumference at the base; the uninjured one was 35 inches long and the spread was 20 inches.

On the following day they started to hunt again in the same general direction, but were compelled to cross three ranges of mountains before they again fell in with any sheep. On this occasion a band of about fifteen, with two good rams, was found. In endeavoring to get upon them, these sheep also became frightened and started to run away. At about 350 yards Elting opened fire and brought down one of the two large rams. This proved to be a very good specimen. The end of one horn, however, was also slightly broken off. This ram was ten years old. The horns had a circumference of 13¼ inches at the base, were 37½ inches long and had a spread of 20½ inches.

Having killed two good specimens, and finding sheep very scarce, Elting decided not to try for a third ram, and they moved back again to their main camp, from which, as well as from a side camp, they hunted the ridges between the Killey and the Funny Rivers for moose, of which a great number were seen. In three successive days' hunting in different directions from camp, so that probably none of these bulls was reckoned twice, Elting counted thirty-three, thirty-two and thirty-one bulls. None of them, however, was taken.

While stalking a moose on the ridges one morning, Elting and Ben caught a glimpse of a large black bear which had just come out of its den to sun itself. One shot broke its neck and the bear fell back into its very artistically constructed den several feet down underneath an old root, from which it was dragged out with a great deal of difficulty. This pelt also was in very excellent fur.

On one of these days, while returning from a day spent hunting moose in the vicinity of Funny River, Elting had a rather exciting experience with a brown bear. This occurred about a mile and a half from where Ben and Elting were side-camped. Just after sundown they had climbed to the top of a high ridge to look over the surrounding country for moose and they stood for some few moments on the exposed summit of this ridge. Having located the moose, they followed a moose trail from the high ridge to a lower one and when the trail reached the lower ridge, it passed along its side instead of over the top. Ben was walking just ahead of Elting and both were looking over their right shoulders in the direction of the moose. In order the better to see these moose they left the moose trail and went eight or ten paces farther up the side of the ridge. While they were thus making their way through the patches of alders and willows, Ben casually turned his head to the left and saw

a full grown brown bear standing erect on her hind legs
in the edge of a patch of alders about six feet the other
side of the trail and about 40 or 45 feet from them.
When Elting saw the bear a fraction of a moment later,
she was just swinging down from her standing position
to start running at him.   Ben, who was unarmed, made
up the ridge toward some down timber and succeeded in
getting about six feet off the ground.   As the bear came
on, Elting swung his 9 mm. Mannlicher from the shoulder
and luckily having a shell in the barrel, had only to
throw the safety catch and be ready for action.   By the
time that this was accomplished, the bear was about
25 feet away, coming straight on.   Without taking much
time for any aim, he fired as nearly as he could at the
right forward shoulder and the bear broke down on this
shoulder with a blood-curdling combination of bawl,
growl and howl.   The force of the shot turned the bear
almost 90 degrees away.   Before he could throw another
shell into the chamber, the bear with its remaining three
legs jumped into the alders and disappeared.   Elting ran
to the top of the ridge and in the dusky twilight had
occasional glimpses of the bear making her way slowly
through the alders.   She fell down three times, but each
time got up and went slowly onward.   Ben, who was in
a position to see the whole episode, stated that at the
crack of the gun, three cubs jumped out of the thicket
at the summit of the ridge about seventy yards farther
on and the wounded female made every effort to follow
these cubs.   Feeling sure that the bear was fatally hit,
and not wishing to encounter her in the darkness in a
thicket, they went back to camp expecting to pick up
the trail in the morning and find the carcass.   During
the night six or eight inches of snow fell and in the morn-

ing it was possible to trail her but a short distance in the alder thickets, but she was followed far enough to determine the fact that the bullet had passed from the point of the right shoulder backward through the left lung and had come out of the left side, for the brush was marked on the left side with abundant lung blood. Some two or three days later, Ed Crawford, Elting's packer, cut the trail of the three cubs going back alone in the direction from which they had come, which was sufficient proof that the mother had succumbed.

The explanation of this rather unusual experience, in the opinion of Elting and Ben, was the fact that for about ten days prior to this incident the weather had been very cold and all of the streams in the vicinity had frozen so that it had become impossible for the bears to fish. The mother and cubs, becoming hungry, had then started for the moose country to secure some food. It is a well known fact that brown bear, when hunting for meat, are very apt to select the early morning or the late evening. On this occasion the bear undoubtedly saw Ben and Elting on top of the neighboring ridge and saw them leave this ridge along the moose trail. Depositing her cubs in a thicket on top of the lower ridge, she went down the trail about seventy yards to meet them, and instead of waiting for them in the trail, stood up in the alders about six feet from the trail. Elting was convinced that she did not recognize the difference between human and moose meat, but was simply hungry and wanted them for supper. Except for the fact that they left the moose trail, that Ben happened to look around and see her as he did, and the further fact that Elting smashed her shoulder with a relatively large caliber bullet, the Doctor felt certain that one and possibly both

Photos. Dr. A. W. Elting

SHEEP AND DOGS IN THE KENAI PENINSULA

Above: Dr. Elting and one of his mountain sheep on the snowfields near the head of Killey River.

Below: A dog-team which Dr. Elting was obliged to use in coming to Seward after a heavy snow-fall had suspended traffic on the Alaska Northern Railway.

THE KENAI PACK TRAIN
Photo, A. M. Collins

Elting, Collins and Lovering started into the Kenai hunting country from the same point and this photograph was taken on the trail between Skilak Lake and the Killey River. From left to right the men are: Bergard, Kusche, Revell, Tolman, Vaughn, Scotty, Sweeny, Lovering, Crawford.

of them would have been very badly mauled, if not killed.

In conjunction with this, it might be of interest to relate the experience of a rancher named Peterson, about three weeks before this. Peterson lived within three miles of the village of Seward and just at dusk was going from his ranch to that of a neighbor when he was suddenly and unexpectedly attacked by a very large brown bear. Elting saw Peterson in the hospital on his return to Seward and secured from him a statement of his experience. He said that when he was attacked he realized that he must, if possible, keep the bear away from his abdomen, and so he made every effort to lie flat on his stomach. Fortunately he had on several shirts as well as a leather coat. The bear mauled him frightfully and left him apparently for dead. Peterson started to get away and the bear returned and mauled him a second time and again left him for dead. Again Peterson endeavored to get away before the bear was sufficiently far off and the bear again returned and gave him another mauling. As a result of these three performances, he was very badly mutilated. He stated that the bear endeavored to crush his skull, for she kept trying to get his head in her mouth, but could not open the jaws quite wide enough to get sufficient purchase to crush the skull. The result of this was that the teeth kept slipping continually on the skull and had torn the scalp in every conceivable direction. With either the teeth or a claw she took off the entire left ear and mastoid process, and in the same manner cut all of the muscles in the back of the neck which extend from the skull to the shoulder. Luckily none of the fangs penetrated the intestines or the lungs, but the muscles about the chest, the loins and groins were very badly lacerated. That the man ever lived to tell the story is the most remarkable part of it. After the third mauling that the bear gave him, he said he knew enough to keep quiet for some time until the animal had had abundant opportunity to get well away. He then managed to rise to his feet, although he could not hold up his head because of the loss of the muscles in the back of the neck. Supporting his head in his hands he made his way to the home of his neighbor, who brought him into Seward, where Dr. Baughman cared for him and where, when he was seen by Elting, most of his wounds had nearly healed.

On his way out of the Kenai, Elting met another man, a prospector, who also had been charged by a bear within two weeks, but who had had a better advantage in that he saw the bear coming for about fifty yards and succeeded in killing him just as the bear got up to him.

These incidents would seem to indicate that in the Kenai Peninsula, at any rate, the brown bear is somewhat more ferocious than he is ordinarily assumed to be.

Considerable snow having fallen, Elting moved his camp back across Killey River and established himself on the King County trail at the little cottonwood, where he spent several days hunting moose and killed a good specimen. These horns were extremely heavy, but they stood up in the air so that the spread was only 56 inches. The palms were 15 inches across and 30 inches in length, with 28 points. One moose being all that Elting wished, they then moved the camp down to the terminus of the King County trail on Skilak Lake expecting to make their way leisurely back to Seward.

Because of a very violent storm with head wind, they were marooned on the edge of the lake for two and a half days and finally, when the storm abated somewhat, they started up the lake against the wind and succeeded in getting as far as the upper end of the lake and part way across toward the mouth of the Kenai River. While out in the middle of the lake, a sudden increase of the wind from the glacier flats kicked up a tremendous sea so that they were compelled to put their dory about and run before the wind toward the other side of the lake. They were fortunate in finding a somewhat protected inlet where they camped for the night. At daylight they managed to get across the lake and started up the Kenai River. Having lost so much time and wishing to get a certain steamer from Seward, it was necessary for them to make a rapid journey up the river, and so Elting took the end of the tow line and walked the entire length of the Kenai River, towing the boat. They made the journey in two days, which was almost record time. Snow kept on falling and by the time they had reached mile 23½ on Kenai Lake, there was 15 inches of snow on the summit and no prospect of a gasoline car to bring them in. From Al Roberts at mile 23½ Elting secured a dog team and in about five hours actual traveling made the journey from this point into Seward.

Lovering told us the following story of his adventures with Collins:

"The last that we saw of Scull was on the thirtieth day of September, when his two dories faded away in the darkness on Lake Skilak. Long after dark we arrived at a point about opposite the mouth of King County Creek and made camp on the shore of the lake.

"The next day all our men, with the exception of 'Scotty,' the cook, packed a part of our equipment and enough food for three or four days to a point about twelve miles in from Skilak Lake and about a mile from Killey River, while Collins and I took a short hunt which proved very interesting. The fact that we saw six moose at close range made us realize that at last we were on the borders of what probably is the best moose country in the world.

"The following day, after a hearty breakfast prepared by our noble cook 'Scotty,' and consisting of raw bacon, coffee, and oatmeal which was cooked for ten minutes, we all shouldered our packs with the 'Bungalow' as our destination, to which our men had packed the duffle the day before.

"The 'Bungalow' belonged to a trapper and prospector, Frank Staniford (a bully good fellow he was). It consisted of a 10 x 12 tent pitched over a permanent frame, and equipped with a stove, cooking utensils and all the comforts of home. Staniford used this camp while tending his line of traps in winter, and at this time was living in a large cabin on King County Creek, situated not far from our camp on Lake Skilak.

"Our next day's march of nine miles took us across Killey River to a small lake 150 yards in diameter, which nestled down in a little pocket on the side of the mountain, at about the timber line, and within three miles of Funny River.

"This was to be our permanent camp, but we had arranged with our packers and guides to carry one tent and enough provisions for several days only, so that we could make good progress on the trail, which was uphill all the way. Our idea in making our arrangements in this way was to have the men leave us alone in this camp while they went back and relayed the rest of the outfit in.

"I will not dwell on the joys of carrying a pack on

one's back over a rough wilderness trail, after having
been cooped up on a ship for three months, further than
to say that if you have tried it you will know that we
appreciated even 'Scotty's' deliciously prepared meals.
Now we were without even 'Scotty,' and I agreed to
incubate the grub if Collins would rustle the wood and
water.

"We had made this same arrangement while hunting
on the Alaskan Peninsula, so we knew what not to expect
of each other.   We had also spent three months together
on the 'Abler' in a stateroom that measured just 6 x 6
feet, and as I am over six feet tall and Collins not much
shorter, the reader can imagine that we were pretty
familiar with each other's faults (although I was never
quite able to find any faults in Collins except once,
when I nearly burned the tent up by allowing it to come
into contact with a very hot stove pipe, and he accused
me of being careless).

"Although we saw no moose on our way to the permanent camping grounds, we did see plenty of fresh signs
at almost every step.   As soon as we had straightened
things up around camp the guides left us.   Before we
had washed up the dishes a young bull moose walked
out in plain view on the opposite side of the little lake,
and we enjoyed watching him while he surveyed us
and then strolled off at a leisurely gait.   Before it was
time for supper we took an hour's walk and saw three
more moose close to us, and at no great distance from
camp.

"It was the intention of us both not to shoot a moose
until we had an opportunity to see a number of them,
if possible, and in that way get some idea of their size
in this particular part of the country.

"I quote from my diary under date of October 4th: 'This sure is some moose country. It has been a beautiful day. "Bunkie" (that's Collins) and I hunted from 7 A. M. till 3 P. M. We saw twenty-eight moose, five of of them, including one nice bull, within nineteen measured paces of us.'

"On our return to camp we found the two guides and packers already arrived, and after this time we hunted either alone or with our respective guides.

"The next day Crit Tolman, my guide, and I started out to find a place to make a temporary camp from which to hunt the white sheep (*Ovis dalli*) that abound in. the mountains at the head of Killey River and Funny River. It was my intention to hunt sheep while Collins hunted moose, and *vice versa*, as in that way we should not bother each other.

"Crit and I had been gone from camp an hour, and were walking straight up the mountain south of camp when we looked around and were surprised to see Elgin Vaughn, one of the packers, evidently trying to overtake us. We knew something must have gone wrong, but were not prepared to hear that 'Scotty' had shot himself through the left thigh with Crit's 22 calibre six shooter.

" 'How did he happen to hit himself in the leg?' I asked Elgin.

"But Crit, who did not think much of 'Scotty's' cooking, replied, 'Because he is a poor shot, I guess.'

"After some talk with Elgin I decided that the wound didn't amount to much, and therefore that I would continue my hunt and that Crit and Elgin could doctor the cripple up with supplies from my emergency kit. The thing worried me though, and really was the cause of spoiling a lot of sport I might have had in hunting sheep.

"Along towards ten o'clock I had worked my way well to the head of Funny River, and was surprised to see a man walking more or less in my direction on the other side of the stream. In a few minutes I heard three shots in rapid succession and saw a bunch of moose come up out of the canyon, going as though they were late for an appointment in the next county. The man who did the shooting proved to be one 'Windy,' a trapper. He said, when I came up to him, that he had been shooting at a wolverine, but those moose were in a fine place to leave a bear or fox bait, and I rather think the wolverine story was told on account of some very bad shooting.

"I told 'Windy' that I was looking for a sheep camp and got from him the location of a cabin on Watch Creek, and for a consideration persuaded him to go back to camp, tell them where I had gone, and return next day with Crit, some grub and my bed.

"Watch Creek heads just over the divide southward from the head of Funny River. It is a small creek and descends from the mountainside most abruptly. About half way down it has cut a deep chasm in the mountain, and just at the top of a beautiful waterfall the trail crosses the creek and in a few hundred yards leads to a little hunter's cabin made of cottonwood logs, and built in a pocket on the mountainside just below timber line.

"On my way to the cabin, which I reached in the late afternoon, I saw seven sheep and was close to a herd of ewes. Upon my arrival at the cabin I had practically to drive a young bull moose from the door before I entered. I found a sheep-skin robe in the cabin and a few handfuls of rice, and was soon enjoying a supper of rice cakes and a ptarmigan, which I had killed on my way down the mountain.

"Sitting there in the door of this little cabin, eating my supper, and looking over the great mountains above me, was a treat I'll not soon forget. Above the green timber there was a lot of snow, and off to the right, on the other side of Indian River, a great glacier split the mountainside. While I looked over this grandeur a band of a dozen sheep walked out from behind a point of rock about a quarter mile from where I sat. The binoculars showed them to be ewes and lambs, and I sat watching them till darkness closed down. It was a beautiful sight.

"Next morning, October 5th, I was on my way back to the main camp as soon as it was light enough to travel, for I was worried about 'Scotty' and thought it possible that I might have to take him back to Seward. If this was the case, I argued, and I was going to get a sheep head, I must take what I could get that day.

"Climbing to the mountainside I spotted twenty-one head of sheep within an hour's tramp from the cabin, but saw no good rams. Just as I topped a long, narrow ridge, and looked down on Watch Creek near its source, I saw before me a bunch of rams some four hundred yards away, walking slowly up the opposite side of the ridge from where I stood on its crest. A hasty glance at the band with the glass from behind a boulder was all that was necessary for me to decide that there were two in the lot that looked good enough to me in the circumstances. A hasty retreat of a few feet to get under cover of the hill, and then a sharp run of several hundred yards, brought me to a point where I felt that

A VERY LARGE MOOSE AT CLOSE QUARTERS

Photo. Wilson Potter

After taking this photograph amid the bare snags of the Kenai Peninsula, Mr. Potter tried vainly for four days to find this animal again, as it carried the widest antlers he had ever seen.

MAN IN THE WILDERNESS

Photo. A. M. Collins

Packing over the snow fields near Watch Creek, Kenai Peninsula. When dogs and horses are not available, man must take on his own back the necessities of life and carry them with him. All authorities agree that this necessary evil tempers the pure pleasure of roaming in Alaskan solitudes.

the distance between the band and myself had been decreased enough to chance a shot, provided the sheep had not increased their rate of travel. I crouched low and came out directly on top of the ridge with no cover available. Sure enough, there they were, not quite two hundred yards ahead of me, traveling slowly and in the same direction as I had last seen them. The moment I came in sight of the band my binoculars were on them for a last look, and before I took the glasses from my eyes they were off up the mountainside at top speed.

"I only wanted to kill the two largest rams in the bunch, and naturally chose the largest for my first target. The first shot brought the big fellow down, stone dead. I thought the next shot was intended for the largest remaining head, but unfortunately the band was now running diagonally away from me, and at the instant I pulled the trigger a very small ram jumped up beside the one at which I had aimed and got killed for his pains. After my hard run I was winded badly, and the disgust with myself for killing such a little sheep all went to spoil my aim, and I am willing to confess that I made several beautifully clean misses before I downed the fellow I was after.

"The sheep that range on the Kenai Peninsula are apparently of a pure white color, but against a background of snow they show up rather yellow at a distance. The report of my rifle had apparently disturbed band after band of sheep on the mountainside that had been invisible to me before I fired, for now the slopes rising abruptly in front of me seemed literally covered with little yellow specks moving rapidly towards its summit.

"I took the heads of the two largest sheep on my back,

together with a little meat, after having cut off the hind quarters of all of them, and started for camp. On my way back I met Crit and 'Windy' coming up with my bed and provisions. They continued on to the Watch Creek cabin to leave the food there for Collins, while I took my bed from Crit and continued on my way with the largest head. I arrived at camp just before dark and ate two big suppers before rolling up in my blanket.

" 'Scotty' was not much the worse for wear, but was not altogether what one might call active on his feet. So one of the packers was despatched in search of Frank Staniford to bring him back to cook for us if possible. Luckily he came and stayed for a week till 'Scotty' could get about again, and during that time we all enjoyed the very best of camp cooking.

"During my sheep hunt Collins had been industriously hunting moose. He had not found one large enough to suit him, but said that he had seen twenty-nine the day I killed my sheep. That's the way it went. Every day we saw from five or six up to twenty or thirty moose. The average was around twenty, I suppose, but Collins saw close to a hundred head in one day.

"Up to this time we had very good weather indeed, as in fact we did during our whole trip, with the exception of a few snow storms, which were to be expected at this time of year.

"On October 10th Collins and Colonel Revell took a small tent and light equipment with them to hunt the down-timber country between Killey and Funny Rivers north of our camp.

" 'The Colonel,' a great big, strapping fellow, would be an addition to any hunting party. He was always jolly and full of fun, and nothing that he could do to make our hunt a success was too much trouble for him. One of 'The Colonel's' chief amusements in camp was to cut up perfectly good clothing of one sort or another and remodel it after his own particular ideas. The results were usually disastrous. One day 'The Colonel' decided that he must have a pair of puttees. He had discovered that Collins had an extra pair of these leg bandages, but didn't quite like to ask for them. So, after supper one night, without saying anything, he walked out to his bed, took from it one of the two blankets of which it was composed, and marched into the cook tent where we were all sitting. After folding one end of the blanket around his leg, and studying the effect for awhile, he asked Elgin for a knife. Elgin asked him what in hell he was going to cut up his bed for, and 'The Colonel' innocently replied that he was going to make him a pair o' them puttees, and made a bluff at beginning operations on the blanket.

"At this point Collins jumped up, protesting violently that he should do nothing of the sort, and produced his extra pair of puttees before 'The Colonel' had actually commenced operations. I imagine 'The Colonel' has since had many a laugh over that little game.

"Late on the afternoon of October 11th Collins got back to the main camp with a fine moose head he had secured the night before. Its spread was sixty inches. The horns were very symmetrical, as well as having good heavy beams and large palms.

"Collins now decided to try for sheep and leave to me the moose country that could be hunted from our main camp. He, therefore, proceeded to the little cabin on Watch Creek for a three days' hunt, at the end of which time he returned with three fine sheep heads. He reported seeing a great many sheep and had but little difficulty in securing his trophies, although he was forced to shoot at very long range, as the big fellows were quite wary and hard to approach.

"One incident that occurred during their sheep hunt might easily have proved serious had it not been for prompt action on Collins' part. He and 'The Colonel' were stalking a band of sheep. Leaving 'The Colonel' under cover of a large boulder while he made the final stalk, Collins crept along to look the band over at closer range. He found none of the heads large enough to suit him, so after a time came back to pick up his guide again. It was very cold on the mountain that morning, but in the exertion of the rough climb the hunters had perspired freely. 'The Colonel,' lying quietly behind the boulder for an hour, had become thoroughly chilled, and, when he got up to continue the hunt with Collins, found that his feet were numb. He said, 'My feet are frozen.' Without further argument Collins helped him off with his shoes and stockings. The feet were nearly white. Collins realized there was no time to be lost. He rubbed the feet in snow and worked over them as best he knew how with little result, till, opening his shirt, he placed 'The Colonel's' feet against his body. Luckily they had a dry pair of extra socks, and after a time, with the heat of Collins' body and the dry socks, feeling again returned to the members, and they were soon continuing the hunt. But both realized the narrow escape the guide had had.

"In regard to the weather at this time, I quote from my diary: 'Oct. 14, 1913. The temperature here this

A. M. was three above zero, and I washed in the cook tent for the first time.'

"On October 15th I started out early to hunt alone. After seeing and getting close to a number of moose I decided to cross over Funny River and hunt down the ridge on its west bank. Nearing the top of the ridge I spotted a bunch of four bulls apparently just looking for a good place in which to lie down for the midday siesta.

"For the last few days we had noticed that the bulls and cows were keeping apart more and more. In fact, only occasionally after this time did we see the male and female accompanying each other; and when we did see them together the bull was always a young one who had probably been unable to compete with his stronger fellows during the height of the rutting season.

"After a very careful stalk, during which time the four bulls I had seen had lain down, I managed to approach within about forty yards of them. The band consisted of one small bull, two with heads that would probably measure fifty inches, and another with a peculiarly deformed set of antlers. The latter animal was truly a giant in stature, and when I compared his antlers with the others they seemed to me as large in proportion as his body. So after some hesitation, on account of the peculiar formation of the horns, I shot him just behind the shoulder. I saw the blood come where my bullet entered his body and also some hair fall away, but the big beast didn't go down. I raised my rifle again and aimed at the spot my first bullet had made, and pulled the trigger. The only effect of this shot, which hit within two inches of the first, was to make the moose start off at a more or less uncertain walk down towards Funny

18

River. I knew he must fall in a short time; so, as he was going towards camp, I walked along behind. I was not moving fast, but within a very short time I had diminished the distance between us to fifteen yards, when the great animal wheeled like a flash and with hair standing on end made straight for me. After two shots more he finally fell within ten yards from where I stood. When measured, the spread of his antlers proved to be only sixty inches, but I was well satisfied with a fine day's sport.

"The rest of my time in the Kenai Peninsula was now spent in a vain attempt to secure a brown bear. Although I saw some sign of them, I was unable actually to come up with any. After I had left our main camp in search of bear, Collins one day visited the carcass of the moose I had last killed. By that time considerable snow had fallen, and he said that the country in the vicinity was literally covered with bear tracks. There must have been by his account, five or six bears in the immediate neighborhood of the carcass and he was lucky enough to get a fine specimen that had lingered too long over his dinner of moose meat.

"On October 30th I overtook Scull at the lower end of Kenai Lake and we went into Seward together, Collins and Elting following in the course of the next day or two.

"It would be unfair to omit stating the fact that our guides and packers were fine fellows, and added very materially to the enjoyment of our never-to-be-forgotten hunt in the Kenai Peninsula."

CHAPTER XVII

OUR ship put in at Latouche, Valdez and Cordova, took on copper ore at Ellamar and Fidalgo Bay in Prince William Sound, gave us a glimpse of a dead boom town at Katalla, and then passed out into the Pacific headed for Yakutat.

We now approached the central part of the remarkable glacial belt of Alaska, which pivots about the great upthrust of Mt. St. Elias and its neighboring peaks.

The glaciers of the Pacific coast of Alaska are extraordinary for their number and their size. For a thousand miles the main collection extends along the slope of the coast range, and the central portion, between four hundred and five hundred miles long and eighty to one hundred miles wide, has been described as one great field of ice and snow. Thousands of glaciers from one to fifteen miles in length fill the crevices of the mountains. More than a hundred almost reach the sea. The Valdez Glacier, which lies back of the town of that name in Prince William Sound, is thirty miles long and rises at an altitude of 5,000 feet. Many glaciers discharge into rivers which carry the ice to the sea. Of these the Childs is a famous example. It flows into the Copper River above Cordova and discharges into the swift stream icebergs which have been likened to a block of city houses. At frequent intervals during the entire summer the discharges take place with reports resembling heavy artillery.

Farther east, in Glacier Bay, the celebrated Muir Glacier discharges ice at the rate of 30,000,000 cubic feet daily during the summer, and is the most notable example of a tide-water glacier. It has an area of three hundred and fifty square miles, and the main trunk which is thirty to forty miles broad is supplied by twenty-six tributaries, twenty of which are each greater than the Mer de Glace in Switzerland; the ice stands about one hundred to two hundred feet above the water at the mouth and reaches down probably a great distance beneath its surface. Unfortunately for the pleasure of many tourists, however, the Muir Glacier was badly shattered by an earthquake and the bay choked with ice.

But the greatest of all Alaskan glaciers we were presently to witness in its sublimity, for after we had left Yakutat and stood out to sea again to make the head of the Inside Passage, the sun melted aside the screen of clouds which hid the vast range of mountains and we looked back upon the dazzling white peak of Mt. St. Elias and its kindred, rising apparently directly from the sea about a hundred miles distant. For almost a hundred miles this cluster of lofty mountain tops rises 15,000 to 20,000 feet above the sea level. On the seaward face of their giant Mt. St. Elias, long considered to be the loftiest summit in America, we could see the vast Malaspina Glacier, covering an area of 1,500 square miles (nearly a tenth the total area of Switzerland), fronting the sea for more than fifty miles of width, bearing on its surface layers of earth and forest. One of its tributaries, the Seward Glacier, is itself more than fifty miles long and three miles broad at its narrowest point. The fortunate glimpse of that spectacle, as the morning sun illumined the realm of ice and snow, is one which I shall never forget.

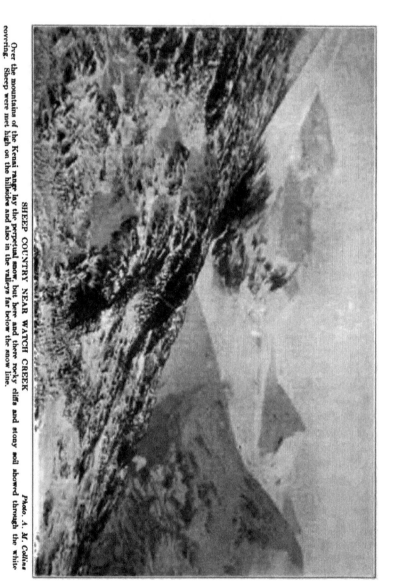

SHEEP COUNTRY NEAR WATCH CREEK

Photo. A. M. Collins

Over the mountains of the Kenai range lay the perpetual snow, but here and there rocky cliffs and stony soil showed through the white covering. Sheep were met high on the hillside and also in the valleys far below the snow line.

THE HEAD OF WATCH CREEK, KENAI PENINSULA

Photo. Gilpin Lovering

This drainage system flows into Cook Inlet through Tustumena Lake, whereas the Killey and Funny River, beyond the divide, enter Cook Inlet by another parallel route, through the Kenai River. Collins and Lovering found sheep on these hills.

But with our passage into Cross Sound, between the mainland and the north end of Chichagof Island, we entered again the waters of the Inside Passage, which we had already once navigated on our journey from Seattle to Skagway.

The Pacific coast of Canada and Alaska is fringed so thickly with islands that vessels sailing from Seattle, Vancouver or Victoria need scarcely be exposed to rough ocean weather in making the passage to that southeastern portion of Alaska from which access is had to the interior through the Yukon Basin.

More than one thousand of them belong to United States territory and many to British Columbia. A voyage through the Inside Passage, as this route is called, is one of the most enjoyable voyages that the world affords the traveler for pleasure. In some respects the Norwegian fiords rival it, but not in quiet charm of landscape and hardly in grandeur.

There is a freshness hanging over the wooded slopes of these Alaskan islands; they are untouched by the axe and ignorant of modern improvements. Here and there a village of Indian huts is in keeping with the atmosphere; a salmon cannery, or a rare town occupied by white men, these are but welcome signs that relieve what would otherwise be too great a loneliness.

Narrow channels, deep carven by the sea into the rock, wind among shores that call to mind the beautiful lakes of Scotland; but towering above the dense growth of evergreens, a ridge of bare peaks crested with snow may wake the lazy dreamer to a realization that he is in the rigorous North.

The tide sucks malevolently through many of the straits and many a vessel is spitted upon the abounding rocks. Fog often casts a threatening pall over the region and makes navigation perilous. Three ships were wrecked in these waters during the summer of which our story tells.

Great fiords also lead from the Inside Passage far into the rugged coast line, but in these the steamers plying to Alaska have no business; except at the north end of the course, where the town of Skagway lies at the head of Lynn Canal.

Collins had been on the vessel which landed the first band of prospectors to pitch their tents on the beach and found the town of Skagway, about sixteen years before. It had suddenly flamed into a large lawless, shifting port. But now its greatest tide of humanity had long since receded, and left it with merely the moderate activities of a terminus for the little White Pass Railway.

Let stout-hearted Mrs. Pullen stand typical of the town. This woman, respected by all Alaskans, came with the early rush, a widow with three children. She ran pack teams over the trails towards the Klondike and kept her little family from the first with her profits from this business. We found her, a tall Amazon of middle age, with one son a physician, the other a finished engineer. During the hard struggle she had laid the third in his grave. And now the frenzy of bread-winning had turned to a placid existence as owner of the best hotel in the town.

A few hours from Skagway we drew near to Fort W. H. Seward adjoining the town of Haines near the head of Lynn Canal, where two companies were stationed. Almost the whole garrison was on the dock to welcome us. "If it weren't for the diversion of ships stopping here," said Colonel McClure, "we would have many a homesick man."

We turned many corners before entering Gastineau Channel on which Juneau is situated. Lying on a scant bit of low land, backed by lofty mountains, nearly a mile high, the situation of Juneau is very picturesque. We found it a busy place, the center of a population estimated at 5,000, for in its immediate vicinity were the most productive deep rock gold mines of Alaska. On Douglas Island, nearly opposite the town, a landing was made to let us go through the famous Treadwell gold mine which had been producing for many years. Other promising mines of the same character were being opened up on the main land near the town, and these enterprises, employing many hundreds of men and certain for years to come, gave Juneau a stability that no other Alaskan city had shown us, and doubtless had helped to make it the capital of the territory. We had here secured from Governor Strong the hunting licenses for our summer's trip and to him we must make reports of our deeds in the chase. All other game except moose was accounted for by affidavits made to the local game wardens, but in order to export heads of the great deer of the Kenai Peninsula it was necessary to secure shipping licenses from the Governor in addition to the hunting licenses which we had already secured, as the strict regulations surrounding the killing of the moose in that locality were jealously observed.

The larger islands of the Alexander Archipelago, notably Chichagof, Baranof and Admiralty Islands, were the homes of numerous Alaskan brown bear. They had been hunted systematically by Charles Sheldon of New York, and the types described by Dr. Merriam of the Biological Survey.

Between the closely fitting shores of Chichagof and

Baranof Islands lay, however, the entrance to the town
of Sitka. The passage of Peril Strait, turning the north
end of Baranof Island, was spectacular. The current
raced around corners at an alarming speed. We seemed
to make little headway past the land at times, but eventually came to dock in the rarely beautiful island-dotted
harbor of Sitka.

The wild heart of Baranof, the old Russian Governor,
chose well when he fixed his residence upon this lovely
spot. For practical purposes it was more accessible to
Siberia than any other in southeastern Alaska, and its
port was admirably sheltered by Kruzof Island and the
numerous rocky patches that showed above water. In
natural beauty it was unrivaled. Mount Edgecumbe
raised its white cone eternally opposite the town and the
great wooded hills of Baranof Island clothed the slopes to
the water's edge.

On a little knoll commanding the harbor the governor
of the Russian Company fortified a castle and lived out
his turbulent life. Upon the site now dwelt Professor
Georgenson, the government's expert in charge of the
more peaceful arts of agriculture in the territory.

Sitka remained the capital of Alaska for nearly forty
years after its purchase from Russia. Then the course
of trade left it apart from the currents of activity, to
drowse away in its present beauty and past importance.

Again we went through Peril Strait and this time
three large porpoises played for miles under the prow of
the ship. They swam up past the cutwater like a cat
scratching its back, turning on their sides and showing
the white belly. Then with powerful up and down
strokes of their graceful tails they went ahead a few
fathoms to dive and repeat the sport.

After the careful captain had crossed the smooth bosom of Frederick Sound and entered again the narrower waterways between the mainland and the islands we felt ourselves especially fortunate in having no mist to mar the view or cause anxiety for safety at Wrangell Narrows, where the swift current treacherously endangered many a ship and wrecked some on its reefs. It had become the custom to go through it at slack water and by day, but circumstances sometimes willed otherwise, and many a vessel had to attempt it in the frequent thick fogs.

Wrangell, a town near the mouth of the Stikeen River, was formerly an important post under the Russians but had lost much of its affluence. Hundreds of gold-seekers outfitted here in the days of the Klondike rush and went up the Stikeen River, either to battle through the hard mountainous country toward Dawson, or to find fresh fields in the northwest corner of British Columbia. But all that had long passed, and the rickety town had settled to a smaller, though still profitable, occupation of fishing and mining on a small scale.

From Wrangell was the usual route for entering the hunting country near the head of the Stikeen River. Arriving at Wrangell about the middle of August the travelers would engage a motor boat and go three days up the river to Telegraph Creek, thence making a trip of thirty to thirty-five days in pursuit of moose, caribou, grizzly bear, sheep and goats.

Ketchikan, the port of entry for Alaska, is the center of a considerable fishing industry, but to the ordinary tourist the numerous totem poles are of greater interest.

A totem pole is the carved trunk of a tree set up in front of an Indian's house to give his pedigree and family history. It has no religious significance. The Tlinket Indians divide themselves into two main clans, that of the Raven and that of the Wolf. Each of these in turn is subdivided into branches under the symbol of some bird, beast or fish. Two persons of the same clan cannot marry. Doubtless this widespread custom explains why the myths of the principal northern races have so many points of resemblance—their conveyance by marriage. On the face of the totem are carved in high relief the various emblems drawn from family history or legends of the owner's clan. Recent generations have held the art in light esteem and erected but few new poles.

Only a few hours' run from Ketchikan is a splendid example of a life devoted to others in the history of William Duncan, missionary and practical leader of the Metlakatla Indians. We met the white-haired little man among his people at the new Metlakatla, Annette Island.

All in all, the Metlakatla community presented a prosperous appearance. A good cannery was operated by the natives and other industries were run on a mutual basis. They were apparently very contented and peaceful. But this question could not find an answer: What would become of these 700 souls when their leader was no longer with them? Would one of their number rise in like power, or would the precept and example grow dimmer and finally fade away?

Now we were out of Alaska, and as if to emphasize the healthful character of that great country, Elting and I both caught malignant colds in the head, whereas we had been entirely free from such complaints during the summer.

While vast wealth has been carved from this huge Arctic territory, much greater riches are likely to be found there in the future. The new government railway and more adequate land laws will doubtless stimulate discovery and trade to an extent previously unknown.

The town of Prince Rupert is the most northern port of British territory on the Pacific. It lies near the southern border of the thin strip of coast belonging to Alaska and is the terminus of the Canadian Grand Trunk Pacific Railway, which was not yet completed. This raw town was most interesting. It was the foreshadowing of a future great city, yet it had a bare 7,000 inhabitants and rough board houses, served by plank roads that ran past many a tree stump and over many a hillock. Here we were permitted consciously to see that rare thing, an important city in the days just following its foundation. The rich country tapped by the new railway, the cheapness of its trans-continental haul, the quicker route to Japan, the excellent harbor, all determined beforehand that Prince Rupert must some day be reckoned with the large ports of the Pacific Coast. It is a fiat city, deliberately placed on its present location after exhaustive search of the coast for the best site, laid out and surveyed by the best civic architects, furnished with a model municipal government. When all this work had been done it was handed over to the inhabitants by the process of auctioning the lots, and these were purchased alike by speculators all over the world and by confident residents. One corner, 50 x 50 feet, unimproved, not yet graded, still full of stumps, was held for sale at $42,500. They had discounted the future for some time to come.

Leaving the zealous real estate agents of Prince Rupert, we boarded a special train and rode nearly a hundred miles up the large Skeena River, by which the railway found an easy gradient to cross the watershed. Lunch was served at Terrace, a paper town, the future metropolis of a farming region. Fabulous prices for town lots and higher values on farms than obtained in the thickly settled Atlantic states were freely quoted and gave a fictitious atmosphere to the cautious visitor.

A large fish-packing factory was opened to our inspection on the water front of Prince Rupert. Thousands of salmon and halibut were brought here daily by the fishing boats, dressed and cooked in cans or frozen or mild-cured in brine. We walked through the great refrigerating rooms where thousands of tons of fish were laid up in shelves to await a favorable market. The manager pulled a big halibut out and dropped it on the cement floor. "It won't break," he reassured the ladies, as the grotesque thing bounded on the pavement with a clatter like a wooden bowl.

One of the reception committee to welcome our party at Prince Rupert was Frank Mobley, a tall man of few words. He appeared to know all the game of North America and after a time we asked if he had ever tried to get musk-oxen.

"Oh, yes," he replied, as though he would not have referred to it unless it had been mentioned in the conversation. "I was one of a party that made a trip for musk-oxen. The trip took us a year. We went down the Mackenzie River about 2,000 miles, employing native guides. These led us purposely away from the game until we discharged them, because they feared a curse if we took the animals alive out of the country, as there was a tradition to this effect. Finally with our own efforts we sighted a herd and set our dogs loose. The musk-oxen were soon bayed up in a circle, their heads

NEW AND OLD CAPITALS OF ALASKA

Above: Juneau, present capital, a thriving town of 5,000, surrounded by extensive deep-rock gold mines.

Below: Sitka, for many years the seat of government, situated on Baranof Island and surrounded by beautiful wooded hills and snow-capped mountains.

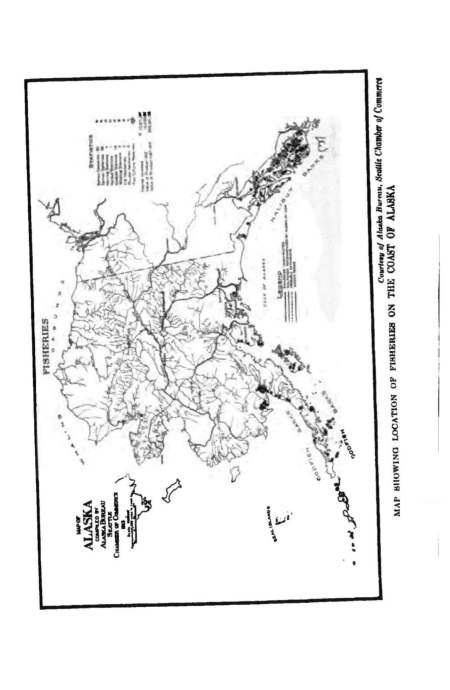

Courtesy of Alaska Bureau, Seattle Chamber of Commerce

MAP SHOWING LOCATION OF FISHERIES ON THE COAST OF ALASKA

outward for defence. We succeeded in roping five rather young ones. The rest got away. We had to make the return march with great difficulty, keeping watch on our back trail against the revengeful natives, whom we knew we had mortally offended. After passing the Indian country we relaxed our vigilance, only to find one morning that all of our musk-oxen had their throats cut. The tracks of one of our guides told the story. He had dogged us for weeks. We followed him for several days but never caught him. He knew enough to travel fast for he had done us out of $25,000. No musk-ox was in captivity at that time and we had orders for these at $5,000 apiece, from zoological gardens."

It took us in all eight days to reach Seattle from Seward, and a home-stretch of 3,000 miles across the continent was accomplished in less than four days more, of actual running time.

Upon November 21st we reached home after an absence of five months and one-half, during which time we had traveled nearly 17,000 miles. The excursion, as we looked back on it, was satisfactory. It had involved some little personal inconvenience, necessitated bits of hard work now and then, and had resulted in a few trophies which we would take pleasure in contemplating with a reminiscence not of scenes of slaughter, but of a summer's travel in varied scenery with good companions.

APPENDIX

DIARY AND DISTANCES

	Date.	Miles between Points.	Total Miles.
Philadelphia....................	June 15	.....	.....
Seattle..........................	19–21	3,050	3,050
Vancouver.......................	22	156	3,206
Seymour Narrows................	23	126	3,332
Prince Rupert...................	24	428	3,760
Terrace.........................	24	94	3,854
Prince Rupert...................	24	94	3,948
Metlakatla......................	25	103	4,051
Ketchikan.......................	25	17	4,068
Wrangell........................	25	109	4,177
Wrangell Narrows...............	26	43	4,220
Petersburg......................	26	3	4,223
Sitka...........................	27	195	4,418
Treadwell.......................	28	219	4,637
Juneau..........................	28	1	4,638
Haines..........................	29	112	4,750
Skagway.........................	29	17	4,767
Caribou Crossing................	30	68	4,835
McRae..........................	30	35	4,870
Pueblo Mine....................	30	7	4,877
McRae..........................	30	7	4,884
White Horse.....................	30–July 1	8	4,892
Lake LaBarge...................	July 1	25	4,917
Hootalinkwa.....................	1	65	4,982
Five Finger Rapids..............	2	136	5,118
Rink Rapids.....................	2	6	5,124
Selkirk.........................	3	50	5,174
White River.....................	3	98	5,272
Stewart River...................	4	10	5,282
Dawson..........................	4	70	5,352
Bonanza.........................	4	12	5,364
Dawson..........................	4–5	12	5,376
Forty Mile......................	5	53	5,429
Eagle...........................	5	49	5,478
Circle City.....................	6	190	5,668
Fort Yukon......................	6	85	5,753
Fort Hamlin.....................	7	152	5,905
Rampart.........................	7	91	5,996
Tanana (Fort Gibbon)............	8	80	6,076
Hot Springs.....................	9	70	6,146
Tolovana........................	9	63	6,209

	Date.	Miles between Points.	Total Miles.
Minto	9	50	6,259
Nenana	9	15	6,274
Chena	10	65	6,339
Chatanika	10	45	6,384
Fairbanks	10	45	6,429
Chena	11	12	6,441
Tanana	11	275	6,726
Ruby	12	163	6,889
Koyokuk	12	112	7,001
Nulato	13	20	7,021
Kaltag	13	40	7,061
Anvik	13	165	7,236
Holy Cross	14	47	7,283
Russian Mission	14	11	7,294
Andreafsky	14	88	7,382
St. Michael	15	181	7,563
Emma Harbor (Siberia)	18–20	(335*) 415	7,978
Penkegnei Bay	21–26	(95*) 125	8,193
Welen	27–28	(150*) 170	8,273
Position where rudder broke	29	(40*) 95	8,368
Teller	July 31–Aug. 8	155	8,523
Herald Island	14	(425*) 550	9,077
Irkaipy (Cape North)	20	(175*) 430	9,503
Cape Serge	24	(200*) 310	9,813
Deshnef (East Cape)	25	95	9,908
Nome	26–28	150	10,058
St. Michael	29	120	10,178
Nunivak Island	Sept. 2	300	10,478
Scotch Cap (Unimak Pass)	5	380	10,858
Pavlof Bay	7–18	(140*) 200	11,058
Pirate Cove	19	70	11,128
Seward	26–Nov. 5	(775*) 850	11,978
Latouche	5	80	12,058
Valdes	6	80	12,138
Cordova	6	91	12,229
Cape St. Elias	7	200	12,429
Yakutat	7	233	12,662
Juneau	9	280	12,942
Ketchikan	10	240	13,182
Seattle	12–15	742	13,924
Philadelphia	21	3,050	16,974

* Direct.

REGISTER OF GAME

POLAR BEAR

Owner.	No.	Sex.	Date Shot.	Locality.	Length of Body.	Length of Skin.	Width of Skin.
Scull......	1	Female	Aug. 12	Herald Id.	7′ 5″	7′ 9¼″	7′ 7½″
Collins....	2	Male	" 13	" "	8′ 1″	8′ 7″	9′ 4″
Lovering..	3	Female	" 17	" "	7′	7′ 7″	7′ 4″
Elting.....	4	Female	" 17	" "	4′ 4″	.....	.....
Collins....	5	Female	" 17	" "	6′ 10″	7′ 6″	7′

GRANT'S CARIBOU, SHOT AT PAVLOF BAY, September, 1913

(As measured six months after killing)

Owner.	No.	Length of Horns.		Circumference at Burr.		Points.		Spread.
		Right.	Left.	Right.	Left.	Right.	Left.	
Lovering..	1	52¼	53¼	5¼	5¼	16	11	38
" ..	2	43¼	38¼	4¼	4¼	13	20	40¼
" ..	3	39¼	44¼	5¼	4¼	16	11	35¼
Collins....	1	43¼	43¼	6¼	7	9	10	39¼
"	2	53¼	55¼	6	5¼	12	9	37¼
"	3*	39¼	38¼	4¼	5	17	8	24
Scull......	1	52¼	53	5¼	5¼	18	17	37¼
Elting....	1	50	49	7	7	17	21	41¼

*In velvet.

FEMALE BROWN BEAR OF PAVLOF BAY

Shot by Dr. Elting

Length of body, from nose to tail, 6 ft. 8 ins.
Width of skin, across forepaws, 6 ft. 5 ins.

Walrus

(All measured six months after killing)

Owner.	No.	Sex.	Date Shot.	Locality.	Total Length of Tusks.		Length to Gums.		Girth at Gums.		Greatest Girth.	
					Right.	Left.	Right.	Left.	Right.	Left.	Right.	Left.
Collins......	1	Male	Aug. 19	Cape Vankarem	32⅜	30	23⅜	22⅛	7⅞	8	..	..
Elting......	2	"	" 19	" "	25	25	19	19	..	..	8	8
Lovering....	3	"	" 20	Cape Irkaipy	27⅞	27½	19⅝	19	8⅝	7⅞	..	..
"	4	"	" 20	" "	28¾	30	21⅞	22⅝	8⅞	8⅞	..	..
Scull.......	5*	"	" 20	" "	34$\frac{1}{16}$	33½	25⅝	25⅝	10⅝	10⅞	11	11½
"	6	"	" 20	" "	29$\frac{1}{16}$	30	22	22⅝	7⅝	7⅝	..	..
"	7	"	" 20	" "	28⅜	25½	20⅜	18⅝	7⅜	8¼	..	..
Lovering....	8	"	" 20	" "	..	..	..	..	..	..	..	..
Elting......	9	"	" 20	" "	24	23	18	17	..	..	7	7½
Collins.....	10	"	" 20	" "	30	26⅝	21⅞	19⅜	7⅞	8	..	..
"	11	"	" 22	" "	24⅛	23⅝	16⅝	16	8	7⅝	..	..
"	12	"	" 22	" "	31⅝	30⅝	23⅜	23	8⅛	8¼	..	..
Lovering....	13	"	" 22	" "	26⅝	27⅝	19	20⅜	7⅞	7⅞	..	..
"	14	"	" 22	" "	28⅜	30⅜	20¾	21¼	9¼	9¼	..	..

* Weight of tusks: right, 11 lbs. 9 oz.; left, 11 lbs. 14 oz.; total, 23 lbs. 7 oz.

White Sheep of Kenai Peninsula

(As measured five months after killing)

Owner.	No.	Spread.	Girth at Base.		Length Outside Curve.		Age.
			Right.	Left.	Right.	Left.	
Lovering . .	1	17	12¾	12¾	25¼	25½	
" . . .	2	19¾	12½	13	33½	34	
Elting . . .	1*	20	13	. .	35	. .	9 years
" . . .	2*	20½	13¼	. .	37½	. .	10 years
Collins. . . .	1	19½	13⅝	12⅞	34⅞	36	
"	2	21⅞	12⅝	12⅝	32⅝	32	
"	3	18⅝	12¾	12¼	31¾	32½	
Scull.	1	20⅝	13⅜	13⅝	38⅝	38⅝	
"	2	20¾	12¼	12⅝	34⅝	35½	
"	3	17⅝	11½	12¼	33¼	33	

* Measured when killed.

Kenai Moose

(As measured five months after killing)

Owner.	No.	Spread.	Girth at Base.		Points.		Length of Blade.		Width of Blade.	
			Right.	Left.	Right.	Left.	Right.	Left.	Right.	Left.
Elting . . .	1*	56	. .	. .	Total 28		Larger 36		Larger 15	
Collins. . . .	1	63½	9¼	9⅜	9	10	26½	28½	21½	15½
"	2	58⅝	7⅝	7⅜	11	10	. .	. .	. .	. .
Lovering . .	1	51¼	7¾	7¼	10	10	27	24	13	12
" . .	2	58¾	8⅝	7⅞	15	9	. .	. .	. .	. .
Scull.	1	52¼	7¾	7⅝	12	12	33	32	15	14
"	2	50½	7½	7¼	13	10	37½	38¼	16½	14¾

* Measured when killed.

Kenai Brown Bear

Shot by A. M. Collins

Length of skin, 6 ft. 10 ins.
Width across forepaws, 7 ft. 8½ ins.

KENAI BLACK BEAR

Shot by Dr. Elting

No. 1. Length of body, nose to tail, 4 ft. 2 ins.
No. 2. Length of body, nose to tail, 4 ft. 10½ ins.

Shot by E. M. Scull

No. 1. Cub. Length of skin, 3 ft. 5 ins.
No. 2. Cub. Length of skin, 3 ft. 5¾ ins.

NOTES ON CONTRIBUTIONS

By Dr. G. B. Gordon

Director of the University Museum
University of Pennsylvania

The ethnological specimens presented to the University Museum by
Mr. E. Marshall Scull, collected by him among the maritime and reindeer
Chukchee and from the Eskimo on the Siberian and Alaskan shores, are
characteristic of the cultures of the hyperborean peoples of the Asiatic
and American side of Bering Sea. The model of a Chukchee dwelling,
constructed by a native, reproduces the methods of house construction
which still persist in that region in spite of many innovations growing
out of the whaling industry and trading stations. Many articles of native
clothing have also survived on account of their superior fitness for the
climate; such, for instance, are the sealskin boots or mukluks used by the
Chukchee as well as by the Eskimo. The Eskimo kayak is another inven-
tion which seems to survive on account of its inherent qualities and
adaptation to native needs. Its native design still answers better the
needs of the Eskimo hunter in his short excursions by water than any
civilised innovation.

In the matter of weapons, however, and the methods of procuring
food, the change that has taken place among the Eskimo is very complete.
The bows and arrows, spears and spear-throwers and heavy harpoons are
no longer in general use and have become difficult to procure as museum
specimens. The repeating rifle has taken the place of the primitive
armory.

On the whole, as Mr. Scull's collecting shows, the native Chukchee
culture has greater permanence and stability than that of the Eskimo.
This is due to the fact that the reindeer herds on which the one depended,
have continued to be their mainstay, whereas the natural food supply
of the other, namely, the great sea mammals, has, in the first place,
always been more uncertain and, at the present time, has become so
diminished that it can no longer be relied upon.

The reindeer, herded as they are in large numbers and serving as
draft animals in domestication, as well as for food, do not involve the
exigencies of the chase, but are slaughtered as domestic animals are
slaughtered. The taking of the sea mammals, on the other hand, requires
great hardihood and skill and is fraught with danger as well as with

uncertainty. The hunting of the whale, the walrus or the seal by native methods requires a variety of weapons, each specialized to its particular use and each requiring a special knowledge and skill in its use. It can easily be understood, therefore, that the repeating rifle appeals to the Eskimo as a great improvement on his armory, answering the purpose of several different kinds of weapons and giving him a greater advantage in the chase. The Chukchee, not being hunters, had not the same use for the rifle.

Another fact illustrated by Mr. Scull's collection is the degeneracy of the native arts in general among these hyperborean peoples. Until a few years ago all the native skin garments were sewn with sinew which now gives place to cotton thread. The characteristic decorative art of the Eskimo, employing as it did pictorial records of the chase and other incidents of native life, is no longer to be found in its purity, but is replaced by pictures in imitation of white man's engraving done on ivory and calculated to appeal to the fancy of the white traders. These pictures sometimes show great skill, but as examples of native art much of their value is lost.

Mr. Scull's energy in collecting these specimens to illustrate present conditions among the natives on both sides of Bering Sea, as well as his generosity in contributing them to the collections in the University Museum, should serve as an example to be followed by all who enjoy similar opportunities, whether the object of their expeditions be for sport or for scientific ends.

INDEX

Lightning Source UK Ltd.
Milton Keynes UK
UKHW020903210921
390928UK00002B/102